An Illustrated History of the
ASHCHURCH TO BARNT GREEN LINE
– The Evesham Route –

An Illustrated History of the
ASHCHURCH TO BARNT GREEN LINE
– The Evesham Route –

R. J. Essery
with contributions from
Philip Jarvis

OPC

Oxford Publishing Co

Half title page:
At Evesham, Ivatt Mogul No 43046 is about to couple to the train it has worked there from Birmingham. The locomotive has run round the train, and after coupling to the coaches it will draw forward into the up platform in readiness to depart for Birmingham. This 1962 picture also provides a good view of the old Great Western Railway's sidings and station. The LMS signalbox is the 1934 replacement for the one shown in the c1920 view. The safety points that protect the passenger lines should be noted. *M. Mensing*

Title page:
A Midland Railway-built Class 4F, No 43975, heads a Class D express freight train on the up line by Redditch South signalbox in 1960. There is a 20mph caution sign adjacent to the signalbox that is just visible. The train is quite short, made up entirely of vans, and could well be the 'Beckford' as described in Chapter 1. Generally speaking, enginemen believed that the old Midland Class 4s, the '38s', '39s' and '40s', were better than the later engines that were built at a number of works by the LMS after 1923 but I have no explanation why this should be. By now, what is known is that an LMS old standard tender has replaced the tender that was originally coupled to this engine. *M. Mensing*

Below:
This splendid picture illustrates Ivatt 4MT No 43036 at Hinton on 15 May 1959 with a three-coach set made up of two third brakes and a composite coach forming what is probably an Evesham to Ashchurch train. Passengers crossed between the platforms by way of the barrow crossing where the rear of a 'Beware of Trains' warning board can be seen on the right. *R. J. Sellick*

First published 2002

ISBN 0 86093 562 0

All rights reserved. No part of this book may be reproduced or transmitted in any form or by any means, electronic or mechanical, including photocopying, recording or by any information storage and retrieval system, without permission from the Publisher in writing.

© R. J. Essery 2002

Published by Oxford Publishing Co

an imprint of Ian Allan Publishing Ltd, Hersham, Surrey KT12 4RG

Printed by Ian Allan Printing Ltd, Hersham, Surrey KT12 4RG

Code: 0204/A2

Contents

DMUs came on to the line in the 1950s. At Redditch, on 18 June 1960, a two-car Metro-Cammell unit forms the 2.30pm from Birmingham with No 51177 leading. *M. Mensing*

Introduction

This book is about a length of railway that was usually referred to by the railwaymen who worked over it as the Evesham branch. The line began at Barnt Green Main Line Junction on the Birmingham & Gloucester Railway and ran via Redditch, Alcester and Evesham to Ashchurch, where it rejoined the Birmingham & Gloucester Railway.

It is not my intention to chart every proposal, Act of Parliament or other event that took place during the construction of the railway, nor do I seek to make any case for the retention of such rural lines as part of a modern railway system. Instead, I have tried to paint a picture of this fascinating stretch of railway, which I knew and enjoyed from the footplate during my time in the Evesham Link at Saltley Motive Power Depot.

The steam era was, for those members of the working classes employed in railway service, not an easy life. In the early days it was usually a case of long hours of work coupled with conditions of service that would be totally unacceptable today; conditions where the infant trade unions sought to improve the lot of their members. Readers of early copies of *The Railway Magazine* would find references to trade union and worker relations as seen from the employers' and shareholders' standpoint. From these references, together with other records of the negotiations which took place during the Victorian and Edwardian periods, it will be recognised that the railway workers of that era usually had a genuine case for grievance, but after the end of World War 2, the balance tipped the other way. As a very junior employee in 1948 I saw some of the things that were happening but at the time I did not understand what lay behind them. Some of these events have been recorded in the pages that follow.

I have mentioned this simply to ensure that readers are aware that in Chapter 1 they are likely to read a rather different story from that which is normally found in a line history. Some authors conduct a very thorough research into the historical facts but fail to explain in detail how the railway was worked, while others appear to only see and record the story while wearing rose-tinted glasses. I hope that I do not fall into either category.

In Chapter 1, in order to set the scene, I have recorded some of my recollections of when I was a fireman in the Evesham Link at Saltley MPD in 1950-1. They have not been embroidered and are intended to be a true record of the events that took place. The railway was not built as one, and in the beginning three separate undertakings made up the length of railway between Barnt Green and Ashchurch, so in Chapter 2, I have attempted to explain how this came about. Chapter 3 is a description of the railway, station by station along the line and I have made use of the surviving signalling and inspection reports that make fascinating reading. Unfortunately, these records vary; some stations, which were subject to a number of changes, are well documented while in the case of others little or nothing at all has survived. This is probably due to the lack of change, other than minimal signalling alterations, during most of the stations' lifetime. Therefore, although there is a lack of balance between the various stations I felt that it was better to record everything that my researches had uncovered rather than to try to achieve an overall uniform level. Chapter 4 is an analysis of the traffic carried on the railway at selected dates during the lifetime of the Evesham branch. This information is also related to the track and signalling plans in the previous chapter. Finally, I have concluded with some Appendices that readers may find to be helpful in understanding how the railway was operated.

Many readers will be railway modellers, as indeed am I, and I hope they will find the track layouts, signalling plans, traffic working information and other details helpful in the construction and operation of working three-dimensional railway models, for both their enjoyment and that of others. Although the railway preservation movement has worked wonders by restoring and demonstrating the hardware associated with the traditional Victorian steam railway, it is only through accurate models that the complete picture can be seen.

Acknowledgements

Two of my friends made an outstanding contribution to this book and I am eternally grateful; they are John Edgington and A. E. Overton. In addition to supplying a number of photographs, John went through the manuscript a number of times and eliminated what would have been errors, in particular with the timetables reproduced in Chapter 4. A few years ago, A. E. Overton introduced me to the world of MT6s at the PRO Kew, and together we have been collecting Midland Railway signalling information, the first fruits appearing in this volume. I think that readers will agree that his drawings are excellent.

Others who have assisted in one way or another are: Roy Anderson and Roger Carpenter for the loan of a number of historical pictures, Roy Burrows for his specialist help with historical matters, Phillip Coventry and Alan Foxall of the Redditch Pictorial History Society, Philip Davis at the Redditch Library, M. A. Hastilow for certain details at Barnt Green, Stuart Morris for information regarding the Beckford cattle markets, John Tilsley for local research on the line, and Mike Christensen and John Hinson for signalling details. Finally, I must acknowledge the immense contribution made by Philip Jarvis who many years ago started the project with me.

Bob Essery
Rolleston on Dove, Staffs
2002

Above:
The view from the footbridge that connected the platforms at the Birmingham end of Barnt Green station. Photographed in 1949, it shows the junction of the branch with the former Birmingham & Gloucester Railway after the widening had taken place and the up platform had been moved further southwest towards Blackwell. The ground signal in the lower centre of the picture controlled setting back movements from the branch into the small goods yard where the cattle dock and goods shed can be seen. Although the staying wires for the branch home signal are not visible here, they were attached to the post by the end of the barrow crossing. *Joe Moss*

1
The Evesham Link at Saltley, 1950-1

The Evesham Link comprised 12 sets of enginemen who were based at Saltley Motive Power Depot in Birmingham. This was one of eight links that were part of what was known as 'the bottom road group'. The official name was Group 3 and the individual links were described as Link A, B, C etc, but the links were always referred to as the 'Little Bristol Link', the 'Evesham Link', etc. There were 96 drivers and 96 firemen in the group. The Evesham Link had a total of about six weeks out of 12 working various goods trains from the Birmingham area to and from various destinations on the line. The remainder of the period comprised one week covering the link's rest days and about five weeks' work on local trip work within the Birmingham area, but not on the Evesham line. This arrangement of about half the link's work on the line that carried the link's name and half elsewhere was typical of the working arrangements at the depot at this period. Even in the top link at Saltley, the Carlisle Link, enginemen enjoyed two or three weeks out of 12 confined to their local area, a welcome change from working long-distance freight trains that sometimes involved lodging away from home.

When firemen became the senior men in a link, they moved up to the next link until they reached Group 3. Thereafter the system changed somewhat. Because several years could elapse before he was the senior man in Group 3 he was moved in May each year from link to link within the group in order to widen his experience of the various roads that Saltley enginemen covered as

From 1 April 1897 New Street station, Birmingham, was jointly owned by the LNWR and Midland Railway companies, both becoming constituents of the LMS at the Grouping in 1923, but even so, the station remained divided between the Western and Midland divisions as two separate operating entities. The opening up and partial rebuilding of the Western Division side of the station after World War 2 gave New Street a very different look from what was in effect the larger part of the old joint station. (The work took several years to complete and is described by Richard Foster in his book *Birmingham New Street — LMS Days*, published by Wild Swan Publications.) The Midland Division's 'half' of New Street remained largely as built until the total reconstruction of the station took place. Most, but not all, passenger trains that travelled over the Evesham branch, commenced or terminated their journeys at Birmingham New Street station, so we begin this chapter by including two pictures of trains that worked over the branch.

Left:
During the final years of the branch the Ivatt Moguls, introduced just before Nationalisation, were in regular use on the line. They were excellent engines and this picture shows No 43049 on 14 August 1958 with the coaches that had formed the 4.25pm from Ashchurch. The train is standing at Platform 7 and the fireman has altered the locomotive's headlamp code to 'empty coaching stock' prior to departing for Saltley carriage sidings where the stock will be left, the engine then running light to its home shed at Saltley. *M. Mensing*

Right:
Photographed on 17 September 1958 Ivatt Mogul No 43046 is shown with the 6.20pm passenger train from Birmingham New Street to Evesham, standing at Platform 10. Although this is the Midland side of the station, the signals are examples of LNWR design. To the left of the picture, behind the screen, lay the fishbays, but at this time of the day there would be little activity in this part of the station. Those familiar with New Street in those days will recall the smell of fish from this area of the station was present at all times. *M. Mensing*

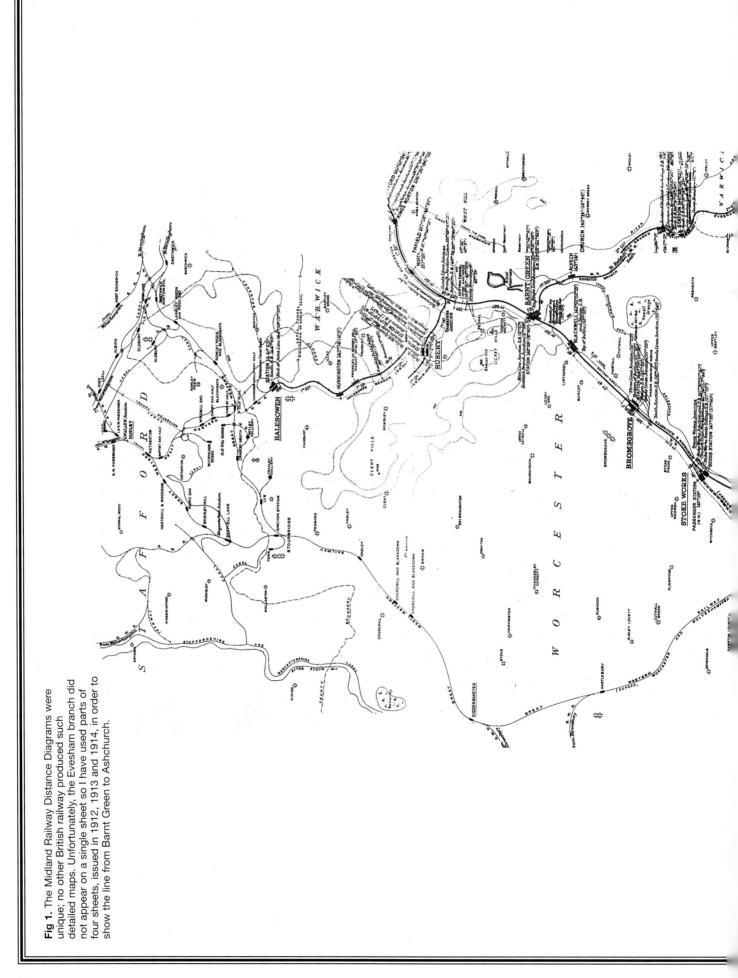

Fig 1. The Midland Railway Distance Diagrams were unique; no other British railway produced such detailed maps. Unfortunately, the Evesham branch did not appear on a single sheet so I have used parts of four sheets, issued in 1912, 1913 and 1914, in order to show the line from Barnt Green to Ashchurch.

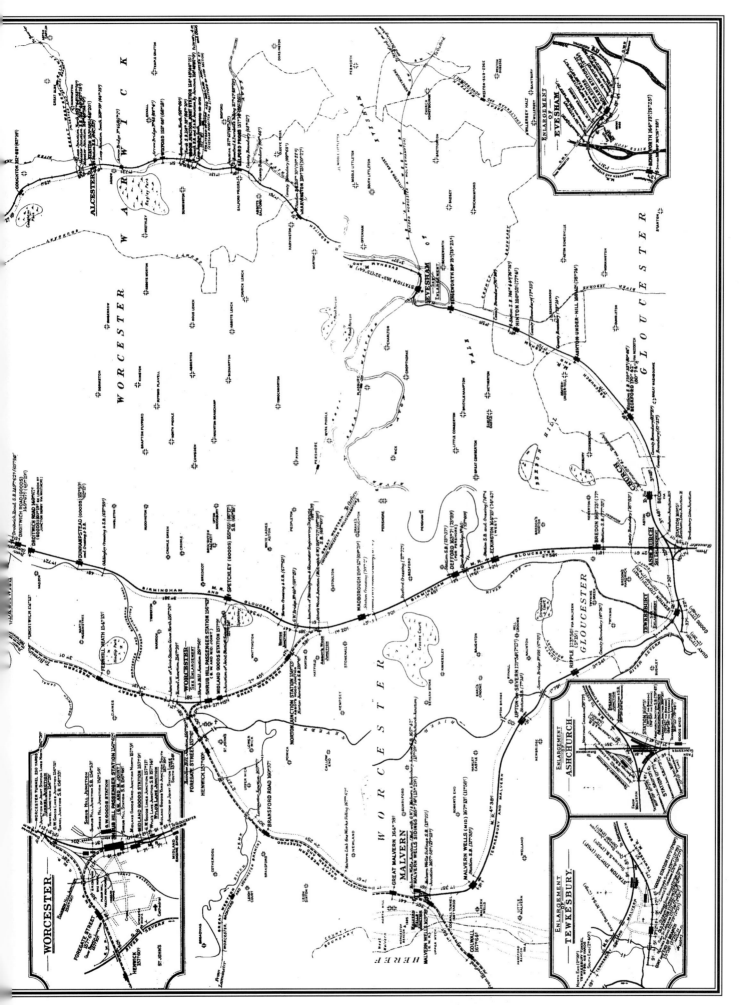

In the final years of the branch, as the Johnson 0-4-4Ts were withdrawn, they were replaced by LMS Standard Class 3F 0-6-0Ts for the Ashchurch to Evesham and Ashchurch to Redditch services. No 47308 is seen at Alcester in 1962 on an up passenger train for Redditch. *J. M. Tolson*

part of their daily work. The link promotion system was complex and, as I have said, it was based upon seniority. The bottom link for firemen was the Washwood Heath Link and when a fireman became the senior man his next move was into the Bank Pilot Link. Thereafter he went into the Control Link, the Special Link and then the Trip Link. The Trip Link had about 18 sets of men and the Control and Special links some 30-36 sets of men in each. Therefore, by the time a fireman reached the bottom road group he was an experienced engineman. When he became the senior man in the bottom road group the next move for a fireman was into the passenger links in Group 2. This was made up of three sets of 12 men known as the Top, Middle and Bottom Passenger links and finally he went into the top group of freight links, Group 1. When he was the senior man in that group he became a passed fireman (fireman passed for driving), and he started at the bottom of the links again.

My first introduction to the Redditch or Evesham branch, the two names given to the line, came in the spring of 1950. At the end of April I was one of the senior men in the Trip Link and at the beginning of May I found myself in the Evesham Link with Driver Charles Reay. Our first week's work was to be on the 'Night Redditch'. The work was straightforward: book on at Saltley, prepare an engine, run light engine to Washwood Heath Down Sidings, commonly referred to as the west end, to work a train to Redditch. This train would be made up largely of coal wagons for the gas works, local industry and domestic users. After we arrived at Redditch we would shunt the sidings; this was something that the guard did without assistance, as there was no local staff on duty. When the shunting was complete we were booked to work a train of empties back to Washwood Heath Up Sidings and then to return light engine to Saltley shed where the engine was 'put away', a railwayman's term for the disposal of a locomotive at the end of a duty. That was the booked work, but we never completed this tour of duty during my time in the link. Relief was usually on hand at Landor Street Junction, just a few minutes' walk from our home depot at Saltley. By the time we reached this point we were on overtime, thanks mostly to Charlie's wangling, whose outlook upon life was to maximise the opportunity for overtime each day. The crew that relieved us

Saltley motive power depot, c1951. This picture was taken on a Sunday from the south end of the shed yard; note the number of locomotives on shed. The allocation of the depot was such that when the three roundhouses were full, many engines were stabled in the open yard. At times, more than one set of men were employed on marshalling duties moving locomotives from the yard to the inspection pits in readiness for the men who prepared the engines for their next turn of duty. *Collection R. J. Essery*

would probably belong to the Control Link and they would work the train forward to Washwood Heath Up Sidings and then return light engine to Saltley where they would dispose of the locomotive.

Charlie Reay, my new driver, was quite a character. Later I was to learn that as a fireman his drivers were not too impressed with his firing skill and I do not think that I learnt anything from him in this regard — rather the reverse! It would also be true to say that he could be described as a woman hater; I think his wife and daughters always nagged him, which given his outlook on life was probably understandable! He was at his happiest when we were on overtime, preferably at time and three-quarters, but since this applied only to Sunday work it was more likely, on the 'Night Redditch', to be at time and a half or even time and a quarter.

To those readers more familiar with regular hours of work, five days a week, no weekend or bank holiday work, with less than an eight-hour working day, the conditions about to be described may come as something of a shock. From the earliest years of railway history difficult working conditions had existed, but by the early 1950s it was considered that a tremendous improvement had taken place when compared with what had gone before. In the past the working conditions included a 'non-guaranteed day', which meant that if there was no work then the railwaymen were sent home without pay. Indeed, those who tend to view railways through rose-tinted glasses may think otherwise if they actually had to work to the accepted conditions of this period, or even worse, from an earlier era. In these circumstances I suspect their views may change somewhat.

Left:
The Class 3 0-6-0 goods engines were universally popular with enginemen. They were free steaming and while not as powerful as the larger Class 4s, they were often preferred for many turns of duty. This picture, taken in September 1936, shows No 3624 at Saltley with 'wait orders' chalked on the bufferbeam. The railwayman on the extreme right of the picture is also waiting for his next turn of duty! *Collection R. J. Essery*

Lower left:
This picture, taken on 14 June 1961, shows an Evesham to Washwood Heath stopping freight train hauled by Class 3 No 43529 from Saltley shed at Broom Junction. The signalman is about to collect the tablet from the enginemen who is on the driver's side of the locomotive (it is probably the driver who can be seen with the hoop and the leather pouch that contains the train tablet). As the signalman does not have a similar hoop, it appears that after giving up the tablet the engine will set back into the sidings alongside the main line. *Collection R. J. Essery*

Right:
Evesham station, looking north. This was the platform where the 'Beckford' used to stand while the train was being made up with additional vehicles. The water crane is just visible at the far end of the platform, beyond the footbridge. *Collection R. J. Essery*

In 1950, we had a guaranteed eight-hour day, which meant we were paid for eight hours' work regardless of whether we were gainfully employed for the entire period. At one time the 'day' was 12 hours. This was reduced to 10 hours and then to eight hours. The 'week' was originally made up of six days but by 1950 it was a 44-hour week that comprised an 11-day, 88-hour fortnight. This meant that an engineman worked six days during one week and then five days the next. The five-day week included a rest day. Therefore a link of 12 men would have 11 weeks' work covering booked turns of duty while one set of men worked the link's rest days. Generally the work was arranged so that the rest days were 'day work', which needs an explanation.

Signalmen and others who worked the three-shift system knew railway time as days, afternoons and nights. Subject to local arrangements, days would be shifts that booked on at 6am, afternoons at 2pm, and nights at 10pm. Generally speaking, enginemen booking on duty from about 3am would consider this to be 'days', but a starting time of 6-8am was seen as an ideal time to sign on duty. The term 'afternoons' usually applied to work that started at about 11am and by the time 6-7pm came it was the start of night work. These were not official times, rather how railwaymen referred to them. From this point onwards I propose to use the railway time that applied then. Therefore, for example, 6.0 is 6am and 6/0 is 6pm. I am not sure when this system began, probably with the introduction of the control offices c1907-9, but for simplicity I have used it throughout the tables in Chapter 4, and in the text, as it is much quicker than any other way of indicating am or pm. No use was made of the 24-hour clock; this was something that the Army did, and it had no place on railways!

Engine crews went round the link on the basis of week one being a six-day week while week two contained five days' work plus a rest day on the Monday. Week three would be a six-day week followed by week four, a five-day week with a rest day on the Tuesday, and so on. We often had a long weekend when we finished on a Friday, with a rest day on the Saturday, no Sunday job and then we were booked for a late pm turn on a Monday. Not all the links were quite as tidy as this, but most were. Usually,

the rest days were on the morning turns while the pm turns were of six-day duration and we would work alternate am and pm weeks. It was unusual to find you had a rest day during a pm week. In addition to the descriptions given above, some others were used. 'Bankers hours' were jobs where you booked on at around 8-9am; 'Day jobs' were when you booked on between say 5.0 and 8.0. As I have said, in most cases, afternoon work described any job which saw the crew booking on from about 11.0 to 1/0, and this was greatly disliked, as you could not do much in the morning before going to work and frequently overtime ruined any prospect of social activity after work had finished.

Payment varied depending upon the hours worked. If crews did not go on to overtime, the basic rates for the guaranteed eight-hour day were: normal time was paid for all work between 6.0 and 10/0 and time and a quarter for work between 10/0 and 6.0, which was considered to be night work. When on overtime during the period when normal time was applicable, overtime was at the rate of time and a quarter. If you were on overtime between the hours of 10/0 and 6.0, then the rate was time and a half. Therefore, it would be possible to go (as we did on the 'Night Redditch'), from day rate at 'time' to time and a quarter, from 10/0 until the end of our eight-hour day. Then we would go on to time and a half (overtime rate until 6.0 when the night rate ended) and thereafter at time and a quarter, overtime at day rate.

On the other hand, all Sunday work, applicable from midnight Saturday, regardless of how many hours were worked, was at the rate of time and three-quarters and it was during this time that money could be made! As I have already mentioned, there was 12 weeks' work in the link and it took three months to go 'round the link'. There were two Sundays with work booked to the link during the 12 weeks, plus the opportunity to get additional Sunday work. This was the position in terms of work and pay when I joined Charlie Reay and we began our first week's work together on the 'Night Redditch'.

We started by arriving on shed at least 20 minutes before our booked time of 7/37. For some unaccountable reason this time has remained fixed in my memory. If we had, as we usually did, a Class 8F or a Horwich Mogul, commonly referred to as a 'Crab', allocated to the job, then we were allowed 60 minutes to prepare the engine. The allowance for the Class 4F 0-6-0, which was the booked locomotive for the job, was only 45 minutes. I should explain that each operating district had the local, or as it was usually known, trip work, in a separate operational document. This Trip Book set out the class of locomotive, all working times and trips to be undertaken. Therefore, by being early we were allowed to book on at 7/22 instead of 7/37.

The fireman's duties were straightforward and can be summarised as follows: collect the engine headlamps, bucket, four spanners, tin of detonators and a firing shovel. All the other tools should have been on the engine. These comprised a coal pick and three fire-irons, namely a clinker shovel, straight dart and a rake. In addition there should be a water gauge lamp and a slaking pipe. More often than not some of these were missing and they had to be found before we could leave the shed. First I would look at both water gauge glasses to check they were giving a true reading and then I would examine the fire. Usually it was in a heap under the firedoor with nothing beyond the middle of the firebox. At the same time I could see that the brick arch and tubeplate were in good condition and no firebars were missing. I would also fill and trim the lamps and make sure the smokebox door was tight, brushing off any ash that may still have been on the platform. I had to check that the coal was safely stacked on the tender and examine the sandboxes, making certain they were filled and the sand was running freely. In addition, there was the need to prepare the fire by spreading it across the firebox and adding fresh coal as the steam pressure began to increase.

These were some of the tasks undertaken by the fireman. While he was fulfilling these duties the driver would examine and oil the engine, and it was during this examination that Charlie would begin to run late! His normal complaint would centre on

BARNT GREEN.

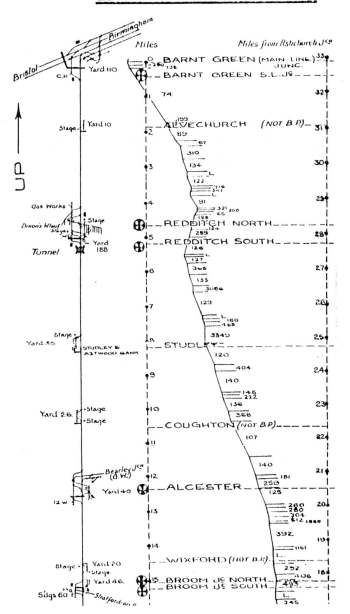

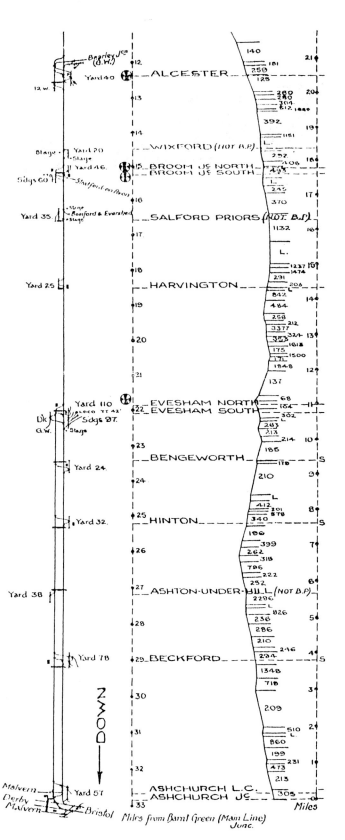

Fig 2. This LMS diagram probably dates from the 1930s and shows the gradients from Barnt Green to Ashchurch, the mileage as calculated from both ends of the line, the single and double track, the block posts, stages, etc. Some of these diagrams have been enlarged and used with the individual stations that are described in Chapter 3. Finally, readers should be aware that some of the other plans used in this book may show variations from these c1930s diagrams, in particular the signalbox changes that took place over the years.

the engine brakes. It would be most unusual for him not to request a fitter to 'take up the brakes', and since this took time it almost certainly meant a late departure from the shed. In Chapter 4 I have used the times that came into effect in June 1951 and by then I was in the Little Bristol Link, so readers may detect some variations of times between those in that chapter and my personal recollections given here.

As a result of such a request, we would arrive late at the front fan at Washwood Heath West End Sidings, which usually meant that by the time we were coupled to our train and ready to leave we were in the way of more important trains due to depart from the sidings. Therefore we were 'set aside', so that our eventual departure was delayed even further. Finally, we were allowed to depart and having lost our original path we crawled along the goods lines to Duddeston Road Junction where, with our bank pilot, we awaited the right away for the run over the Camp Hill line westwards to Barnt Green. We could at times be as much as two hours late at this point in the journey, but it was all good news to Charlie Reay.

Our journey from King's Heath, where our pilot ceased to provide rear-end assistance, to Barnt Green Main Line Junction, along the goods and slow lines was at best sedate. Eventually, we were turned on to the branch, collecting the tablet at Barnt Green Single Line Junction signalbox. Upon arrival at Redditch, having surrendered the tablet at Redditch North signalbox, shunting commenced. It seemed to me as if we always shunted the entire yard, but this may be a slight exaggeration. Suffice to say that eventually the yard was shunted to the guard's satisfaction and our train of empties was assembled ready for the departure, which would be tender-first back to Birmingham. Now it was time to have our 'snap', a term used to describe the brewing, or to quote the railway term, 'mashing' of tea and to eat our evening meal, which in my case was sandwiches. Some engine crews used to prepare a more elaborate feast by frying bacon, eggs and sausages on the firing shovel that was turned into a hygienic frying pan by cleaning it with the slaking pipe, the boiling water and steam quickly cleaning the surface. After producing a 'fry up', bread was soaked in the bacon fat to complete the meal.

The timing for our departure called for considerable skill on the part of the driver and guard, who needs to be introduced. Charles Fennel entered railway service too late to go on the footplate — he was too old — so he became a goods guard. The goods guards also worked in links of 12 and by good fortune, three of our 11 weeks' non-rest day work were with Charlie Fennel. In addition to the 'Night Redditch' he was with us on the Beckford to Lawley Street goods and 57 Trip, one of the weeks when we were not on the Evesham branch. On the 'Night Redditch' Charlie Reay and Charlie Fennel would confer and because we were, in railway terms, 'out of course', there was no booked time for our departure from Redditch. There was an important train due through Redditch and the trick was to time our 'ready to depart' to the signalman when there was insufficient time for our train to travel from Redditch to Barnt Green Main Line Junction. It was only here that we would join the slow and goods lines to King's Norton and thereby be out of the way of more important trains. If the timing was right then we were not allowed to go and we had to follow this train which further increased our late running, not that Driver Reay worried overmuch. The problem arose if we were so late that by the time we finally arrived back at Saltley we had been on duty for more than 12 hours. Then we usually 'gave the company the time' and booked off showing just 12 hours' work. If we were not able to 'catch the job' we would be spare and goodness knows what work we would undertake. In retrospect it was all very wasteful, and poor management allowed the train crews to get away with it. Therefore the costs of train working soared which was a factor that contributed to the decline in rail freight traffic, but the 'Charlie Reays' didn't see it that way, and who could blame them? In their minds the 'job' of enginemen, at the top of the working class league pre-World War 2, had declined so much that a better weekly wage could be received by sweeping the floor of the local car factory. A number of Saltley drivers retired at 65 on a Friday and on the following Monday started new jobs, generally at a wage that was higher than their basic railway pay when employed by British Railways.

The Beckford goods was totally different, and although like the 'Night Redditch' its hours were somewhat antisocial, I enjoyed the week's work. The duty began with the train crew, driver, firemen and guard, booking on at about 1/20 and travelling to New Street in order to catch a passenger train to Ashchurch which departed at about 2/10. We went 'on the cushions', a term meaning that we travelled as passengers to Evesham where we took charge of our engine. This locomotive had worked down from Birmingham earlier in the day and following its arrival at Evesham had been in the care of a set of Evesham men who cleaned the fire, oiled the motion and brought some coal forward. When we arrived there wasn't too much to do as far as I was concerned. The Evesham men had prepared the fire so it was merely a case of waiting for orders. By 1951 the arrangements for this train had changed and it is these workings, rather than those that I knew, which are shown in the 1951 timetables reproduced in Chapter 4.

Our train was booked to start from Beckford at 6/0 but we went there only if there was traffic to collect. Usually there was, but on the few occasions when there wasn't anything to pick up we waited at Evesham where our train was made up prior to the departure time of 7/0. However, for the sake of this story I will assume that there was something to collect from the yard at Beckford station. In order to do this we ran from Evesham to Beckford tender-first propelling our brakevan in which Charlie Fennel travelled. Upon arrival the guard and local staff marshalled the train; the traffic was fruit and vegetables, usually loaded in covered goods vans plus open goods wagons that were sheeted over. On one occasion I recall it comprised just one van while at other times, in the height of the fruit season, it could number a dozen vans or so. We returned to Evesham with the train and with the engine standing in the up platform road by the water crane the train was made up.

We conveyed traffic from the LMS, or as it was then, British Railways London Midland Region, goods depot but, to use a railway term, the 'Great Western Man' also transferred traffic from the old GWR sidings at Evesham via the 'slip' or transfer road on to this LMR train. Finally, with the brakevan attached to the rear of the train, we were complete and ready to go. Before departing, Charlie Fennel advised Charlie Reay of the exact load and details of our next stop for traffic.

As far as I was concerned the run to and from Beckford had not required too much effort on my part but the run from Evesham could not be taken lightly. I always prepared a decent fire in readiness for this work. I cannot recall ever having any locomotive other than a Class 4F 0-6-0 on this turn which worked from Evesham to Birmingham Lawley Street, picking up at Broom Junction if required, although many of our runs were straight through from Evesham without collecting any vehicles from there. During the height of the fruit season this train could easily load to 40 plus vehicles from Broom, usually fully laden and consequently it would be a heavy train. It needed a good fire and a boiler full of water to run to time with a full load and I was usually very pleased to reach Barnt Green where I surrendered the final single line token to the signalman at Barnt Green Single Line Junction signalbox.

On this line the tokens were carried in a small pouch, which was attached to a wire hoop that could be hung on a coat hook in the cab. The method of making the exchange was for the fireman to stand on the top step between the engine and tender, throwing the tablet with the hoop on to the ground as he approached the signalman and scooping up the new tablet with one arm while he clung to the engine with the other. I cannot recall the official handover speed but I do recall Charlie's instructions: 'Throw the tablet down and try not to hit the signalman, but be bloody sure you get his tablet.' Many are the tales that have been told of tablet exchange problems, but regrettably, I don't have any. As far as I am aware I never hit the

Advertisement for Easter holidays 1935

Left:
Before car ownership became commonplace most people travelled by train. This shows part of the LMS programme of half-day excursions on Good Friday, Easter Sunday, Monday and Tuesday 1935 for passengers from the Birmingham area, including Coventry. The arrangements are straightforward, and provided the arrival at Weston-super-Mare was on time then passengers would have had about six hours at the resort.

Above right:
Football specials were a regular feature of excursion traffic and this shows the half-day arrangements for the game between Redditch and Evesham on Good Friday, 19 April 1935.

signalman and I scooped up all tablets offered to me. Furthermore, although I examined each and every one, they were always correct and applied to the section of line we were about to enter.

At Barnt Green Main Line Junction we joined the main line and usually we had a good run to Lawley Street. The route was over the Camp Hill line to Duddeston Road Junction where our train was backed into the yard prior to being shunted. Much of the traffic we conveyed was to be worked forward by the evening and night fast freights whose journeys commenced from either Lawley Street or Water Orton sidings. If the traffic was to go forward by a train originating from Lawley Street then it was merely a case of shunting the wagons we had brought with us onto the appropriate sidings set aside for that particular train. Traffic to be worked forward on trains starting from Water Orton had to be taken there and this was a job for a connecting trip service.

This was, without doubt, the most interesting week's work in the link. I also recall we had two weeks' work on the Kingsbury branch, which was the furthest point north I was to travel while in the Evesham Link. In addition to the work already mentioned, there were other local jobs, but it was all freight work; the branch passenger trains to Redditch, Evesham and Ashchurch were handled by others. Many of these trains were worked by men from Bournville shed, although I had worked some of these passenger trains when I was in one of the spare links at Saltley.

Before leaving the story of the Beckford goods trains I can still, in my mind's eye, visualise standing on the tender back of a Class 4F at Evesham station while it was taking water, and watching the GWR pannier tank at work. This locomotive would be propelling vehicles from the Western Region sidings to increase the length of our train, prior to our departure. Then the scene changes and we are approaching Broom Junction where we have a dozen or so covered goods vans and wagons to collect from the sidings at this station. On northbound trains these vehicles were left in the sidings by the old, long-closed turntable and it was the guard's job to couple the wagons together and to ensure that our train was complete before we started away on the next part of our journey. Although all this happened almost 50 years ago it remains fresh in my memory.

Studley was a fascinating place; another story from my time in the link involved shunting an empty wagon train that we were working to Washwood Heath Up Sidings. Our train engine was a 'Crab' 2-6-0. For some reason Control wanted us 'inside' at this station. This made sense because, as can be seen from the track plan, there was no passing loop and a train was to pass us at this station. We had a long train of wagons, probably 50 or so, and it took a little while to shunt them into the sidings in order to ensure that everything was 'inside clear' of the main line. It also took quite a while to reassemble the train before we could continue our journey.

Another recollection is the tunnel at Redditch, which was a nasty little bore, very tight for space. Going north in the up direction, in other words towards Birmingham, trains were on a falling gradient and as we approached the tunnel I always shut both the damper door and firedoor, putting the blower on full to prevent a blowback. As a further precaution the driver and fireman tucked themselves into the front corners of the cab if the train was moving quickly. I can recall a trip with a Class 3F 0-6-0 that must have had a warped damper door. We were running at speed as we entered the tunnel and we produced a blowback, which I was later to associate with the Cape Canaveral rocket launches when featured on television. The tongue of flame from the firebox came right across the footplate and flattened itself against the tender front — frightening if you were not used to it, but accepted by enginemen working the line. Once a train had run through the tunnel you were almost into the station at Redditch before the final pull up to Barnt Green. At Barnt Green Main Line Junction the hard work was over and I enjoyed some splendid runs over the branch. These were a foretaste of the long-distance freight work with Class 4s that was still to come, mostly on the west road from Birmingham to Gloucester and Bristol.

Other work on the branch included a daily stopping freight from Washwood Heath, which terminated at Evesham, conveying traffic for all stations from Alvechurch. There wasn't usually much traffic for Alvechurch but at this station I have always understood that wagons could only be detached from westbound trains, so any traffic for Alvechurch from the Redditch direction, was taken to Barnt Green and detached there. The next down train would collect the wagons from the sidings and work them back to Alvechurch. However, some of the

timetables reproduced in Chapter 4 show goods trains that stopped at Alvechurch in the up direction. The Midland Railway 1908 Appendix gave Alvechurch as being one of three places on the Evesham branch where tow-roping was permitted. This practice will be explained later.

All in all it was a delightful line; a 'steam and brake' railway was how Charlie Reay described it. To me it seemed as if there was scarcely a level stretch on the line but the gradient profile tells the factual story. There was no shortage of curves either. As Charlie remarked, 'you could shake hands with the guard at a number of points if you had a mind to.' He had another amusing saying, which I can recall. He said, and I quote, 'I'm sure they put a pig down at Barnt Green and told it to go to Ashchurch. Then they laid the rails down where it wandered.' Why a pig I don't know, but my memory of the line is mostly of the ups and downs, curves and tablet exchanges. What Charlie, and I suspect the majority of railwaymen who worked over the line, didn't know was that it was built in three separate sections, as we will record in due course.

It would have been nice to have seen the line in its Edwardian heyday including Broom, with its SMJ engines and stock, and Alcester with its junction with the GWR. It would even be nice to run over it again, but with the rails lifted it has gone for ever. The track is still in place at Barnt Green Main Line Junction and this is a fitting point to end my personal recollections of the Evesham branch, with a story of how I nearly caused a major accident. We had a train of coal empties, which we were working to Washwood Heath with the 'Night Redditch', and our engine was a 'Crab' 2-6-0. We were running tender-first and we had a full train. As we struggled to get away from Redditch Single Line Junction signalbox, where we had been brought to a stand by signals, we slipped continuously as we made our way along the platform towards the junction. As we approached the main line junction I'm sure that through the smoke I could see the signal at clear, which meant we had the road across the junction. Charlie was too busy opening and closing the engine regulator in an attempt to keep the train from stalling to look, as we were slipping so much, and he took my word for it. As we finally passed under the signal both Charlie and I saw the signal was on so he closed the regulator and stopped the train before fouling the main line and promptly set back inside the home signal. I was furious and went to the signalbox where the 'bobby' wanted to know what we were doing. I said that we had seen the peg (signal) at clear, but he said it wasn't. I will never know the truth, but I suspect, and Charlie agreed with me, that we spent so long crawling past the platform that the signalman replaced the signal to danger having been offered another train from Blackwell. Charlie Fennel the guard was not able to help as there was too much steam and smoke to enable him to see the signals at all. If I had not been so angry I should have looked at the train register to see what was recorded, but I did not think about it until much later.

Before leaving the Evesham Link perhaps I should recall a final story about Charlie Reay and his wangling. We had two Sunday jobs booked during the 12 weeks it took a set of men to go round the link, and, wherever possible, he tried to get us extra Sunday work. The normal procedure followed by the time-keeper's office at Saltley was that as men booked off on a Saturday morning they would be offered the available following Sunday's jobs not covered by crews booked to work that day. By midday all these jobs were generally allocated, so when Charlie and I booked on at 11.0 Saturday for a trip working we knew that we wouldn't finish until 7/0 that night, long after all the extra Sunday work had been allocated. Furthermore, we were due back at work again on Monday morning at 3.0, but this did not deter Charlie, who,

I'm sure, had 'an arrangement' with the foreman's assistant who allocated the work. We used to book off at 7/0 Saturday, return to work at 7.0 Sunday morning, book off at 3/0 Sunday, in time to take our 12 hours' rest in order to catch our 3.0 Monday morning job, a trip working on the Kingsbury branch. At Saltley, on these extra Sundays, our work was 'on shed' disposing engines and it was considered that the disposal of six locomotives constituted a day's work if you were on contract work. This meant that you would be prepared to dispose of six engines and when this was done, regardless of how long it had taken, you booked off under the guaranteed day arrangements, once you'd put 'six away'.

Having introduced the expression 'contract work' I ought to explain how it worked. Some sets of men were prepared to be available to work for eight hours disposing engines for men who were on overtime when they arrived at Saltley shed. At the start of a shift the men who were on contract work took the first engines awaiting disposal, if possible the driver and fireman taking one each. On Sunday mornings it was not unusual to see 12 or more engines, one behind the other, on the two arrival roads. When a driver and fireman took two engines they were usually coupled together.

As soon as all the contract men were at work any other engines that were to be disposed, that is coaled, tank filled, fire cleaned or dropped, ashpan raked out and smokebox emptied, were taken by the men not on contract work. If they were lucky the contract men who booked on at 7.0 could be on their way home by midday or even earlier, while the non-contract men would, or could, be there for eight hours. Whereas the contract men

disposed of six engines, the other men would consider themselves to be unlucky if they 'put away' more than two locomotives during their shift. Often, they may have disposed of just one locomotive and spent the rest of their shift marshalling engines in the shed yard area. It was a case of either hard graft, equal to 14 hours' pay for an actual 4½-5 hours' work, or easy work but staying on duty for eight hours, while also being paid for 14 hours (eight hours at time and three-quarters).

Naturally, Charlie Reay always opted for contract work but as usual he wangled it so that when we got our pair of engines and took one each, he always took the smaller one. He usually managed to have the Class 2F or 3F 0-6-0s while I always seemed to have the 'Crabs', Class 5s or 8Fs to deal with single-handed. But since I was 21 and he was close on 60 I guess it wasn't too unfair. I do recall the hours of work played havoc with my social life, but then he was quite a man and I enjoyed firing for him.

This is the 'Beckford' at Evesham during the late 1950s. The engine is No 43940, one of Saltley's ex-Midland Railway Class 4Fs but now running with an LMS Old Standard tender which has replaced the original Midland Railway design. Here, the train is quite light, with just nine vans and there is a man at the end of the train, but I am uncertain what he is doing, although he could be uncoupling the brakevan. The crossover is set for the train to shunt back into the sidings and the guard, standing in the 'four foot', a railwayman's term for the track, appears to be advising the driver what has to be done. I believe the train has just arrived from Beckford and that it is about to be made up along the lines that I have described in this chapter. *Milepost 92½ Library*

2
An Historical Review

It would be surprising if many of the railwaymen who worked on the Evesham branch knew that it was not built as a single railway. I recall wondering why the northern end of the line, from Evesham to Barnt Green was single with passing loops, while the southern end was double track. Furthermore, the single line seemed to carry more traffic, but the words, "Twas ever thus' summarised all the answers that I received whenever I asked any of my drivers about various historical aspects of the railway. I knew that it was the LMS until the end of 1947 and that in the far distant past it was the Midland Railway, but that company had ceased to exist before I was born. It was not until many years later that I found the study of the origins and development of the various railway companies answered many of the hitherto unanswered questions that I had had when I worked on the railway. It is for this reason that I recommend that those who wish to enjoy a serious study of the British railway system should go back in time and study the origins and development of the network.

This railway, from Barnt Green to Ashchurch, was really three separate undertakings and we will consider the origins of each, beginning with the Redditch Railway. The Act that authorised the construction of this part of the railway received Royal Assent on 23 July 1858 and it was opened to passengers on 19 September and to goods on 1 October 1859. Built as a single-line railway, it ran from the junction at Barnt Green, on the Midland Railway's Birmingham & Gloucester Railway, to the terminus in Redditch. The estimated cost of £35,000 was deemed to be the capital and it was divided into 3,500 £10 shares with powers to borrow a further £11,500. The company was leased to the Midland Railway on incorporation and it was dissolved and transferred to the Midland in 1863, merging with the Midland under the Midland Railway (Additional Powers) Act 1874.

According to the Act the connection with the Midland Railway at Barnt Green had to be effected in a substantial manner by rails and points to the satisfaction of the Midland Railway engineer. The necessary signals at the junction were to be erected and worked by watchmen, switchmen and others appointed by the Midland Railway, the cost to be borne by the Redditch Railway. There were some detailed clauses in the Act that protected the rights of the proprietors of the Worcester & Birmingham Canal, which was crossed by the railway at Alvechurch.

The rates that could be charged for the various traffics make interesting reading: first class passengers were carried at 3d per mile, second class at 2d, and third class at 1d. The free luggage entitlements were 120lb, 100lb and 60lb respectively.

The second railway to be built was the Ashchurch & Evesham Railway. This line was built by the Midland Railway from the junction with the Birmingham & Gloucester Railway at Ashchurch to the terminus at Evesham under the powers granted by the Midland Railway (New Lines) Act 1861. The railway was opened to goods on 1 July and to passengers on 1 October 1864. The contractors were Brassey & Ballard and the resident engineers were Messrs Hall and Bird.

The Evesham & Redditch Railway filled the gap between the two railways. The powers that authorised the construction of this line were those granted under the Evesham & Redditch Act 1863. The railway was leased to the Midland Railway upon incorporation and vested in the Midland by the Midland Railway (Additional Powers) Act 1882. The opening dates were: between Alcester and Evesham for goods on 16 June and

The Worcester & Birmingham Canal was crossed by the Redditch Railway at Alvechurch but no pictures of the original bridge have come to light. This picture, taken in March 1909, shows the new bridge that was built by the Midland Railway to replace the original structure. *Collection V. R. Anderson*

The Redditch Railway was the first part of the Evesham branch to be opened and is now the only section still in use. The total distance from Barnt Green Main Line Junction to the terminus at Redditch was about five miles and there was only one intermediate station, at Alvechurch. This station remains open today, but on a different site from that shown here. This undated picture of Alvechurch was taken when the photographer was facing towards Redditch. The far end of the platform is at a higher level and the slope between the two levels can be seen. I have not been able to establish when the platform was extended and it is possible that the far end was the original platform; the stationmaster's house was at that end of the station. There was also a stile and footpath at the south end of the station. *Collection R. J. Essery*

The first terminus of the Redditch Railway was in Clive Road and this early 1900s picture shows the exterior of the building. Another view of the closed station will be found in Chapter 3. *Collection Philip Jarvis*

The tunnel to the south of Redditch, on the Evesham & Redditch Railway, was the major engineering work on the line. This 1962 picture shows an Ivatt Class 2MT 2-6-0 at the head of a passenger train for Evesham and Ashchurch. The gradient of 1 in 120 before and then through the tunnel was not a problem for passenger trains, but for a mineral train, which had to stop for water at the end of the platform, it was a different matter. *M. Mensing*

The section from Evesham to Alcester on the Evesham & Redditch Railway was opened in 1866 and the line from Alcester to Redditch was opened on 4 May 1868. For almost two years Alcester was the terminus of the line from Evesham and Ashchurch. The station building at Alcester, with the stationmaster's house, was a generous building and this 19 April 1959 picture shows the exterior from the approach road. *H. C. Casserley 18639*

passengers on 17 September 1866, and between Redditch and Alcester to all traffic on 4 May 1868.

A number of historical papers about these three railways have survived and they form the basis of this chapter, beginning with the Redditch Railway. On 26 August 1859 a letter was sent to the Board of Trade together with a copy of an agreement that 60% of the shareholders of the Midland and Redditch railways had assented to at a special meeting held for that purpose. This agreement has been reproduced in full.

The copy of this agreement, which was on file at the Board of Trade and is now at the PRO Kew, is not dated but the reply from the Board has been found. This was dated 26 August 1859 and it gave approval to the agreement that detailed the working arrangements for the railway.

Memorandum of Agreement Between the Midland Railway Company and the Redditch Railway Company

1. The Midland Railway Company shall work and maintain the Redditch Railway for the term of ten years from the opening of the line for traffic.
2. Except in cases arising from faulty construction the Midland Railway shall be responsible for any accident which may occur in the working of the traffic.
3. The Midland Company shall out of the gross receipts of the Redditch Company pay the interest upon the debenture debt of £11,500 of the Redditch Company which shall be the first charge upon such gross receipts and shall after retaining the said interest pay £50 per cent [sic] of such gross receipts to the Redditch Company but should such £50 per cent [sic] be insufficient to pay the said interest in any year the Midland Company shall retain the same out of the receipts of any subsequent year until the arrears of interest shall be fully paid. Should the Midland Company not have received the full amount of the said interest at the expiration of this agreement the balance shall be a debt due from the Redditch Company to the Midland Company.
4. That the daily number of trains to and from Redditch and Alvechurch shall be settled from time to time according to the requirements of the traffic.
5. The Midland Company shall pay all rates and taxes except Government duty, which shall be deducted from the gross passenger receipts.
6. Any disputes arising under this agreement shall be settled by arbitration in the way provided by the Company's Clauses Consolidation Act 1845.

The Ashchurch to Evesham railway was both promoted and built by the Midland Railway and the Board of Trade inspection report makes interesting reading. The file opens with a letter from the Secretary's office of the Midland Railway to James Booth, Secretary, Railway Department Board of Trade, Whitehall, London. Dated 16 May 1864 it was the normal month's notice that the railway companies were required to give prior to opening a new railway. Captain Tyler, Royal Engineers, in the company of E. M. Needham, Superintendent of the Midland Railway, Mr Ballard of the contractors and a number of other officials, inspected the line on Saturday, 8 July. The report was highly critical. On 11 July 1864 the Board of Trade sent the Midland Railway a copy of the report and confirmed the company should postpone the opening of the line for a period of one calendar month. Before setting out Captain Tyler's report it is worth recording what a contemporary newspaper, the *Evesham Journal*, had to say.

At the time that they went to press the inspector's report had not reached them but they were able to state that the contractors at the waiting rooms of Evesham station provided a sumptuous repast prepared by Mr Butler of the Star Hotel. The guests included the various railway officials and Captain Tyler. The newspaper reported that the line was open for goods traffic and that it was expected to be open for passenger traffic the following week. The congratulatory theme continued about prosperity for the town, the hope to see the line carried forward to Redditch, and finally they recorded an accident that had occurred on Friday the 8th inst, at Ashchurch. A 45-year-old navvy named Wood of Eckington who was employed upon ballasting the line near to the new station was moving between two trucks when he slipped and the truck moved and went over both of his legs. One of his legs was nearly cut through and the other was slightly injured. He was taken to Cheltenham Hospital where one leg was amputated. There was always a human cost to be paid in both the construction and running of the British railway system.

We come now to Captain Tyler's report; this is what he had to say.

Harvington was the first station from Evesham on the Evesham & Redditch Railway and this c1900 picture shows the station with the goods loop and short siding that ran behind part of the platform. The two cattle wagons can be recognised by the lime wash used to disinfect the vehicles; the others are various Midland Railway covered goods wagons. *Collection R. J. Essery*

'The junction at Ashchurch is temporary and the accommodation of a very inferior character. It is intended to form a permanent junction with the Tewkesbury line in the west as well as that to Evesham on the east of the present station: to complete the triangle by a third side directly connecting these two branches and crossing the main line on the level on the north of the present station, and to build a new station also to the north of the present station. The line to Evesham starts in the meantime from a very short platform with a single line for the arrival and departure at the back of the east platform at Ashchurch, and joins the main line north and south of that station; and if the incoming train from Evesham was to overrun the platforms by a few yards it would foul the main line. It is necessary that some better temporary arrangements should be made at this point, if the line is to be opened before the completion of the permanent junction. At Evesham also, a second line should be laid to the temporary station, by the side of the short portion of single line, which is now interposed between the double line in the station and the double line on the branch.

'The permanent way is of a substantial description. It is laid with double headed rails, 20ft long, weighing 80lb to the linear yard, and fished at the joints. The chairs are cast iron, weighing 34lb each and are secured to transverse larch sleepers by wrought iron spikes. The sleepers are stated to measure 9ft long by 10in x 5in and are placed 3ft apart. Some of the fish-bolts are missing, and many of them do not come through the nuts, and some keys are missing.

'The fencing is post and rail and is rather low in some places, as well as the gates and styles. They should all be made up over the whole line to a minimum height of 4ft.

'The different bridges under and over on the line have been carefully and substantially constructed, and they appear to be standing very well. The principal work is the viaduct over the

Avon, comprising two openings of 123ft 7in each on the skew and constructed with iron girders upon masonry abutments and a pier comprised of three cylinders in the river. These girders yielded deflections of about ¾in under rolling loads of rather more than a ton to the linear foot, including a permanent set about 1⁄16in. I have recommended a few extra cover plates should be added to this and one other new bridge.

'The intermediate stations on the line are admirably completed and the line is with the above exceptions in a very creditable condition; but I am obliged to report in this account that it cannot be opened, by reason of the incompleteness of the works, without danger to the public using it.'

There was a further exchange of correspondence between the Midland Railway and the Board of Trade and on 5 September 1864 the Midland Railway wrote to say the line was 'ready for the safe conveyance of passengers' and requested that an officer be appointed to conduct an inspection. The Board of Trade appointed Captain Tyler who made his inspection on 16 September 1864; part of his report has been reproduced below.

'I find that the temporary station at Ashchurch has been improved by the addition of a second line of rails, and a second platform, so that the trains arriving from Evesham will not now be in danger of fouling the main line. A buffer stop has also been

Above:
In Capt Tyler's report he stressed concern about the viaduct over the River Avon and this picture shows the structure that he reported had 'two openings of 123ft 7in on the skew'. The original timber deck was replaced in 1928/9 when the LMS strengthened the viaduct and installed a concrete floor. This picture, taken 8 April 1924, also shows, in the right background, the GWR engine shed at Evesham. *Collection V. R. Anderson*

Right:
This c1904 picture was taken from the Redditch end of Evesham station. The 'six wheels coupled' goods engine's lamp holders are in the post-1903 position. The home signal on the short post, shown in Fig 43, on the platform side of the overbridge, cannot be seen in the photograph on page 93. *Collection R. J. Essery*

Right:
The reporter of the *Evesham Journal* who said: 'they are equal in point of accommodation the appliances for the comfort of travellers, to any in the kingdom', praised the stations on the Ashchurch to Evesham line. They were certainly well built as this exterior view of Ashton-under-Hill, taken on 8 May 1945, shows. *H. C. Casserley 58528*

Above:
Ashchurch was the starting point of the line that the Midland Railway built to Evesham and this view, dated 8 September 1949, shows the branch with the single platform face on the right of the picture. The Birmingham to Gloucester main line, mostly hidden behind the signalbox, is in the centre, while the line to the left is the branch to Tewkesbury and Malvern. *H. C. Casserley 58530*

Left:
The line between Evesham Junction and Tewkesbury Junction was opened on 1 October 1864 and crossed the Birmingham & Gloucester on the level. Although originally built as double track, it was singled by 1927. This picture shows Fowler Class 4MT 2-6-4T No 42326 on this line on 9 September 1949. *H. C. Casserley 58560*

Left:
If there had been an engine shed at Ashchurch then it would probably have been close to where this locomotive is standing. This picture was taken on 18 June 1960 and shows Class 4F No 44180 from 15D Bedford after arriving with the 5.10pm passenger train from Birmingham. It seems likely that the foreman at Saltley 'borrowed' the engine for this turn of duty. This also shows the platform that was used for Evesham branch arrivals and departures. Empty stock between duties could be stored in the siding as shown, although some pictures show that carriages were also kept in the siding by the goods shed. *M. Mensing*

provided at the end of the new line, and a crossover road by which the engines may be disengaged from the carriages on arrival of the trains.

'The fish-bolts have been changed which were too short, and the fencing has been improved, as well as the gates and styles by being lifted or otherwise increased in height. A little more improvement is desirable in this respect in a few places, and is to be at once carried out.

'The line has been doubled near the Evesham station as I recommended. No alteration has been made in the cover plates of the wrought iron bridges. After further consideration and discussion in this subject, having regard to the particular construction of the bridges and the difficulty of satisfactorily making the alteration, I am not disposed to press it in this instance, though I should be glad to see this difficulty that I have pointed out avoided in the future.

'Some short portions of fencing at one of the stations which were too near the rails are to be removed tomorrow morning, and adjusting screws [the wording is not entirely clear, but in effect it was to improve the working of the wires to the distant signals]. I am now able to report my opinion that this section of railway may be opened for traffic without danger to the public using it.'

The newspaper coverage of the opening of the line for passenger traffic was a single paragraph; this is what it said:

'The difficulties hitherto in the way of the opening of the Evesham and Ashchurch Railway for passenger traffic have been overcome and it is now finally decided that the line will be formally opened on the first of October next. The new iron bridge over the River Avon was the greatest obstacle to the passing of the line by the government inspector, Captain Tyler. Yielding at length, however, to the representations of the engineers and officials of the Midland Railway Company, and to the opinions of other eminent engineers as to the safety of the structure, Captain Tyler again went over the line yesterday, and has consented to it being used for passenger traffic. Arrangements will therefore be made for the opening on the day as above stated.'

The official records show that the Midland Railway opened the line for goods traffic on 1 July 1864 and these reports explain why it was not opened for passenger traffic until 1 October. Before leaving this railway it is worth recounting the article written by a reporter of the *Evesham Journal* who went on the first passenger train to travel over the line. He began by praising the quality of the work carried out and wondering why the inspector was not able to pass the iron bridge over the River Avon on his first inspection. He made some interesting statements, saying, 'in terms of accommodation at the stations this little branch line is truly described as a 'pattern line'.' He went on to say: 'If the Redditch extension is carried out in the same style the district would be fortunate and may boast of a railway equal, in point of accommodation and the appliances for the comfort of travellers, to any in the kingdom.'

At Evesham, where there was a temporary station, the reporter stressed that while the public appreciated what had been achieved so far, success would only be complete when the line was extended through to Redditch. I have not determined when the permanent station was opened, certainly it was not on 1 October. His report continued with a description of the railway south from Evesham to Bengeworth. The station, less than two miles from Evesham, was in the parish of Hampton. It appears that the local inhabitants did not like what the reporter

described as 'the arbitrary suppression of the name Hampton and substitution of the name Bengeworth because there were a great number of stations with the name Hampton on the Midland lines.' There was in fact only one in Warwickshire. From his report it appears that the opening of the line was cause for much celebration, with bands, floral tributes, church bell ringing, feasting, dancing and speeches.

We can now consider the railway that was to provide the link between the northern and southern branches, namely the Evesham & Redditch Railway Company. By good fortune, a copy of the Heads of Agreement between the Evesham & Redditch and Midland Railway companies has survived, but first I must record the background to the story.

Dated 20 April 1867, this document was submitted to the Board of Trade by the solicitors acting for the Evesham & Redditch Railway Company. The covering letter confirmed that the Heads of Agreement had been approved by the shareholders of both companies and that it was not proposed to execute any formal agreement in as much as the agreement would simply be a copy of the Heads with the omission of the last clause. The letter continued by saying that, as Mr Bullen was now dead, the last clause was inoperative. The writer, whose signature appears to be Jasmond, continued by asking that the Board of Trade treat the Heads as an agreement and to limit it to a term of ten years from the date of the Heads of Agreement.

I have reproduced the extract from the *Daily News* of 12 February 1869 that shows the agreement was approved at a

half-yearly meeting of the Midland Railway held on Monday, 22 February 1869.

Although the Midland Railway owned the line from Barnt Green to Ashchurch, two other railway companies formed junctions with it. The most important was the Stratford-upon-Avon & Midland Junction Railway which was formed on 1 January 1909 by the fusion of the East & West Junction, the Stratford-upon-Avon, Towcester & Midland Junction and the Evesham, Redditch & Stratford-upon-Avon Railway companies. After 1909, the Midland Railway Distance Diagrams describe this railway at Broom as the Evesham, Redditch and Stratford-on-Avon Section of the Stratford-on-Avon Junction Railway. In 1892, when the events about to be described took place, the line was shown on the company letterhead as East & West Junction

There was a small engine shed at Tewkesbury which was about two miles from Ashchurch. This was the servicing point for engines that required to visit a shed, although most locomotives on turnback passenger work from Birmingham would stay at Ashchurch. Johnson '3F' 0-6-0 No 43506 was on shed, 9 September 1949. *H. C. Casserley*

Although not of the best quality, this picture is historically important. It illustrates SMJR 0-6-0 No 14 at Broom Junction about to depart for Stratford-upon-Avon. The method of working was simple. The Stratford line train arrived in the up line platform and the passengers with their luggage alighted from the train and waited on the platform. The train was set back onto one of the sidings by the turntable and the locomotive was turned and recoupled to the coaches. While this was taking place the up and down Midland trains arrived and their passengers for stations on the Stratford line alighted and the passengers from the Stratford line joined the Midland trains. After the Midland trains had departed, the SMJR train ran into the platform and while the passengers joined the train the engine ran round and was coupled to the train in readiness to depart for the Stratford line. *Collection R. J. Essery*

and Stratford-on-Avon, Towcester & Midland Junction Railway.

Although the line between Evesham and Redditch was opened in 1868, the junction at Broom was not built until 1879 and the date that the station was opened for non-advertised passenger traffic is generally accepted as being 2 June 1879. It is clear from Major Marindin's report that at first the method of working was rather primitive to say the least. This is not really surprising, as some of the early British railway operating practices as far as brakes, signalling and interlocking were concerned, were very dangerous. It was the 1889 Regulation of Railways Act that finally brought about the end of working methods similar to those referred to in the report.

On 20 October 1892 the Midland Railway wrote to the Board of Trade to request that the resignalling arrangements at Broom Junction be inspected. The Board replied on 22 October advising that Major Marindin had been appointed to carry out the inspection. His report, reproduced here, makes interesting reading and again reveals some of the very primitive practices that still applied to parts of the British railway system at the beginning of the final decade of the 19th century.

Major Marindin wrote:

'I have inspected the resignalling arrangements at Broom Junction on the Midland Railway. At this junction the single line from Stratford-on-Avon to Broom joins the Midland Railway Company's single line from Redditch to Evesham.

'At the time that the line from Stratford-on-Avon was made a loop was constructed on the Midland Railway with an island platform and the junction was formed as a double junction; but this loop has never been used as a passing loop and the Midland traffic has been conducted along one line, the Stratford trains running across the Midland line to the other side of the platform. The Midland line was worked with a train staff, but Broom was not a staff station, while the staff working on the Stratford line ended at the junction. Consequently the Stratford train came on to the middle of a staff section of the Midland line once used for the purpose of putting the engines round their trains.

'In order to put an end to this dangerous mode of working Broom Junction has now been made a passing loop, train tablet working has been adopted on the Midland line, and the station has been resignalled so that trains run upon their proper lines.

'The North signal cabin contains six working levers and two spare levers and the junction cabin, a new one, contains 20 working levers and four spare levers. There have been no alterations in the connections with the permanent way. I can recommend that the use of the new resignalling arrangements may be sanctioned.

'My visit to this place was hurriedly arranged, I did not have any notice of the East & West Junction Railway Company, the owners of the line from Stratford, but the attention of this company should be called to the state of their lines at the Junction, to which my inspection did not extend. On the few

Double-headed trains on the Evesham branch were not usual and I suspect that this occasion, captured at Broom Junction, was to 'save a block'. This was a railwayman's expression to describe economical working whereby two engines travelled as one train. The train engine is an 0-4-4T, the pilot is a Class 2 0-6-0, originally described as a 'single-frame goods engine'. The coaches are Clayton bogie vehicles. There is another goods engine on the sidings to the right and this is probably the SMJR train about to return to the platform where it will run round before returning to Stratford-upon-Avon. It is worth noting in this c1923 picture that the line to the turntable is in good condition. *Collection Roger Carpenter*

lines of which I did inspect I noticed two very bad rails, quite unfit for use, and one joint with one fish plate bolt missing and a second with two missing, both are one side of the joint, a most dangerous condition of things.'

On 29 November the Board of Trade wrote to both the Midland and East & West Railway Company. The Midland were told that the work was sanctioned and the East & West were asked what steps they proposed to take to remedy the dangerous condition of things to which their attention had been drawn. This letter was acknowledged on 30 November and a second letter dated 3 December 1892 confirmed 'the portion of this line referred to has been re-laid with new steel rails'.

The other junction on the line of railway between Barnt Green and Ashchurch was at Alcester where the Alcester and Bearley branch of the Great Western effected a junction to the north of the station. Originally known as the Alcester Railway it was authorised on 6 August 1872 and it was opened on 4 September 1876. From the outset the Great Western Railway worked the line and this included running powers into the Midland Railway station. The Alcester Railway was finally taken over by the Great Western on 1 July 1883.

Above:
This Redditch street scene dates from c1905 and is a view looking down Alcester Street. *Collection Alan Foxall*

Above right:
This picture of Alcester Street was taken c1905 and the photographer was looking towards St Stephen's Church. The row of shops on the right is still there today. *Collection Alan Foxall*

Right:
Evesham Street c1905, looking towards The Parade. All the buildings in this picture were demolished to make way for the Kingfisher Shopping Centre. *Collection Alan Foxall*

A number of Fowler Class 3P 2-6-2Ts were used on the branch and this view of No 16 shows a passenger train on the up line at Barnt Green on 12 July 1939. The three-coach set, almost certainly made up of a brake third, composite and brake third, is a Redditch to Birmingham New Street train. *H. C. Casserley 42488*

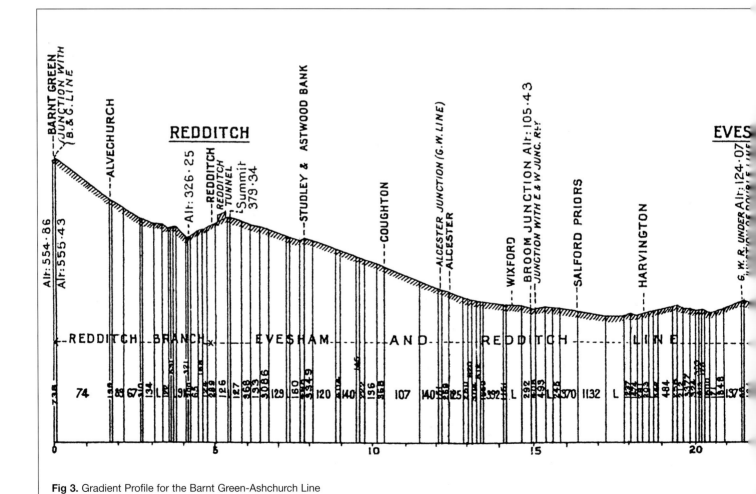

Fig 3. Gradient Profile for the Barnt Green-Ashchurch Line

3
The Railway Described

To enginemen at Saltley the west road from Birmingham to Gloucester and beyond offered a choice of route: the line via the Lickey was the original railway and understandably it was known as the 'old road'; a second route was via Worcester and this took trains over the GWR. To follow this route trains turned west at Stoke Works Junction and rejoined the 'old road' at Abbots Wood Junction. The third line, and the subject of this book, was built as three separate railways and ran from Barnt Green to Ashchurch via Evesham. As we have seen, these three railways were all joined end on to form a continuous route. I have described the origin of these railways in Chapter 2, and for the purpose of this and the final chapter they will be considered as being part of the Midland Railway.

Although it was not an official description, the Evesham branch was the name used by railwaymen and I do not propose to use any other name for this line of railway. From Barnt Green Main Line Junction to Evesham Line Junction, Ashchurch the

line was 33 miles long. The rather busier northern section was mostly single line, while the line south of Evesham to Ashchurch was a double line. In order to describe the railway I propose to use words that a railwaymen would use. Engine crews took a tablet for the single line at Barnt Green Single Line Junction signalbox and gave it up at Redditch North. The section from there to Redditch South was double track where another tablet was taken for the single line to Studley where tablets were exchanged. However, if the signalbox was closed, the tablet was for Alcester. A tablet taken at Studley would cover the section through Coughton to Alcester where there was a passing loop and tablets were exchanged again. Continuing south over the single line trains ran through Wixford before coming to the junction at Broom where there was a passing loop and a further tablet exchange. The section from Broom south through Salford Priors and Harvington was a section and while tablets were exchanged, there was no passing loop at Harvington. The final section was 3½ miles on to Evesham where the tablet was surrendered; the railway was double track for the remainder of the route to Ashchurch.

In summary, there were passing loops at Redditch, Alcester and Broom. The distances were approximately 4½ miles from Barnt Green to Redditch, 8 miles between Redditch and Alcester and 3¼ miles from Alcester to Broom, with a final 6½ miles from Broom to Evesham. Finally, it should be noted that tablets were exchanged at block posts that did not have passing loops. These were at Studley and Harvington, this enabling the headway between trains travelling in the same direction to be reduced. The single-line section between Barnt Green and Evesham was 22 miles of railway in all.

The gradients were considerable and can be seen on the diagram reproduced here. The description of the road, going south, was downhill from Barnt Green to just before Redditch North signalbox where there was an uphill length through the station and then through the narrow single-bore tunnel which lay just beyond the station. This continued to a point where the line began to run downhill again, this continuing to Wixford. The line through Broom and Harvington was mostly level, followed by a dip down and then a climb into Evesham. There was a further climb to a point roughly halfway between Hinton and Ashton before running downhill to Ashchurch. That's roughly the way an engineman would describe the road to a fellow driver and the niceties of the actual gradients would be largely ignored. Coming north, and if asked to describe the road, I would have said that it was slightly uphill from Ashchurch to a point south of Hinton then down to Evesham. From Evesham it was downhill at first and then a steady pull through Broom, steepening to Alcester and up to a point just south of Redditch Tunnel before running down to the platform at Redditch. After Redditch it was uphill to Barnt Green Single Line Junction with the last couple of miles being quite steep. It was a 'steam and brake' railway.

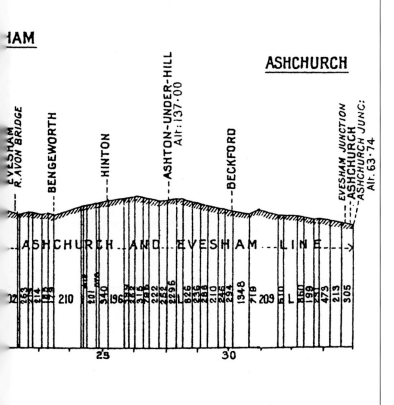

Another operating factor for steam locomotives was the availability of water. There were water columns or cranes at the ends of the platforms at Redditch and Evesham; both stations were a booked water stop for many through trains and this will be seen in the tables reproduced in Chapter 4. In addition, there was also the question of turning tender engines. There was a turntable at Broom Junction, which was used mostly by trains working off the Stratford-upon-Avon line, this going out of use sometime after the mid-1930s. There were no facilities at Redditch after c1903 and any locomotive at that point requiring to be turned would have to go to either Evesham or Bournville although it would have been possible to turn on the curve at Lifford (near Bournville) if need be. For a number of years there was a turntable at Barnt Green but the exact date that it ceased to be used is unknown to me. As soon as suitable tank engines became available for the trains that terminated or originated there it was not required. After the south connection was put in at Broom it was also possible to turn on the triangle which this line created. There was a 42ft turntable at Evesham which remained in service until the final years of steam and finally there was the opportunity to turn an engine on the triangle at Ashchurch.

The line of railway from Barnt Green to Ashchurch via Evesham fulfilled a number of distinct functions. In a purely local sense it provided a route which enabled both passenger and goods traffic from either Barnt Green or Ashchurch or any intermediate station to travel between points along the line. In addition, it enabled both passengers and goods to move from any station along the line to destinations beyond either Barnt Green or Ashchurch and, in the reverse direction it enabled originating traffic from beyond to arrive at destinations on the line. The junction with the GWR at Alcester was very much local in nature but the connection with the SMJR at Broom was always far more important and in particular during the wartime period, after the south junction was installed, was also a valuable part of the

railway. A final use, the value of which cannot be overestimated, was as a relief facility for the operational bottleneck on the old line between Bromsgrove and Blackwell. When the Birmingham & Gloucester Railway was built the line of railway was taken straight up the side of the Lickey Hills, just over two miles of 1 in 37¾, where even today some trains still require rear-end banking assistance. This applies to freight trains worked at night and the banking engine is usually a Class 60. During the era of the traditional steam railway just about everything going 'up the hill' needed a banker and virtually all goods trains in the down direction stopped to pin down brakes before proceeding down the incline. The railway between Bromsgrove at the bottom of the incline and Blackwell at the top was only a double line and there was a limit to the number of trains which could be worked over the section between Blackwell and Bromsgrove in a given time. Therefore it was helpful if some through trains could be diverted away from the Lickey Incline by running over the Evesham branch.

The northern end of the Ashchurch to Barnt Green line was largely single track so it had a lower line capacity than the Evesham to Ashchurch section. Nevertheless it was possible to diagram some through workings in between the local traffic and these through trains bypassed the Lickey Incline. In railway terms the railway was a relief or loop line, which helps to explain the term 'Birmingham to Gloucester loop' that has been used by some to describe this railway.

I propose to devote the remainder of this chapter to a station-by-station description and to travel along the line in the down direction, beginning at Barnt Green. Although most of the descriptions will apply to the latter part of the line's history, during my research into the subject some early material has come to light and this has also been included.

Unfortunately, not every station's early records have survived which explains why the coverage of the stations is somewhat varied.

Barnt Green

The total length of railway from Barnt Green Main Line Junction to Ashchurch was 33 miles. Prior to the opening of the Redditch Railway the name of the station was changed from Barnt Green, used from the opening on 1 May 1844, to Barnt Green for Redditch. This change, dating from 1 June 1857, was short-lived, the name becoming 'Barnt Green for Bromsgrove Lickey' at some date before 1 January 1863. On 1 July 1868 the name reverted to Barnt Green. Although the Redditch Railway opened for passenger traffic on 19 September 1859, the signalbox at the junction did not open until 1869. Until then the signal and point control was as described in Chapter 2.

Above:
This Edwardian period picture shows the up platform with the Midland Railway station sign, 'Barnt Green, junction for Redditch and Evesham'. The letters were painted in white on an ultramarine blue board. The white-painted wooden fence displays a number of enamelled advertising signs typical of this period, and to the right the cattle dock has been freshly painted. The object of the photographer's attention is an express train heading towards Bristol. The pilot engine is a Johnson slide valve bogie single and the train engine also appears to be another of his 4-2-2 locomotives.
Collection R. J. Essery

Left:
This picture was taken from the footbridge that connected the platforms at the north end of Barnt Green station. The photographer was looking northwest towards Birmingham. Although not strictly accurate, enginemen at Saltley referred to the north and west roads when describing the routes they travelled from Birmingham. The Evesham branch was often described as 'down the ditch', derived from the name Redditch. To the right of the picture is the Evesham branch which had a facing connection for down trains from the main line. The pointwork is worth more than a passing glance; note how the connection from the up main line to the up goods line is separate from the connection from the Evesham branch to the up goods line. There is also a trailing crossover from the up to the down main lines, but I doubt if this saw much use. The main line home signal is also interesting; note the lower arms that repeated the aspect shown by the upper arms, ensuring enginemen had a clear view at all times unobstructed by the overbridge. *Joe Moss*

The section of the Birmingham & Gloucester Railway that ran through Barnt Green was opened in 1840 but there was a delay of a few years before Barnt Green station opened. According to Long and Awdry, *The Birmingham & Gloucester Railway*, published by Alan Sutton 1987, it was the gift of land by the Hon Mr Robert Clive MP that lead to the erection of a second class station comprising a station house, platforms, signal posts, stables and a large entrance gate. The district of Barnt Green was sparsely populated at the time and the directors of the Birmingham & Gloucester Railway did not think that a station was worth while. This may help to explain the staggered platform layout at the station and the fact that the connecting footbridge was not erected until 1895, but by that time the sale of land for house building was under way and the population of the area was increasing.

The earliest track plan layout that I have been able to find is similar to the layout reproduced at Fig 3. This, together with the pictures, shows the junction before the widening between Barnt Green and Halesowen Junction that was opened in 1930. There was a connection with the branch from the down main line at Barnt Green as well as a connection from the down slow lines, which also provided the connection with the Barnt Green goods yard. The branch began at the station and later there were two platform faces, both curving and on a falling gradient. The single line of the branch commenced at Barnt Green Single Line Junction signalbox, but prior to 1894 this was not so. In that year an additional 350yd of double track were laid and presumably the second platform face was added. The single line signalbox was first opened in 1883 and a replacement box, further south, was opened on 9 December 1894 following the extension of the running line. The original train staff and ticket working was replaced by an electric train token on 20 September 1891. The Evesham branch began by heading in a southeasterly direction then it turned due east and turning again it headed almost due south towards Alvechurch crossing the Worcester & Birmingham Canal.

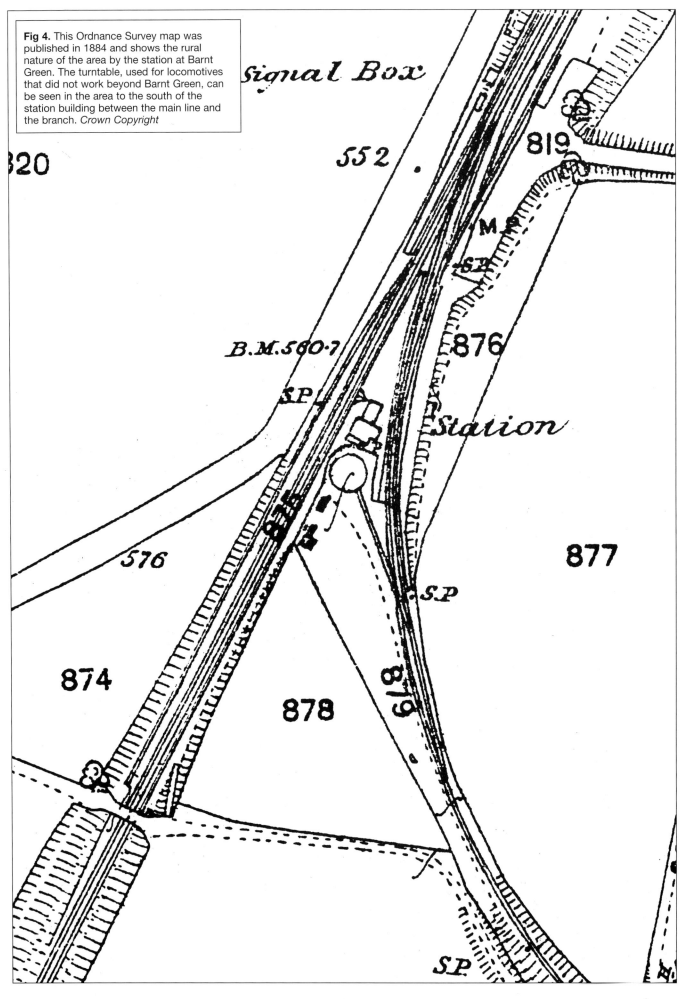

Fig 4. This Ordnance Survey map was published in 1884 and shows the rural nature of the area by the station at Barnt Green. The turntable, used for locomotives that did not work beyond Barnt Green, can be seen in the area to the south of the station building between the main line and the branch. *Crown Copyright*

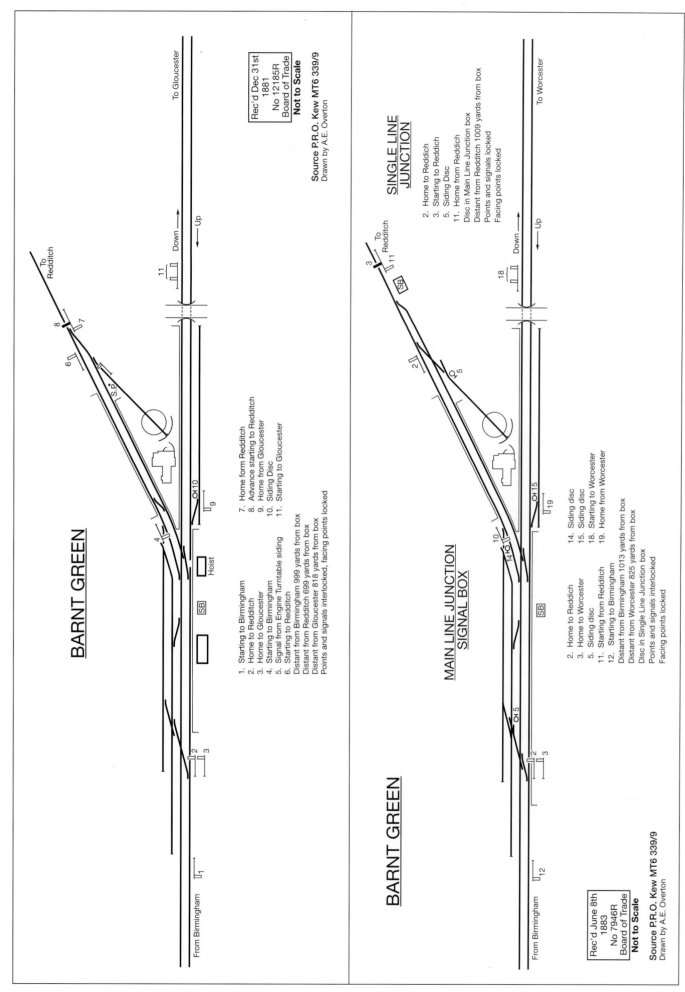

BARNT GREEN

To Redditch

To Gloucester

From Birmingham

Down

Up

SB

Hoist

S.P.

1. Starting to Birmingham
2. Home to Redditch
3. Home to Gloucester
4. Starting to Birmingham
5. Signal from Engine Turntable siding
6. Starting to Redditch
7. Home form Redditch
8. Advance starting to Redditch
9. Home from Gloucester
10. Siding Disc
11. Starting to Gloucester

Distant from Birmingham 999 yards from box
Distant from Redditch 699 yards from box
Distant from Gloucester 818 yards from box
Points and signals interlocked, facing points locked

Rec'd Dec 31st
1881
No 12185R
Board of Trade
Not to Scale

Source P.R.O. Kew MT6 339/9
Drawn by A.E. Overton

Fig 5.

BARNT GREEN

SINGLE LINE JUNCTION

MAIN LINE JUNCTION SIGNAL BOX

To Worcester

To Redditch

From Birmingham

Down

Up

SB

SINGLE LINE JUNCTION

2. Home to Redditch
3. Starting to Redditch
5. Siding Disc
11. Home from Redditch

Disc in Main Line Junction box
Distant from Redditch 1009 yards from box
Points and signals locked
Facing points locked

MAIN LINE JUNCTION SIGNAL BOX

2. Home to Redditch
3. Home to Worcester
5. Siding disc
11. Starting from Redditch
12. Starting to Birmingham
14. Siding disc
15. Siding disc
18. Starting to Worcester
19. Home from Worcester

Distant from Birmingham 1013 yards from box
Distant from Worcester 825 yards from box
Disc in Single Line Junction box
Points and signals interlocked
Facing points locked

Rec'd June 8th
1883
No 7946R
Board of Trade
Not to Scale

Source P.R.O. Kew MT6 339/9
Drawn by A.E. Overton

Fig 6.

Figs 5 and 6. On 30 December 1881 the Midland Railway wrote to the Board of Trade and forwarded a plan, from which this drawing (Figs 5 and 6) has been reproduced. The company sought approval for the new main line connections that it was to install and requested an inspection. These connections were a trailing crossover at the Birmingham end, from the up main line to the down main line and up side sidings. There was also a trailing connection from the sidings to both the down main line and the branch. The other connections for which approval was sought were the trailing crossover between the platforms, the slip points at the junction of the branch with the main line and the new connection between the up lie-by and the up main line.

Major Marindin was in the area engaged upon other inspection work and he wrote to the Board of Trade on 31 December to say that he had inspected this work. The signal cabin contained 22 levers and he wanted some interlocking changes. However, he continued: 'The turntable road to be worked from the cabin, fitted with safety points, and connected to the down not up loop line. A new signal cabin at the loop points is required. The Company should report when the requirements specified in the report have been complied with in order that a re-inspection may be made.' The Board of Trade wrote to the Midland Railway on 2 January 1882 advising the company of the requirements and the railway replied on 7 March inviting an inspection. The plan used to produce Fig 7 was enclosed.

Major Marindin made his inspection in June and his report was dated the 7th. His opening remarks are rather interesting. 'This is one of the places where new connections had been made at various dates since 1871 without being submitted for inspection.' There is evidence that at one time the company was somewhat cavalier in its attitude to the Board of Trade. He continued by saying, 'The loop upon the single line being too long for the facing points to be worked from the station cabin, a second cabin has been erected. The station cabin contains 20 levers of which three are spare, and the new cabin contains 12 levers of which four are spare.' He was satisfied and recommended that the use of the alterations be sanctioned. *(Figs 5 and 6 redrawn by A. E. Overton from original Midland Railway drawings at the PRO Kew.)*

Fig 7. This 1957 plan shows the final arrangements at Single Line Junction. Note the catch points worked by lever 8, with the fouling bar that prevented the points being moved if a train was standing on it. The face discs, described on page 37 have now been replaced by distant signals. Note that the Barnt Green plan, dated 1894, also seen on page 37. This was drawn to show the arrangements prior to the construction of the Up slow lines, by the date of this plan a distant signal, shown as part of the bracket that carries the Up starting signal 10, applied to these slow lines.
Drawing and notes by A. E.Overton

Barnt Green was close to the Lickey Hills, a popular beauty spot for the residents of Birmingham. As a child I remember being taken there by my mother, but rather than travel by train our journey was by tramcar. This evocative view of Barnt Green was taken from the bridge that spanned the main line from Birmingham to the west. To the left is the lie-by siding for up trains and prominent in the centre of the picture is the down platform. The up platform is just visible beyond the overbridge. For many years, Barnt Green was very rural as is evident in this picture. *Collection Jack Braithwaite*

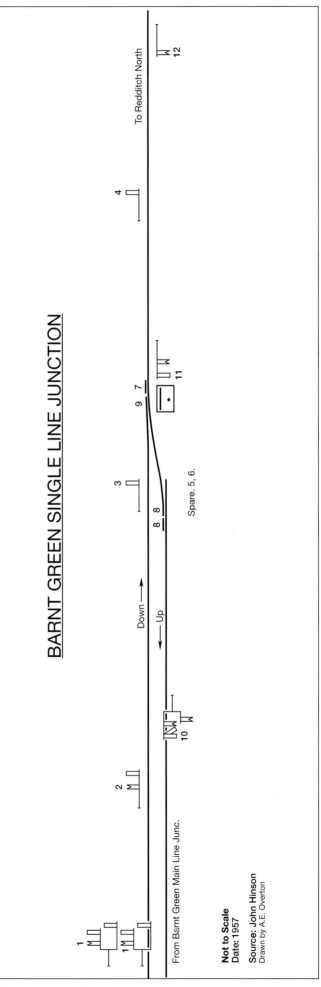

BARNT GREEN SINGLE LINE JUNCTION

To Redditch North

From Barnt Green Main Line Junc.

Not to Scale
Date: 1957

Source: John Hinson
Drawn by A.E. Overton

Fig 7.

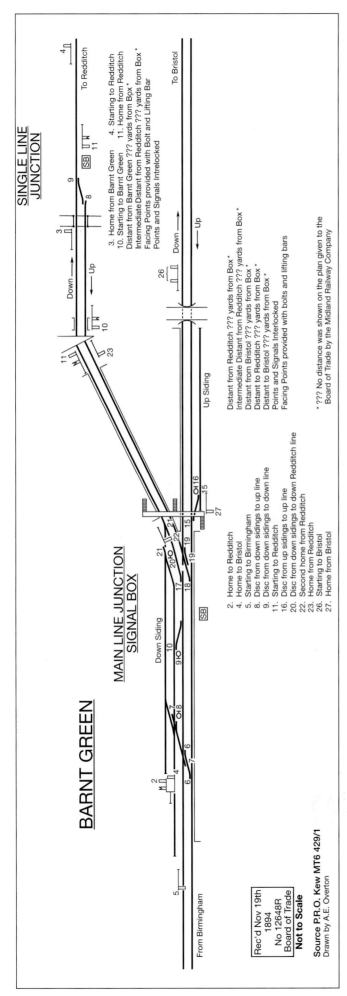

Fig 8.

Fig 8. The Midland Railway planned further changes in 1894 and the Company wrote to the Board of Trade on 16 November seeking approval for connections at Barnt Green, subject to an inspection. The Board of Trade replied on the 20th and confirmed the appointment of Major Marindin. However, there was a delay before the inspection could take place. The Midland Railway had to seek parliamentary powers in order to obtain some of the land required and the final work was delayed. The inspection was carried out on 8 February 1895 and Major Marindin reported that the loop on the single-line branch to Redditch had been lengthened by about 1/4 mile. He continued by stating that the station platforms had been improved, a footbridge connecting the platforms had been built and a new siding connection had been put in. In addition, the signalling arrangements had been revised, a bridge under the Redditch branch with a brick arch of 28ft span had been widened to carry the second line of rails, and he confirmed it was of substantial construction. The new cabin that was built at the end of the loop contained nine working levers with three spares, all correctly interlocked. He concluded by saying that some work still remained to be done on the down branch platform, but this could not be undertaken until powers to obtain the land had been completed. Nevertheless he recommended that the work be sanctioned. There were a number of letters exchanged between the Midland Railway and the Board of Trade and finally, on 28 January 1896, the company wrote to say that the alterations at Barnt Green station had now been completed. Although not specifically mentioned in the report, it would seem that the turntable was removed at this time and no further changes took place until the widening between Barnt Green and Halesowen Junction in 1930.

Note, the original Midland Railway drawing at the PRO Kew did not give the yards for the distant signals. However, the drawing has been reproduced here in a similar form as submitted to the Board of Trade. *Redrawn by A. E. Overton from original Midland Railway drawings at the PRO Kew.*

Face Disc

During the late 1800s on the Midland Railway, many closely-spaced signalboxes on relatively low speed sections of line were provided with 'Face Discs' worked from the signalbox in advance instead of the usual lineside distant signal.

The Face Disc consisted of a flat 5in brass disc engraved with a legend such as 'Down Distant On'. It was mounted on a bracket at windowsill height and when operated would simply flip over, indicating that the signalman in advance had cleared all his stop signals and that the signalman could now clear or pull off his distant signal, having already cleared his stop signals.

Regulations respecting the working of distant signals on a section of line between closely-spaced signalboxes where, due to the distant signal being fixed at a point that did not provide the required braking distance to the home signal, applied at Barnt Green, in so much as the Face Disc replaced the distant signal worked by the signalman in advance. The signalman of the box in rear had to wait for the signalman at the box in advance to clear his distant signal before he was allowed to pull off both his stop and distant signals; otherwise he must first wait for an approaching train to come nearly to a stand at his home signal before clearing it.

At Barnt Green Main Line Junction, as soon as the Face Disc worked by the signalman at Single Line Junction had been operated, the signalman at the Main Line Junction signalbox could, after setting the points for the Redditch branch, clear the down branch distant signal. This meant that the driver of an approaching Redditch train would know that the line was clear beyond Barnt Green Single Line signalbox.

In the up direction, as soon as the disc worked by the signalman at Barnt Green Main Line signalbox had been operated, the signalman at Barnt Green Single Line Junction, once he had cleared his stop signals, could pull off his up distant signal. This meant that the driver of an up train would know that the line was clear through and beyond Barnt Green Main Line signalbox.

In the majority of cases, from the early part of the 20th century, normal distant signals, fixed on posts below stop signal arms, replaced the Face Discs. *Notes by A. E. Overton.*

Above:
An Edwardian view of the junction at Barnt Green shows how the branch curved sharply away from the main line. At this period the goods lines had not been built so there was only one home signal from the branch. The passenger train on the down main line could be heading for either Worcester or Gloucester. *Collection R. J. Essery*

Left:
This lovely Midland Railway era view shows the third signalbox visible behind the people at the end of the down platform. This box was opened on 28 November 1897 and remained in use until 1929 when the replacement was opened, 100yd to the north. *Collection R. J. Essery*

The branch to Redditch from the junction at Barnt Green began with an up and down line between the platforms before becoming a single line. The platform was on a curve and the gradient was falling towards Redditch. When built, the line was single track but later a second platform was constructed with the passenger shelter seen here. In 1894, an additional 350yd of track were laid; the double track ended at Barnt Green Single Line Junction signalbox. This photograph is dated 1949. *Joe Moss*

Above:
In the final years of the branch, British Railways Standard locomotives were used. This undated picture shows 2-6-4T No 80063 from Saltley shed at Barnt Green heading an Ashchurch to Birmingham train.
P. Shoesmith, courtesy Philip Jarvis

Below:
When I was firing on the branch my driver recommended that I collected the tablet by thrusting my arm through the centre of the hoop which was attached to the pouch that contained the tablet for the section ahead. In this 18 June 1959 picture the driver of Ivatt Mogul No 43049, working the 12.57pm Birmingham New Street to Redditch, appears to be about to use the same method. The signalman always held the tablet up and away from himself and when tablets were exchanged at speed it was normal practice for the fireman, who usually did the exchange, to throw the tablet on the ground in front of the signalman. Note the raised platform and protective rail for the signalman. During the hours of darkness the only illumination was from the oil lamp. This arrangement was to be found at all the signalboxes where tablets were exchanged. *Roger Shenton*

Above:
The first signalbox at the junction of the single line was opened in 1883, but when the line was extended, as described previously, a new box was built further south with a 12-lever tumbler frame and was opened on 9 December 1894. This box was closed on 7 September 1969. At first, train staff and ticket controlled the trains between Barnt Green and Redditch, but on 20 September 1891 electric train tablet working was introduced. *Donald Powell*

Below:
The line between Barnt Green and Redditch was curved and on a falling gradient towards Redditch. This picture, dated 1 October 1921, shows the ¾ milepost in the centre of the picture.
Collection Roger Carpenter

Alvechurch

The line from Barnt Green to Alvechurch was on a falling gradient of 1 in 74 and the distance between these stations was 1 mile 66 chains. Alvechurch was opened for passengers on 1 November 1859, a few weeks after the line from Barnt Green to Redditch, which was opened on 19 September for passengers, and on 1 October 1859 for goods. This station remains open today as an unmanned halt. The present station, opened on 19 March 1993, is to the north of the original, which it replaced, on the site of the siding and closer to the road bridge. At Alvechurch there was a single siding capable of holding ten wagons with normal entry via a stage, but only for trains heading in the down direction, that is from Barnt Green to Redditch. Although no documents about Alvechurch appear to have survived, it was usual Board of Trade practice to insist upon entry to sidings that were on a gradient to have the locomotive at the lower end of the train, and this rule should have applied at Alvechurch. However, in the absence of the original Board of Trade inspection report it is possible that the opening of the railway may have preceded this rule and the Board was powerless to insist upon retrospective improvements of this nature. up direction trains with traffic for Alvechurch had to use a tow rope, and this was one of the places where this primitive method of shunting was permitted.

The use of a tow rope to place wagons into the siding from Up trains began with the train being stopped short of the entry into the siding. The guard's brake would be screwed down hard and the wagon or wagons that were to be towed were uncoupled from the train. These wagons would be attached to the engine by a long rope and the engine would move off towards Barnt Green and go beyond the points that made the connection between the main line and the siding. These points would be changed and with the rope pulling the wagons they would move into the siding. It was a dangerous practice and men could be injured if the rope broke under the strain.

When I knew the line, traffic from Alvechurch for destinations north of Barnt Green would be first taken to Redditch where it would be detached prior to joining a northbound service. Traffic from the Redditch direction for Alvechurch would be taken to Barnt Green where it would be detached in order to join the next stopping freight heading in the Redditch direction which was booked to stop at Alvechurch. This was much safer than tow roping.

The accommodation at Alvechurch was basic; the single siding catered for local deliveries or despatches together with agricultural roadstone traffic. At the Barnt Green end of the platform a small warehouse provided accommodation for such parcels and general merchandise traffic being worked into or away from the station, and which could not or should not be dealt with in the open. The only track plan that I have seen is shown here.

Fig 9. Alvechurch was in a rural setting and the line from Redditch, which was on a falling gradient of 1 in 74, eased to 1 in 199, before falling again at 1 in 89 through the station. Entry to the siding was via a ground frame, or as they were also known, a stage; the train tablet unlocked this. The driver, once he had the tablet, was in charge of the only train permitted in the section, so it was perfectly safe for the train to stop for shunting purposes. Furthermore, the tablet could not be recovered from the stage until the points had been returned to the correct position and the section could not be cleared for another train to enter until the tablet was returned to the signalman at the end of the section. The facilities at Alvechurch were very basic; there was a siding with a dock that held 10 wagons, and this was also used as a coal wharf. At the side of the approach road there was a weighing machine. The goods shed was on the platform without direct rail access and it was probably only used for 'smalls' and tariff traffic, while larger loads would be dealt with in the yard, being loaded or unloaded directly into road vehicles. See also the Rating Plan on page 43. *Crown Copyright*

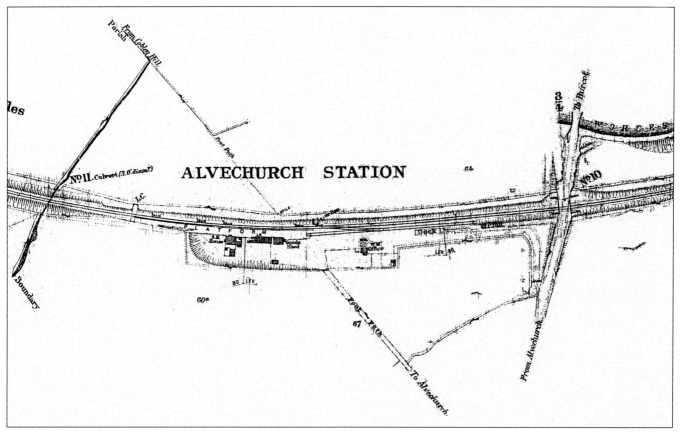

ALVECHURCH STATION

Fig 9.

Upper right:

This is the approach to Alvechurch as seen from the overbridge on the Alvechurch to Burcot road which was to the west of the station. Motor vehicles approached the station from this road but foot passengers from Alvechurch could use a footpath that provided a shorter route. The small goods yard, with the single siding, weighbridge and side-loading dock is clearly visible. Entry into the yard by a down train was made by stopping the train short of the trailing connection, uncoupling the wagons to be detached and pinning down the wagon brakes on the first two wagons at the head in order to hold the train on the falling gradient. Then the locomotive would draw the wagons forward that were to be detached and after the points had been changed they would be set back into the siding. However, if there were wagons to be picked up, they would be coupled to the wagons that were to be detached and all the wagons drawn forward on to the main line. When the engine and wagons were clear of the siding and standing on the main line, the points would be reversed. Then the locomotive would propel the wagons that had been picked up together with those to be detached back on to the train. The wagons that had been picked up would be coupled to the train and the brakes of the end wagon applied. The locomotive would draw forward again with the wagons to be detached, the guard would change the points and the driver would reverse the engine and propel the wagons into the siding. When these shunting moves had been completed the points would be reset, the engine coupled to the train and the wagon brakes released. After the points had been set for the main line the tablet could be removed from the stage and when the guard was ready the train could set off for Redditch. *J. M. Tolson*

Centre right:

Because the station was off the main road a large sign was erected by the overbridge. I don't know if this was a British Railways installation or if it replaced an earlier Midland or LMS sign. The palisade fence appears to have been recently repainted in this 23 April 1958 view. *H. C. Casserley*

The station buildings at Alvechurch are seen in this 11 May 1963 photograph, with the goods shed at the north end of the platform. The building in the centre contains the booking office, booking hall, ladies' waiting room and toilets. The building at the far end is the stationmaster's house. The corrugated iron hut is the stage, or ground frame, that contained the levers which were unlocked by the train tablet and enabled the train to enter the siding. This type of hut was normally used for toilet purposes and a drawing and description was published in *Midland Record 15*. A number of other stations on the line also used this type of building as a stage. The gradient post can be seen to the left of the buffer stops, and the coal merchant's hut carries the name A. Foster. The footpath and walkway, shown on the rating plan, can also be seen. The station nameboard was shown to be of the angled type in a 1929 photograph I have and so at some time it was replaced by the flat board seen here. There was also a chimney stack at this end of the goods shed and the post by the corner of this building originally held a gas lamp. *R. M. Casserley*

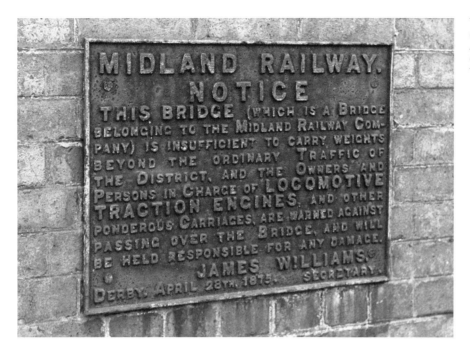

This Midland Railway sign was on an overbridge about half a mile south of Alvechurch station and was still in place there on 28 March 1964 when this picture was taken. *M. Mensing*

The British Railways Standard locomotives were ideal machines for working on the Evesham line as the cab arrangements meant it was not necessary to turn the engine so they could run tender-first. This 23 April 1960 picture shows a Class 4MT 4-6-0 No 75060 hauling the 5.32pm passenger train from Birmingham New Street to Redditch. The train is entering Alvechurch station and the Burcot road overbridge with the station sign can been seen on the skyline. Also visible is the public footpath at the end of the platform with the 'Beware of Trains' noticeboard. *M. Mensing*

Also taken on 23 April 1960, the last weekend of scheduled steam working north of Redditch, hauled by Ivatt 2-6-0 No 43047 the train is approaching Alvechurch station with the 5.10pm Birmingham New Street to Ashchurch ordinary passenger train. *M. Mensing*

Fig 10.

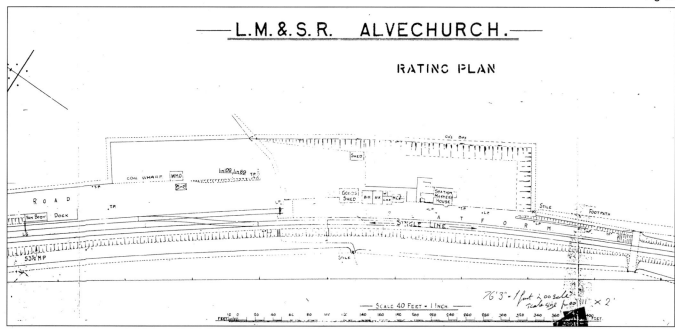

Fig 10. The 1926 Rating Plan for Alvechurch station. See also page 40. *Crown Copyright*

An undated view facing towards Barnt Green shows a deserted station with no staff in sight. There are a number of 16-ton steel-bodied coal wagons in the siding which means this photograph was taken after 1948. It is not clear how the station was illuminated as the three lamp posts do not have lamps on them. The change of platform height, noted in the illustration in Chapter 1, is prominent here. *Collection David Tee*

Baroness Windsor's Model Farm Siding

The Windsors were major landowners in the area and lived at Hewell Grange near Barnt Green. The Midland Railway wrote to the Board of Trade on 7 July 1873 enclosing a plan of a siding connection from its Evesham & Redditch line, for the accommodation of traffic to and from Baroness Windsor's Model Farm and sought permission for the siding to be opened. The Board of Trade replied and appointed Colonel Yolland to make an inspection.

Colonel Yolland's report was dated 14 July 1873. He said: 'I have the honour to report for the information of the Board of Trade, in compliance with the instructions contained in your minute of the 9th instant that I have inspected the siding connection constructed by the Midland Railway Company on their Evesham and Redditch branch line for the accommodation of the traffic to and from the Baroness Windsor's Model Farm near Redditch, and state that the points and signals are properly interlocked with each other, and to recommend that the sanction of the Board of Trade may be given for it's [sic] being opened for traffic.'

The Board of Trade advised the Midland Railway that the siding met with their approval. A reference in the Midland Railway Appendix No 11 issued on 18 April 1878 refers to it as not being a block post and only being opened as and when required. Later practice would have been to use a ground frame that would have been unlocked by a key at the end of the single-line train staff or a train tablet. When the frame was unlocked, access to the siding would have been possible and a signalbox would have been unnecessary. The arrangements would have been similar to those at Alvechurch, described above. I believe this is the signalbox at Alvechurch recorded by John Gough (*The Midland Railway, A Chronology*). He gives an opening date of pre-1 November 1875 and a closing date of 1885. This would have been when the siding and the signalbox were closed.

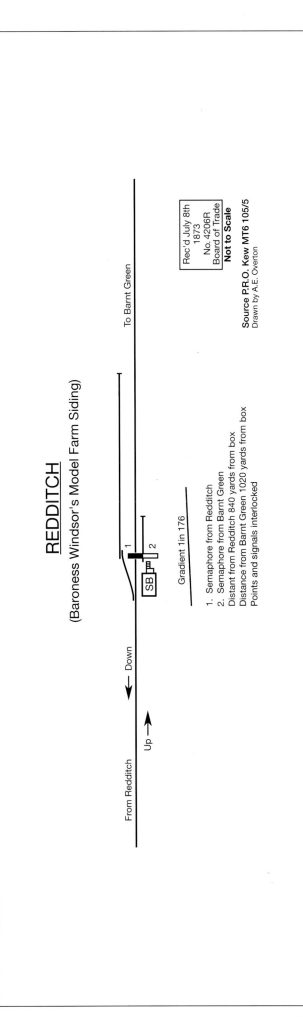

REDDITCH

(Baroness Windsor's Model Farm Siding)

To Barnt Green

From Redditch

← Down

Up →

Gradient 1 in 176

1. Semaphore from Redditch
2. Semaphore from Barnt Green
Distant from Redditch 840 yards from box
Distance from Barnt Green 1020 yards from box
Points and signals interlocked

SB

Rec'd July 8th
1873
No. 4206R
Board of Trade
Not to Scale

Source P.R.O. Kew MT6 105/5
Drawn by A.E. Overton

Fig 11

Redditch

According to the official guide to the Midland Railway, the distance from Redditch to Birmingham was 15½ miles and it reminded readers that the town overlooked the River Arrow. The distance from Alvechurch station to Redditch was 3 miles 19 chains. In the 19th century its principal claim to fame was that it was the centre of the needle and fishing tackle industry and by the early 1900s the population was about 15,000. Later, a large motorcycle and cycle factory was established and by 1951 the population had almost doubled. In railway terms Redditch was a goods, passenger and parcels station capable of handling furniture vans, carriages, portable engines and machines on wheels. I will use this Railway Clearing House classification for other stations because they are precise and spell out what traffic was dealt with at each location. In addition to those categories given above, Redditch could take livestock, horseboxes and prize cattle vans together with carriages by passenger trains. The resident crane power was 1½ tons, later upgraded to 10 tons c1940.

The first passenger station in Redditch was at Clive Road and this was opened on 19 September 1859. It closed when the Evesham & Redditch Railway opened on 4 May 1868, making an end-on junction with the Redditch Railway. The new station, which remained in service until 7 February 1972, was built 22 chains to the south of Clive Road station. In order to show the arrangements at Redditch I have used a number of documents beginning with the Board of Trade inspection report dated 17 October 1885. Colonel Rich RE inspected the new work, and the plan that the Midland Railway forwarded to the Board of Trade, as reproduced here, showed that other than the main line it was mostly new work. This suggests that prior to 1885 the railway was simply a single line from Alvechurch to the Redditch passenger station with just a junction to the gas works sidings. The inspector's report was brief; this is what he had to say. 'I have inspected the alterations at Redditch on the Midland Railway. The line at Redditch is a single line and a facing point connection, worked by means of an Annett's key, has been moved for some distance so as to be under the control of the signalman in Redditch Gas Sidings signalbox. This box contains 12 levers of which five are spare.' He concludes his report by recommending that the work be sanctioned. This plan is shown at Fig 12.

The LMS line diagram reproduced at Fig 13 dates from 1932 and illustrates the track layout during this period, and is the one that I knew. The problem with these diagrams is that they are not to scale, but they do provide readers with a good idea of the track layout, and for this reason they are extremely valuable. The accompanying OS map on page 47 illustrates the railway from the north tunnel mouth to the engine shed and it should be used in conjunction with the line diagram: this is Fig 15. The final plan to be used shows the arrangements at Redditch Gas Sidings, Fig 14. The Redditch Gas Company owned wagons that were painted black with white lettering and were used to deliver gas coal from the colliery to the gas works. I expect that the coke produced during gas making was sold locally and that road transport was used to move it from the gas works to the consumers.

With these various plans and drawings it is possible to see how the railway at Redditch developed. The original terminus was at Clive Road and Redditch ceased to be a terminus in 1868 when

A rare view of the first railway station at Redditch, which was situated in Clive Road. It opened to passengers on 19 September 1859 and to goods on 1 October. It was to remain open for passengers for less than ten years, closing on 4 May 1868, the date the new passenger station in Plymouth Road was due to open. The only facilities to remain in Clive Road were the locomotive shed, the old station building which became a cottage, and the old goods shed. Additional sidings were laid about 1939 to deal with increased traffic to the site at Pound Meadow, the name of the area where the second station was situated and where the goods depot was built after the Clive Road station was closed. *Collection Philip Jarvis*

Fig 12.

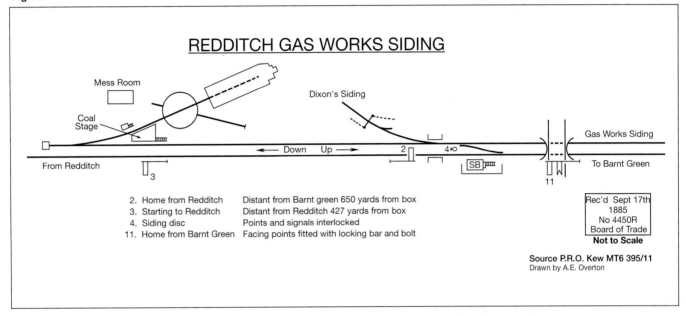

REDDITCH GAS WORKS SIDING

Mess Room

Coal Stage

Dixon's Siding

From Redditch

← Down   Up →

2   4

SB

Gas Works Siding

To Barnt Green

3

11

2. Home from Redditch Distant from Barnt green 650 yards from box
3. Starting to Redditch Distant from Redditch 427 yards from box
4. Siding disc Points and signals interlocked
11. Home from Barnt Green Facing points fitted with locking bar and bolt

Rec'd Sept 17th 1885
No 4450R
Board of Trade
Not to Scale

Source P.R.O. Kew MT6 395/11
Drawn by A.E. Overton

Fig 12. This drawing, based upon an original at the PRO Kew, was submitted to the Board of Trade by the Midland Railway and the substance of the inspecting officer's report is in the text. The line at this point was single and there was a facing connection for trains approaching from the Barnt Green direction. This led to a siding at the Redditch end which gave access to the engine shed where entry was over the turntable, to Dixon's Wharf and the gas works.
A. E. Overton

Right:
Redditch North signalbox was opened on 17 January 1926 and was photographed on 6 June 1976. According to John Gough's *Chronology*, this box was renamed Redditch prior to closure on 10 August 1986.
M. A. King

the original railway was connected to the new line that had been constructed from Evesham. The Redditch signalbox that existed from before 1875 was closed in 1885. The engine shed was opened c1872; the precise date is not known. However, the track layout can be seen at Fig 12. The gas works was rail connected at some date before 1877, and by then the Redditch Gas Works Siding signalbox was in service. A new signalbox was opened on 8 November 1925 and the old box was closed. The replacement signalbox was 120yd further south and the name was changed to Redditch North on 17 January 1926. It was to be renamed

Fig 13.

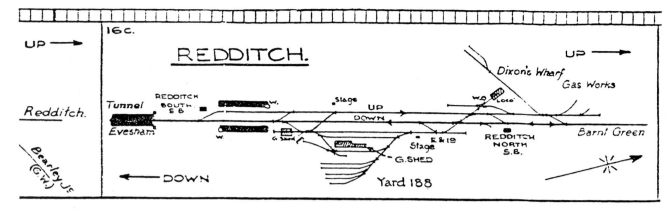

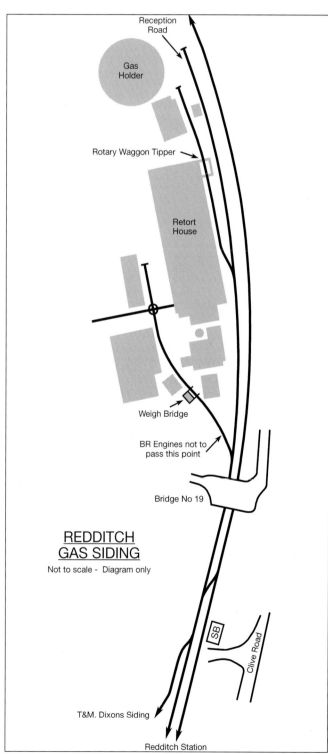

REDDITCH GAS SIDING

Not to scale - Diagram only

Fig 14.

Fig 13. (*Above*) This is an enlargement of the 1932 LMS diagram that illustrates the arrangements at Redditch. Although not to scale, these plans are extremely useful and they provide information about the track layout, position of water cranes, signalboxes and ground frames (shown as stages), siding capacity, etc. What they do not show is any sidings or lines that were not LMS property, for example the sidings in the gas works.

I cannot recall the work that we undertook when on the 'Night Redditch' but the method of working the sidings shown in this LMS diagram is straightforward. Down trains entering the yard would stop in the down platform and set back over the trailing connection into the goods yard running past the old goods shed. There was a run-round loop parallel to the main line so once trains were 'inside' and clear of the main line there would not be any reason to foul the main line when shunting. When the train was on the loop the engine could uncouple and run round the train shunting from the north end of the yard. A train for the down direction would be made up in the yard, drawn back into the shunting neck and propelled to one of the loops. The engines would run round and depart over the connection to the main line at the old goods shed end of the yard.

Up trains entered the yard by setting back over the trailing crossover by the loco shed and on to the loop. This would have the engine at the correct end for shunting and when the train was ready to depart it would draw forward over the crossover to the up line.

Fig 14. (*Left*) An undated drawing showing the arrangements at Redditch gas works. Note that British Railways locomotives were not allowed to go as far as the weighbridge but they were able to shunt wagons up to the rotary wagon tippler.

Fig 15. (*Right*) This extract from the Ordnance Survey map should be compared with the LMS diagram shown above. The engine shed can just be seen at the extreme left of the map and Dixon's Wharf is almost parallel to the main line and not as shown on the LMS diagram. Nevertheless, when both maps are considered together a complete picture can be seen. *Crown Copyright*

Redditch before it was closed on 10 August 1986. There had been a previous Redditch North signalbox that was opened in 1885, replacing the original Redditch signalbox as noted above, but this was closed when the new, larger signalbox opened in 1926 taking over the work previously undertaken by the two smaller signalboxes. When the new signalbox was renamed in 1926 the up loop line between Redditch station and the signalbox was extended.

Redditch South signalbox, shown in Fig 15, opened in 1885 and a replacement box was opened on 23 August 1925. This signalbox became redundant as a result of the closure of the line south of Redditch when the track was severed at the south end of the platform on 29 January 1967.

For a few years Redditch was a terminus and shortly after the line was opened the first goods facilities were in place. These included arrangements for goods and coal traffic, but following the opening of the line to Evesham in 1868 the yard was enlarged. A spacious goods warehouse with two cart porches was

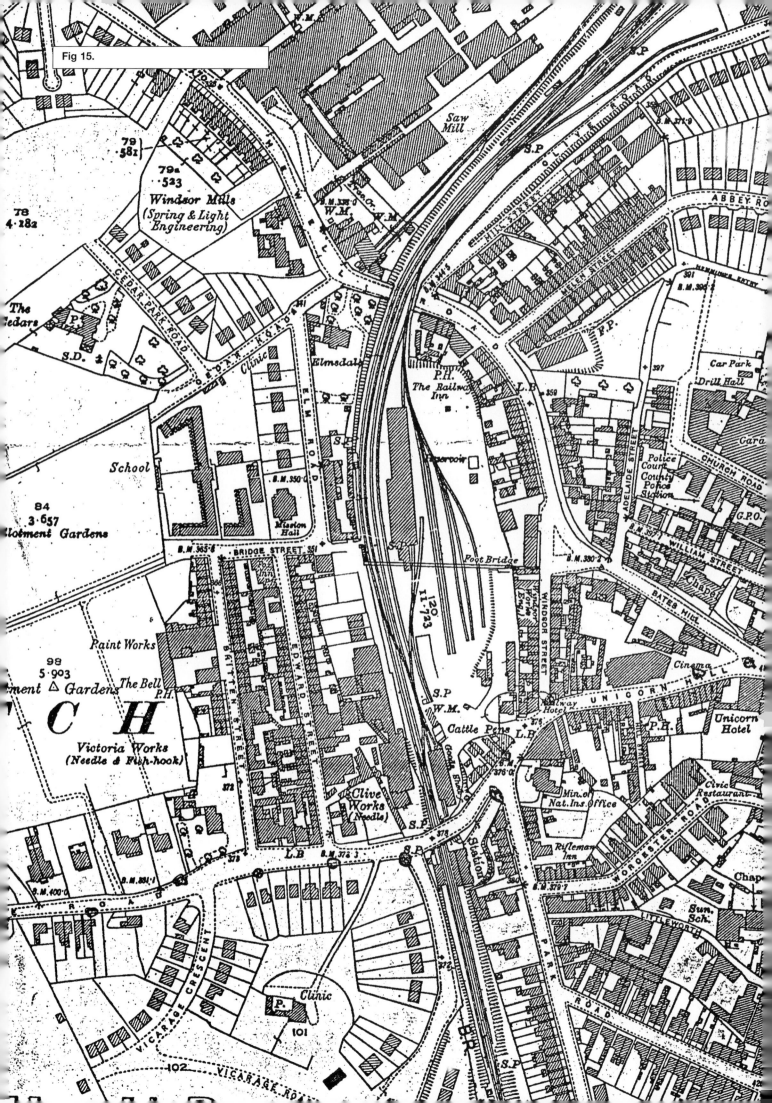

Fig 15.

Above: Redditch South signalbox is seen just before the line closed south of Redditch with the platform for the signalman to stand on when he was exchanging the train tablet with the enginemen. The 20mph speed restriction sign, mentioned previously, is still in place. *Collection R. EJ. Essery.*

Fig 16. *(Right)* At an earlier date there was a ground frame or stage worked connection from the Up to the Down sidings on the station side of signals 17/18. This connection was removed at a date that is not known to the author. There was an unusual arrangement that probably dated from the installation of the ground frame whereby Redditch North down starting signal was slotted by Redditch South. This protected the connection mentioned above. The term 'slotting' describes an arrangement whereby two signal boxes work one signal and until the second lever is pulled the signal will not clear. We believe this was achieved at Redditch by underbolting, a term used to describe the mechanical locking of a lever in a signal box.
Drawing and notes by A. E.Overton

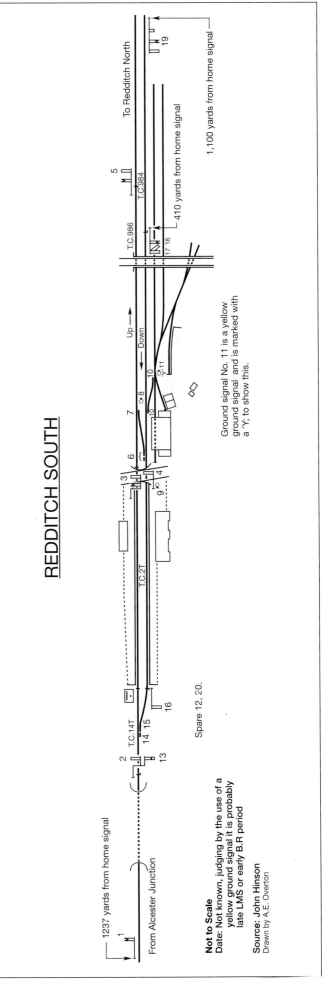

REDDITCH SOUTH

Fig 16.

built on a site known as Pound Meadow. The usual facilities associated with a town goods station were to be found at Redditch. These included cattle pens, coal wharves for private traders, side and end loading docks and a weighing machine at the entrance of the yard. The variety of traffic handled was considerable. In addition to the domestic and industrial coal, which provided the greatest tonnage, the goods station handled bricks, timber and slates for the building industry. Other inward traffic was lime, artificial manure, Peruvian guano and animal feedstuff for the farming community. The needs of what today we would describe as consumers were many and included flour, coffee beans, tea, cheese and salted butter for sale by grocers. In addition there was traffic in fine wines and spirits, Burton beer, Dublin stout and West Country cider. The needs of local industry included the raw materials that was turned into finished products thus providing originating traffic that required transporting away to customers elsewhere.

The steady expansion of the town with its industrial development called for better facilities, in particular crane power, and a degree of remodelling of the depot was undertaken by the LMS prior to World War 2, including additional sidings, primarily for mineral traffic at Clive Road. There were private sidings for T. & M. Dixon, whose principal business was coal traffic, together with the Redditch Town & District Gas Company's siding, both companies owning their own wagons. Local road transport for both collection and delivery was provided by the Midland Railway, later the LMS and finally British Railways. Until the final years horse-drawn vehicles were used on the 'town round' but after the Grouping in 1923 increasing use of motor vehicles was made for the more outlying districts. In later years the LMS Country Lorry Services, continued by British Railways, covered the outlying districts and Redditch was one of the stations that provided this service.

The 1932 line diagram shows that the railway company's own goods yard could hold 188 wagons, but with the additional sidings that were built, this figure was exceeded. Finally, it should be noted that according to the 1935 LMS List of Tariff Vans, Redditch was served by four workings and details of these are given later in Appendix IV.

Redditch station, looking south during the Edwardian period. A' six-wheels coupled' goods engine hauls the train approaching on the up line and the train on the down line is headed by an 0-4-4T. This train comprises seven six-wheel Clayton carriages, but no tail lamp is visible. I suspect the lamp has been removed and is to be placed at the other end of the train, and when the line is clear the engine will run round the train in order to work it back to Birmingham. From other pictures it is clear that some trains terminated at Redditch or worked back to Birmingham departing in the up direction from the down platform. *Collection R. J. Essery*

The passenger train approaching on the up line is hauled by a Johnson single-frame goods engine and will probably precede the train on the down line. A Johnson 0-4-4T, whose number appears to be 1259, heads this train. Note the well-coaled bunker in readiness for a full day's work. I think the date of this picture is c1905 and that 1259 is the pre-1907 number. If so, the engine will become No 1263 in 1907. *Collection Jack Braithwaite*

This Edwardian period picture shows some of the Redditch station staff. The stationmaster is in the centre of the front row and the goods agent is on his left. It is not possible to be sure who the others are, porters, signalmen, etc. *Collection Phillip Coventry*

The inscription at the bottom of the picture reads 'International War 1914, Redditch'. I suspect that these men are Territorials leaving home to go to war, many never to return. *Collection Philip Jarvis*

This c1960 picture shows the north end of the up platform at Redditch and the barrow crossing. A degree of litter that would not have been tolerated in earlier years is evident. *John Maries*

Fowler Class 4MT 2-6-4T No 42337, an engine stationed at Saltley, stands in the up platform on 19 June 1955 with a three-coach set of compartment coaches — two third brakes and a composite. Other than the head appearing from the first coach, the station appears to be deserted. *W. Garbett*

This 19 September 1958 view shows the front of the station at Redditch.
H. C. Casserley 94213

The presence of the locomotive head and tail lamp on No 43714 suggests the locomotive is the Redditch pilot and not the train engine. The outside wall of the goods shed and the yard beyond can be seen in this picture. *John Fozard*

A deserted Redditch station, looking south towards the tunnel with the South signalbox visible at the end of the up platform. The previous water crane at the end of the down platform was one of the swan-neck type, but in this picture the water column is one of the less common standpipe variety. *Joe Moss*

A wintry scene with Fowler Class 4MT 2-6-4T No 42419 on a down freight train. *M. Gregory*

Left:
Although rather a faded photograph, this is the only early view of Redditch goods yard at Pound Meadow which I have been able to find. Later, a larger goods shed was built to the north and both sheds appear on the maps reproduced on pages 46 and 47.
Collection Philip Jarvis

Below:
The Fred. A. Hill wagon was built by the Gloucester Railway Carriage & Wagon Company and was painted black with white lettering. The dimensions were, according to the board, 14ft 11in x 6ft 5in x 3ft 1in.
HMRS 22331

Above:
This c1963 view is looking north and shows the new goods shed and part of the yard. In the foreground there is a rather unusual design of loading gauge. The iron bridge, which can be seen in the background, leads to Poole's fishing tackle factory. This building was demolished in the late 1960s and the site is now occupied by the Driving Standards Agency's Driving Test Centre in Elm Road which was built in 1988. The gas lamp in the foreground was mounted on a short column and was for viewing the floors of cattle trucks.
Collection R. J. Essery

Right:
A weighbridge was an essential part of a goods depot and Messrs Pooley usually made the weighing machinery and the measuring instruments which were inside the building. This weighbridge was by the entrance to the goods yard from Unicorn Hill. *Collection R. J. Essery*

This picture, taken c1955, shows part of the cattle pens and an unidentified ex-Midland Railway Class 3F shunting coaching stock. Note the old loading gauge; the replacement can be seen in a previous view. *Collection R. J. Essery*

The Redditch Gas sidings began as a single road, known at first as Mr Cliff's Sidings. It was built shortly after the line was opened in order to serve his gas making plant. On Thursday, 29 May 1864 there was an accident here when an engine became derailed, but I have not been able to establish any further details of what happened. The growth in demand for gas as the town of Redditch developed meant that over the years the sidings were extended and the diagram shown on page 46 depicts their ultimate extent. They were worked by the Redditch pilot engine, which would propel a rake of about ten wagons laden with gas coal into the reception road. The train was divided so that the first three or four wagons could be drawn forward and then propelled back along the tippler road for passage through the rotary wagon tippler. When the last wagon, i.e. the one nearest the engine had been tipped, the empties were drawn out and returned to the reception road so that three more laden wagons could be attached, the procedure being repeated until the whole rake had been dealt with.

The small, single-line engine shed with a 42ft turntable was to the north of the station but the turntable was removed in 1903. At the same time the coaling stage was repositioned but I am unsure if the shelter was provided then or at a later date, probably the latter. The shed received a new roof c1938 and this totally changed the appearance of the building. From an administrative standpoint Redditch was in the Midland Railway's Birmingham district and later it was to become a sub shed of Bournville, 21B.

There was a water column at the south end of Redditch station platform and it was not unknown for drivers of mineral trains or heavy goods trains travelling in the down direction to stop at the entrance to the station and to uncouple the locomotive after the fireman had pinned down a couple of wagon brakes. The locomotive would run forward to the water column where the tank would be filled. This task completed, they would run back, couple up, release the wagon brakes and be on their way. The reason for this seemingly complex move was simple: it gave the crew a slight run at the 340yd-long tunnel that was a narrow bore on a rising 1 in 126 gradient. More than once on a slow moving train my driver and I have been close to the floor of the engine cab with wet cloths over our faces.

At some date prior to 1873 the line between Redditch and Studley began to be worked by train staff and block telegraph while the line between Studley and Evesham was worked by train staff only. From 1880 the block telegraph came into service, and from 11 October 1891 the line from Redditch South to Alcester Junction was subject to electric train token block working.

I believe this picture was taken from the bridge shown in Fig 14 on page 46 and the date is post-1903, showing the gas works signalbox. There is no sign of the second lamp holder that should be evident at the front of the engine platform if the date was 1903 or earlier. These were removed in 1903 when most British railway companies rationalised their headlamp codes. The locomotive appears to be carrying an express headlamp code. *Collection Philip Jarvis*

Left:
Ivatt Class 4MT 2-6-0 No 43041 approaches Redditch with an ordinary passenger train *c*1961 running in the down direction. The building to the left of the single line is the retort house of the gas works. The signal to the right of the engine is the up starter.
Ian Hayes

Above:
Class 4F 0-6-0 No 44168 was allocated to 21A, Saltley, and here we see the locomotive being prepared for its next turn of duty. The driver is oiling the inside motion which was accessible from the locomotive platform. The fireman will rake out the ashpan when the locomotive is standing over the disposal pit, using the long rake, part of which can be seen, in the foreground. *G. Latter*

A rather splendid view, taken on 2 June 1963, showing Redditch engine shed, the North signalbox and the additional sidings added in 1942, seen here occupied by coaching stock. *J. M. Tolson*

I am not aware of the circumstances that brought a Rebuilt 'Royal Scot' to Redditch, but this picture shows No 46137 *The Prince of Wales's Volunteers (South Lancashire)*, then allocated to 21A, Saltley, on Redditch shed. This picture provides a good view of the shed arrangements, the enginemen's cabin, the gas lamp which provided lighting and the water column with its frost fire to prevent the water from freezing in icy weather. *M. Gregory*

Right:
The engine shed at Redditch received a new roof c1938 and this gave it a modern appearance. This 1952 picture shows the shed entrance without any doors, the inspection pit and the swan-neck water crane; note the replacement crane in the previous view. The enginemen's cabin probably also contained some stores, oil, etc. *Collection R. J. Essery*

Centre right:
The coaling stage at Redditch was very rudimentary and it was probably built without a shelter; this would have been added later. It was all very labour intensive, the coal was shovelled from the wagons on to the platform and from the platform into the tender or bunker of the locomotives. *Collection R. J. Essery*

Fig 17. The gradient for down direction trains was, to use a railwayman's words, 'against the engine', until you were through the tunnel, when the gradient was down, or 'with the engine', to Salford Priors. This Ordnance Survey map shows how the line curved away south from Redditch. *Crown Copyright*

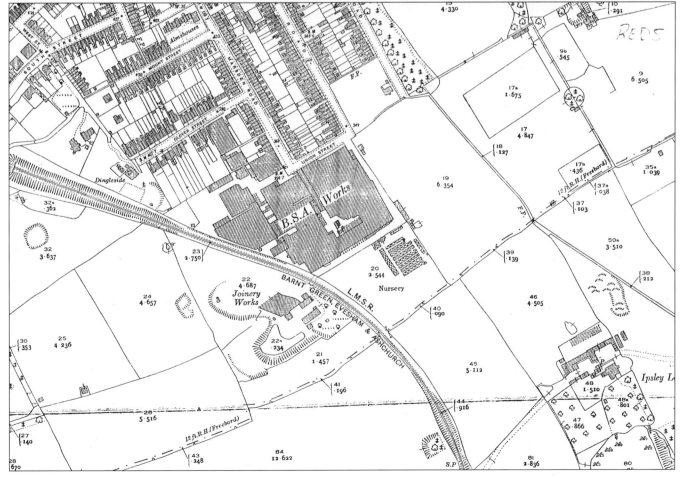

Fig 17.

This undated picture illustrates the north portal of Redditch Tunnel. The tunnel nameboard gives the length as 352yd, which does not agree with the 340yd stated on the Midland Railway Distance Diagram dated 1913. The narrow bore of the tunnel can be seen; there was not much room between the top of the chimney and the roof of the tunnel on a large engine. *Collection R. J. Essery*

The south portal of Redditch Tunnel was similar to the north end, as this 1957 picture shows. *D. Ibbotson*

Studley & Astwood Bank

Studley & Astwood Bank was 3 miles 11 chains from Redditch station and is a good example of a station that served a number of small communities, namely Studley and Spernall, Astwood Bank and Crabbs Cross. The station was opened on the same date that the railway opened and it was closed to passenger traffic on 1 October 1962. Closure to goods traffic was on 6 July 1964. In the final years, commencing 14 June 1954, the signalbox was open only between 7.0 and 3/0 to deal with the local stopping freight train. The LMS 2 October 1944 document that gave the hours of duty for signalboxes shows Studley as being open continuously; I am uncertain what other changes may have taken place between then and the final arrangements in 1954. The first signalbox was opened at some date prior to 1 November 1875 and it was replaced by the signalbox seen here on 25 May 1891.

The LMS rating plan, reproduced opposite, shows the track layout and facilities at the station; there is no record of any other track plan known to me. The three-throw point that served the siding with the paved crossing was removed a few years prior to the line's closure but otherwise I believe this arrangement served Studley for most of the station's life. There was not a passing loop although tablets were exchanged at Studley when the signalbox was open. There was a single platform face with stationmaster's house on the platform, the goods shed was attached to the platform, and the signalbox was just beyond on the Redditch side of the station.

The facilities at Studley & Astwood Bank were similar to those at Redditch except that furniture vans etc and carriages could not be handled. Prior to the arrival of the 10-ton crane at Redditch

This view of Studley was taken in Midland Railway days, believed c1910. At least four members of staff can be seen in the crowd on the platform. The Barnt Green to Ashchurch railway was far from straight and one of the many curves that typified the line can be seen under the road bridge. Although not visible in this picture (the lamp on the platform obscures the view), the station nameboard carried the name in three rows of equal size letters that were in white, attached to a board that was painted ultramarine blue. The post and beading was in Denby Pottery cream. *Collection R. J. Essery*

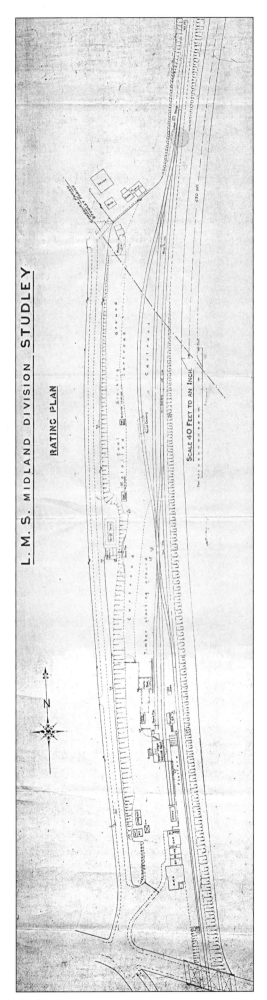

Fig 18.

Fig 18. This has been reproduced from an undated LMS 40ft to 1in rating plan. The platform has a booking office and hall with the toilets between the ladies' and general waiting rooms. There was also a urinal and water closet that was accessible from the platform. The entrance to the goods yard was gated and the goods shed was at the north end of the platform. There was space for a single cart to back up to the shed that contained a 30cwt hand crane. The yard had a weighbridge, a small store, mess room, cement store and cattle dock with an adjacent standpipe. Another gate was at the entrance of the cart road that led to the timber stacking ground, Pratts Petrol Co and the coal stacking ground with small offices for T. & M. Dixon, and the Alcester Co-Op.

Wagon labels were attached to both sides of vehicles, No 1 was for mineral traffic, coal, No 2 was for mineral traffic that was not coal, and No 3 was for goods traffic. The train guard and other yard staff calculated the weight and loading of the train using these labels. The labels illustrated are examples for both coal and goods traffic consigned to Studley and show the sender and consignee often giving details of the route that the wagon was to travel.

Fig 19. A fairly simple station layout that did not include a passing loop. When the signal box was closed, or as it sometimes called, 'switched out,' long section working applied.
Drawing and notes by A. E.Overton

Studley's signalbox was at the north or Redditch end of the station and this picture also shows the rear wall of the goods shed. This signalbox was opened on 26 May 1891. When this picture was taken the box was 'switched out', and on the original print the signals for both the up and down direction can be seen in the clear position.
W. Garbett

the crane power at Studley was identical. The yard capacity was 55 wagons. Entry at the north end was via a stage, released by the tablet, and from the south the signalman controlled the entry. This meant that when the signalbox was not open, entry to the yard was only possible by the stage at the north end. One interesting feature of the plan is the use of a wheel scotch to protect the centre siding. In most respects Studley was a good example of a typical single-line station without a passing loop, and I have already recorded what happened when I was 'put inside' one day when working a northbound empty wagon train that was divided between the various sidings.

The goods facilities at Studley comprised a small warehouse with a single cart porch at the north end of the platform. The arrangement of the cattle pens, loading dock and a weighing machine, together with space for household coal and timber, can be seen on the plan. In addition to T. & M. Dixon, other local merchants were the Alcester Co-Operative Independent Society and G. Shrimpton. A fair amount of agricultural traffic was handled, for example animal feeding stuff in sacks, dried sugar beet pulp and artificial fertilisers. One interesting traffic feature towards the end of July and in September was the considerable amount of unaccompanied passenger luggage, together with bicycles used by the students who were studying at the nearby Studley Agricultural College when they took their summer holidays.

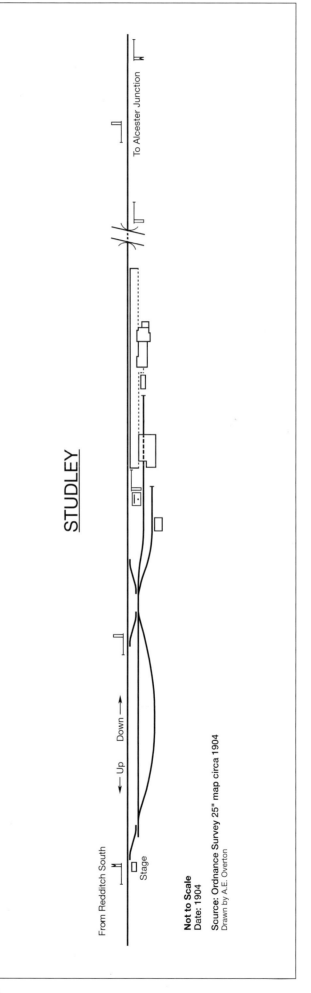

To Alcester Junction

STUDLEY

← Up   Down →

From Redditch South

Stage

Not to Scale
Date: 1904

Source: Ordnance Survey 25" map circa 1904
Drawn by A.E. Overton

Fig 19.

Fowler Class 4MT 2-6-4T No 42417 departs from Studley & Astwood Bank station with a passenger train for Birmingham on 24 March 1962. *J. M. Tolson*

This rather pleasant view of Studley & Astwood Bank station was taken on 22 April 1957 and shows Ivatt Class 4MT 2-6-0 No 43036 on the 5.10pm Birmingham to Ashchurch ordinary passenger train. The station nameboard was a British Railways addition; an earlier LMS period picture does not show a nameboard at this end of the station. *T. J. Edgington*

Stanier Class 8F 2-8-0 No 48700 heads a northbound stopping freight train at Studley. This picture provides a clear view of the modest goods shed with the adjacent office that served the needs of the station. *P. J. Shoesmith*

Coughton

The next station was at Coughton, 2 miles 15 chains from Studley, which was opened on 4 May 1868. It was an early closure, both passenger and goods traffic ceasing on 30 June 1952. From the copy of the OS map it can be seen that it was most beneficial to the owners of Coughton Lodge, but there is little evidence of other sources of traffic in the area. In 1909, generally the busiest year surveyed in Chapter 4, the passenger trains that stopped at Coughton were four down and five up workings each day. There was originally a signalbox, opened at some time before 16 August 1877 that was closed on 11 October 1891, when the home and distant signals were dispensed with.

Coughton had a single platform with minimal facilities. There was a single siding that was connected at both the north and south ends and after the signalbox was closed, entry was via the two stages that were released by the train token, the siding being capable of accommodating 26 wagons. In addition to being both a goods and passenger station, furniture vans etc could be accommodated at the end loading dock that was part of the station and which formed the trap point to the north of the siding. At the south end of the siding there was a trap point that protected the main line from any wagons that may have run away. According to the Railway Clearing House *Official Hand Book of Railway Stations*, livestock could be handled but this must have been either via the dock or by using a ramp. Fig 20 is an extract of the OS map and Fig 21 is a sketch that illustrates the arrangements after the loop was removed prior to closure.

Fig 20. The Ordnance Survey map underlines the rural nature of the area and shows that the nearest building was Coughton Lodge, which no doubt generated some traffic for the railway. *Crown Copyright*

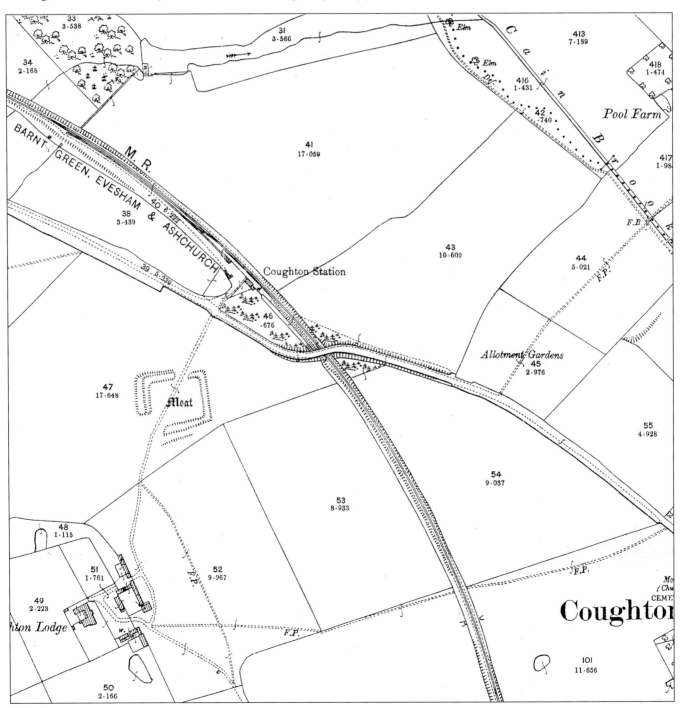

Fig 20.

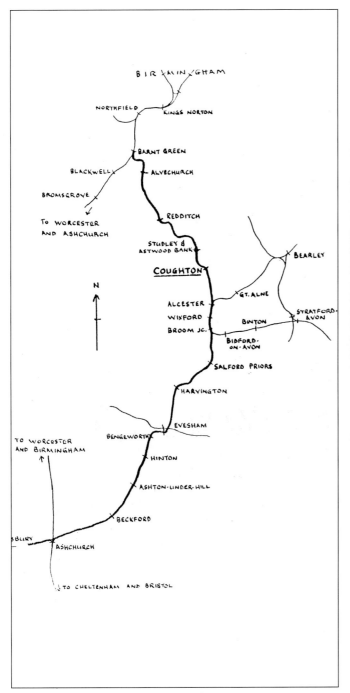

Fig 21.

Above:
Taken on 21 June 1952, just a few days before the station was closed to all traffic, this view of Coughton is looking north. There is now a house on Sambourne Road which is not shown on the Ordnance Survey map. *Joe Moss*

Fig 21. This sketch map show the position of Coughton station that was provided under the terms of an agreement when the line was built, in relation to the other stations in the area. There was a footpath from the Coughton to the Sambourne road which ran alongside the railway, and a road entrance that was gated. Although there was only a single siding in the form of a loop, a weighbridge was provided. At some time the loop was altered as shown in Fig 22 and the two stages, one at each end of the siding, were reduced to one. Access to this siding by a train requiring to attach or detach vehicles would involve the same procedure as that described in the section on Alvechurch.

A c1912 picture of Coughton showing the station building with two members of uniformed staff, the stationmaster and a porter. It is not possible to be sure who the others were, railway staff or passengers. Later pictures show a substantial chimney stack at the north end of the building. *Collection Roger Carpenter*

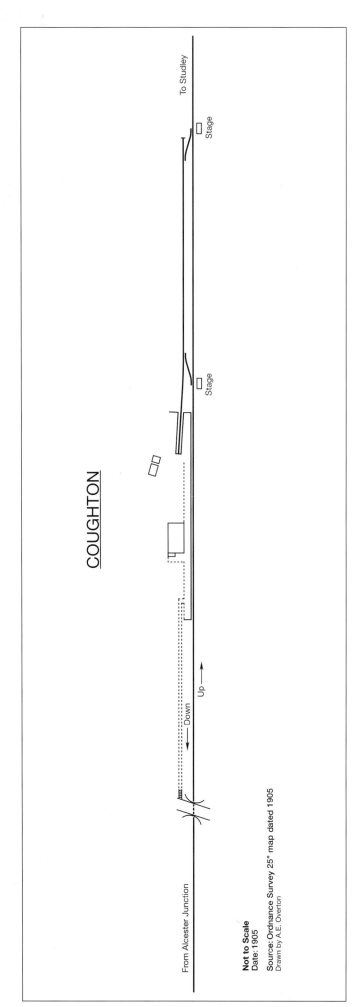

COUGHTON

To Studley

Stage

Stage

Down

Up

From Alcester Junction

Not to Scale
Date: 1905

Source: Ordnance Survey 25" map dated 1905
Drawn by A.E. Overton

Fig 22.

Fig 22. The layout at Coughton was simple, after 1891 there was no signal box, and entry to both ends of the loop was via the points that were controlled from one of the stages the stages that were released by the train tablet. One source suggests that later one stage was removed but I am unable to confirm if this happened.
Drawing and notes A. E.Overton

Above:
Closure to all traffic came to Coughton on 30 June 1952. This picture shows the British Railways closure notice posted on an ex-LMS noticeboard. The last stationmaster at Coughton was Percy Duckett, who was later to become the stationmaster at Redditch. On this occasion he is wearing his LMS uniform and cap badge; it is possible that he had not been issued with new British Railways insignia. *Collection R. J. Essery*

Above right:
Coughton, looking north from the end of the station platform. From the track plan it will be seen that access to the siding was gained via points operated from a ground frame. The north frame is just visible on the original print and was similar to the south frame seen in the picture. This is the same type of frame as the one at Alvechurch, described in the section on that station. The road serving the dock adjacent to the platform is on the left, while the siding appears to be little used at this time. *Collection R. J. Essery*

Right:
Photographed on 21 June 1952, this picture shows the overbridge at the south end of the station. *Collection R. J. Essery*

Fig 23.

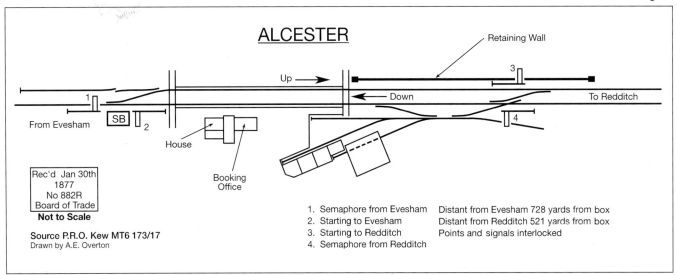

ALCESTER

Retaining Wall

Up →

← Down

To Redditch

From Evesham

SB

House

Booking
Office

Rec'd Jan 30th
1877
No 882R
Board of Trade
Not to Scale

Source P.R.O. Kew MT6 173/17
Drawn by A.E. Overton

1. Semaphore from Evesham   Distant from Evesham 728 yards from box
2. Starting to Evesham   Distant from Redditch 521 yards from box
3. Starting to Redditch   Points and signals interlocked
4. Semaphore from Redditch

Alcester

Alcester was the next station, 2 miles 6 chains from Coughton, and opened for goods traffic on 16 June 1866 and to passenger traffic three months later, on 17 September. A few years before the railway was built, Alcester, an old market town, had a thriving industry that employed almost 1,000 people in the manufacture of needles, but later this industry was absorbed into Redditch. At first it was the terminus for the line from Evesham, the extension to Redditch not opening until 4 May 1868. Later, the station became a block post and also provided a junction with the GWR branch line to Bearley. Although the track plan of the station in 1877 has survived there is no inspection report. This track plan, as reproduced above, was submitted to the Board of Trade for approval. The track layout was interesting: a passing loop with two platform faces and small goods yard and shed with access from both the up and down directions. The additions that were made from the previous layout, no doubt dating from when the line to Redditch was opened, were the connections opposite the signalbox and those shown between signals 3 and 4. I have also reproduced a copy of the OS map (Fig 25) which illustrates the entire station area including the junction with the GWR. A later LMS rating plan gives an identical layout but the line diagram (Fig 27) shows the final layout of the station after the signalbox changes had taken place.

Fig 23. This track plan has been redrawn from an original Midland Railway plan submitted to the Board of Trade. Alcester station was opened for goods traffic on 16 June 1866 and for passenger traffic three months later. At first the line was single with a crossing loop and, according to John Gough's *Chronology*, the extended loop line came into use on 4 September 1876 when the Bearley branch was opened. In *British Railway Journal* No 66, Roger Carpenter, the author of an article on Alcester, states that the Bearley Company paid for the alterations to the track layout shown here. The Midland Railway plan that was sent to the Board of Trade was received on 30 January 1877 but there is no report in the file now at the PRO Kew. Therefore it is not possible to be sure if the Midland Railway was late in submitting the plan or if it had been revised following an inspection by the Board of Trade inspecting officer. What it does show is two new connections: one opposite the signalbox that provided a crossover with a trap point to protect the running line and one between signals 3 and 4. This was a crossover between the up and down lines with a connection from the up line into the siding. No siding discs were shown on the original Midland Railway plan.
A. E. Overton

At first Alcester was just a single-line platform but the loop line, shown on the 1877 plan, was an early addition dating from 4 September 1876. The arrangements for signalboxes are a little complicated. The first signalbox was the one shown on the 1877 plan which had been opened in 1876 or before. The signalbox at Alcester Junction probably opened in 1876 to coincide with the arrival of the Alcester Railway from Bearley. The Midland Railway replaced this box on 28 May 1922 and the LMS again in 1932. It then became the only LMS signalbox at Alcester.

An early Edwardian view of Alcester taken before 17 December 1905 when the signalbox was moved on to the end of the platform. There were a number of signalbox changes over the years at Alcester which are recorded in the text. *Collection R. J. Essery*

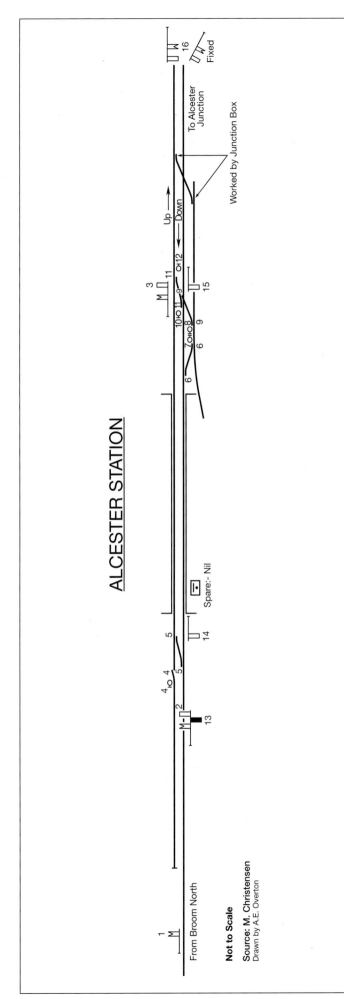

ALCESTER STATION

From Broom North

Not to Scale

Source: M. Christensen
Drawn by A.E. Overton

Spare:- Nil

To Alcester Junction

Worked by Junction Box

Up →
← Down

Fixed

Fig 24.

The station signalbox was replaced on 17 December 1905 and was closed on 24 April 1932 with the opening of the signalbox close to the junction with the GWR. At this time the LMS was engaged in a programme of staff and maintenance cost reduction by eliminating signalboxes where resignalling arrangements would enable this to be carried out. Alcester was not the only station on the Evesham branch where this happened.

Probably the most interesting feature at Alcester was the presence of the small GWR single-road engine shed, together with the fact that the GWR possessed running powers into the Midland Railway station for both goods and passenger traffic. The available records show this junction was opened on 4 September 1876, closed on 1 January 1917 and the rails were removed on 25 March 1917. The connection was restored on 29 July 1923. Closure to passengers for the GWR came on 25 September 1939; for goods, the official closure date was 1 March 1951. However, it seems likely that goods traffic also ceased on 25 September 1939. The map on the cover of the GWR service timetable Section 13 dated 1 October 1945 shows the Alcester branch as 'temporarily closed', the junction being taken out of use on 31 May 1953.

The GWR did not treat Alcester as a connecting point with the Midland Railway if the latter's 1909 working timetable is a case in point. The timetable of that date shows arrivals from the GWR at 9.18, 11.3, 1/25, 5/17 and 7/7 with departures at 8.22, 9.33, 11.18. 2/9 and 6/5, which gives five trains in each direction daily and returns the locomotive to the shed, but few trains offer reasonable connections for onward travel by the Midland Railway. Clearly travellers were coming to Alcester only.

By 1934 there was a GWR mixed train arriving at 10.6 from Bearley and an autocar service from Stratford at 11.56. The departures commenced at 8.0 with an autocar to Bearley followed by an autocar to Stratford at 10.39. A Saturdays-only autocar to Bearley departed at 12/43 while at 2/2, Saturdays excepted, there was a mixed train departure to Bearley. On Saturdays only this service was retimed to depart at 2/5 and ran as an autocar. A further autocar departed to Bearley at 4/2, and at 5/29 to Stratford. During the week it ran as a mixed train, departing at 5/40; this train concluded the daily working from Alcester by the GWR. While I am unsure of the exact GWR arrangements in 1909, it is clear from the 1934 timetable that the service was worked by a locomotive stationed at Alcester which ran either 'auto' or 'mixed' trains as required.

The Great Western Railway used the expression 'autocar'; other railways described them as 'push-and-pull' or 'motor trains'. Amongst the locomotives known to have been stationed at Alcester were '517' class 0-4-2T Nos 569, withdrawn in May 1933, and 1157 withdrawn in November 1935. A '48xx' 0-4-2T, No 4801, was also there for a time.

The total goods yard capacity was 52 wagons — 40 in the yard with a further 12 vehicles able to be accommodated in the short siding to the south of the station which was connected to the up line platform. Alcester was able to deal with goods and passenger traffic, including furniture vans, livestock, horseboxes, and carriages by passenger train. Crane capacity was 1 ton 10cwt. The Alcester Co-op owned wagons that would have been seen in the yard; they were painted medium grey with white-shaded black lettering. A certain amount of traffic was

Fig 25.

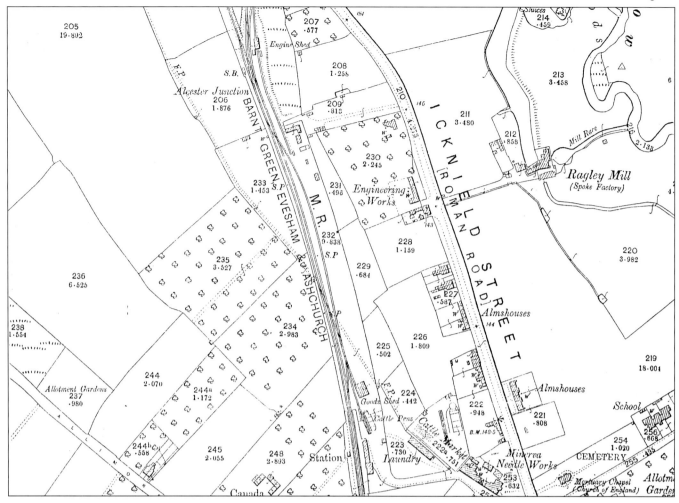

interchanged between the GWR and the Midland or LMS companies. The principal traffic was of an agricultural nature, together with supplies of coal and the empty wagons returning to collieries. There was a large cattle market that held regular stock sales and cattle was moved away from the market to the cattle pens prior to onward movement by train.

Fig 25. An extract from an Ordnance Survey map showing the station area and the junction with the Bearley Railway, together with the two signalboxes, one at the junction and the other to the south of the station. *Crown Copyright*

A delightful period view of Alcester taken c1907, with the photographer looking north towards Redditch. The signalbox on the platform, described as Alcester on the front facing nameboard, was opened on 17 December 1905 replacing the pre-1877 structure. The replacement box was to remain in service until 1932 when, as part of a resignalling scheme designed to cut costs, it was removed and a new box closer to the junction was opened. The train is hauled by a double-frame goods engine, and the headlamp code, three lamps across the front of the engine platform, denotes a through goods or mineral train. There appears to be a fair amount of traffic on the platform awaiting collection and there are at least three members of railway staff, two of whom are holding shunting poles.
Collection R. J. Essery

The GWR Bearley branch train at Alcester station. The GWR had running powers into the Midland station for both passenger and goods trains. The locomotive is 0-4-2T No 203 of the '517' class, built at Wolverhampton in 1876. The locomotive remained in service until April 1920. This picture was taken in 1901 and the coach is a bogie brake third, but it was not unusual to add a four-wheel full brake to this branch passenger train. *Collection R. J. Essery*

A pleasant general view of Alcester taken in the late 1930s, facing north towards the junction with the GWR. The signalbox in the centre of the picture was opened on 24 April 1932 as the replacement for two existing signalboxes: one at the junction, the other at the south end of the station. The GWR branch autocar can be seen, but the locomotive is out of view, probably on shed. *Lens of Sutton*

Photographed c1957, this north-facing view shows the down advanced starter and up inner home signals on a single Midland Railway signal post. The Midland Railway often used this arrangement when it improved sighting for engine crews and it was commonplace for many years after Nationalisation. To the left of the picture is the dead-end siding that was parallel to the single line and was able to hold 12 wagons. *D. Ibbotson*

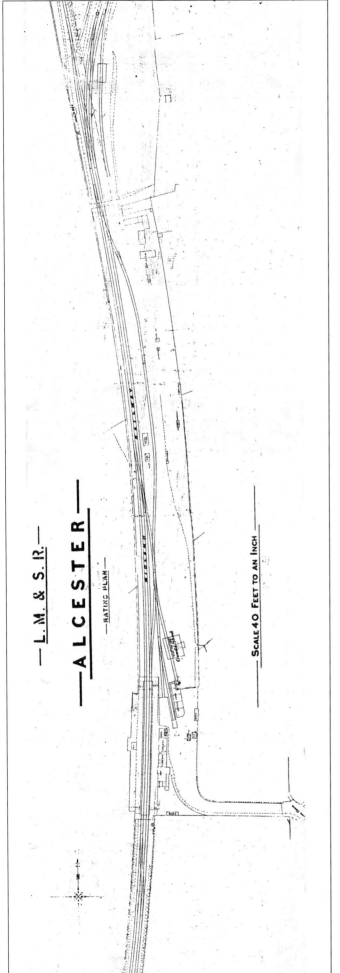

Fig 26.

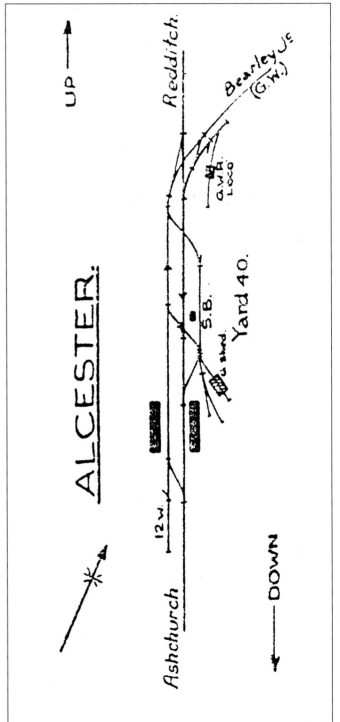

Fig 26. The 1926 Rating Plan for Alcester station. *Crown Copyright*

Fig 27. This LMS diagram of the station at Alcester was drawn after the signalbox at the station was closed and a new box had been opened to the north of the station. Trains travelling in the down direction ran straight through, while up trains ran over the loop line before rejoining the single line just beyond the junction with the GWR's Bearley branch. Working the yard was straightforward: down trains could set back into the yard from the down platform line using the trailing connection and then the locomotive would run round the train in order to shunt the yard with the engine at the Redditch end of the yard; up trains would be set back over the connection by the signalbox and either set back into the yard or along the down line. This would depend on circumstances. For example, there may not have been enough space for a long train if there were a number of wagons in the yard. Departure would be from the yard on to the up loop and then on to the single line.

Fig 27.

Above:
Part of the small goods yard with the loading gauge and the 1932 replacement signalbox can be seen in this 13 June 1954 photograph taken from the down home signal gantry. The goods shed, visible at the end of the platform, was about 50ft long and contained a 30cwt hand crane. The goods brakevan is an ex-LNWR vehicle. *Collection R. J. Essery*

Right:
The small engine shed, which measured 38ft x 16ft, was erected by the Bearley Railway and taken over by the GWR. It could hold one locomotive which was used to work the branch to Stratford. The adjoining tank house was supplied with water from the River Arrow and the water crane was swung clear of the line when not in use. An inspection pit was inside the shed and a disposal pit was on the shed road which was extended beyond the building to a small coaling stage that measured 20ft x 9 ft. This c1953 photograph shows the disused GWR engine shed that I used to see when working trains through Alcester.
Collection R. J. Essery

Above:
Alcester in the final years before closure. Photographed on 19 April 1959, this shows how little the station changed over the years. The barrow crossing at the south end of the station, the substantial stationmaster's house on the down platform and the various offices on the platform remain. These comprised a store, booking hall and booking office, ladies' and general waiting rooms. The station nameboard on the up platform appears to be a British Railways replacement.
H. C. Casserley 18640

The closure notices at Alcester station confirm the end of both passenger and freight traffic on the line with effect from 6 July 1964. *G. Braithwaite*

Flooding was not unknown along this stretch of line, but I doubt if the River Arrow caused this kind of problem very often. The railway crossed the river twice between Alcester and Wixford and this is bridge No 48, just to the north of Wixford station. The photographer was facing north towards Alcester and Ragley Park was to the left of the picture. The photograph is dated January 1901 and the line was closed to traffic while repairs were undertaken. *Collection R. J. Essery*

The hand-written note on the reverse side of this Midland Railway Engineering Department picture states, 'Wixford, July 13th 1915. Top of new Bridge 5, Replaces Bridge 51, 52, 53. Looking towards Alcester.' The previous picture shows the effect of flooding that led to some major engineering work being undertaken on this section of line; this is a further example of what became necessary. *Collection V. R. Anderson*

Fig 28. A drawing based on information kindly supplied by M. Christensen, which I believe shows the arrangement as at c1910. The diagram is to the same orientation as the diagram hanging in the signalbox. There is a question about lever number 12; I think one of the two 12s should be number 11. *A. E. Overton*

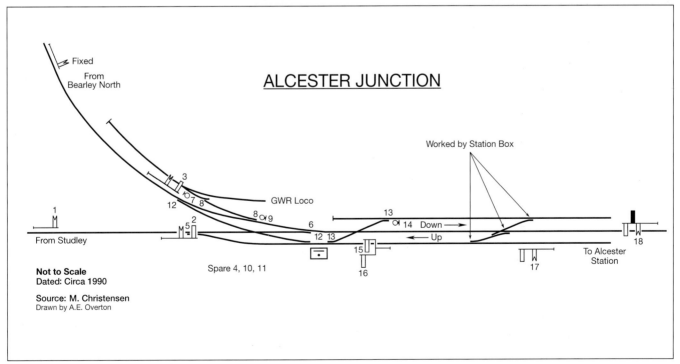

Fig 28

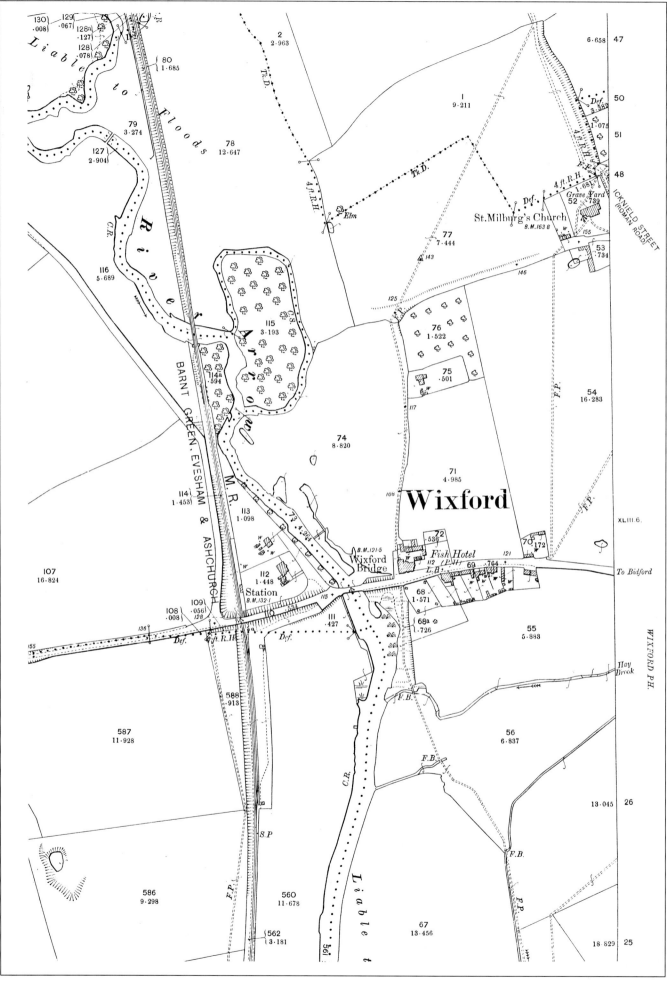

Fig 29.

Wixford

The line from Alcester to Wixford ran almost due south and crossed over the River Arrow twice on the 1 mile 78 chains between the two stations. The small station at Wixford had a single platform face and a siding that could be entered via two stages, one at each end of the siding, that were unlocked by the train token. Entrance to the platform was by an overbridge that separated the station from the goods facilities. Wixford was opened as a temporary station on 17 September 1866, but later it was given permanent status and lasted for more than 80 years before it was closed to both passengers and goods traffic on 2 January 1950.

Other than a loading gauge and a portable livestock loading ramp for use by any cattle, sheep or pigs routed via this station, usually in connection with livestock auction sales held in a field nearby, there were no goods facilities. The siding capacity was 20 wagons and there was road access to the side of the siding through a gated entrance.

Fig 29. This Ordnance Survey map shows the simple nature of Wixford station which opened as a temporary station in 1866. The station was made permanent at a later date and British Railways closed it on 2 January 1950. The map shows that the area north of the station was liable to flooding. In later years, I expect many passengers to Wixford came for the fishing and enjoyed a visit to the appropriately named Fish Hotel, just over Wixford Bridge from the station. *Crown Copyright*

The station at Wixford was a platform with a small wooden building and urinal. Seating was minimal and the station lighting was by oil lamps. This picture, taken on 13 June 1934, shows the siding that ran parallel to the single line and was entered by two stages released by the train tablet. It was worked along similar lines to the one at Alvechurch. The north ground frame was in the wooden hut seen under the road bridge, and the south frame was in a corrugated iron hut similar to that shown at Alvechurch. *Collection R. J. Essery*

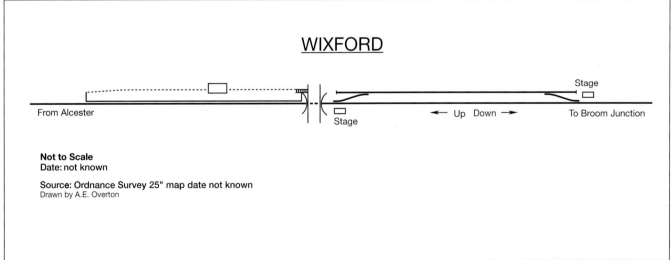

WIXFORD

From Alcester   Stage   ← Up   Down →   Stage   To Broom Junction

Not to Scale
Date: not known

Source: Ordnance Survey 25" map date not known
Drawn by A.E. Overton

Fig 30. This station did not have a signal box, entry to both ends of the loop was via the points that were controlled from the stage, being released by the train tablet. *Drawing and notes by A. E.Overton*

Fig 30.

Taken on 18 May 1930, this photograph illustrates the basic nature of the station. The barrow crossing is unusual as it does not appear to lead anywhere. *Clarence Gilbert*

Although not of the best quality, this picture has been included in order to show the siding that provided the only goods facilities at Wixford. Cattle were loaded at Wixford by using the ramp that can be seen. *Collection Joe Moss*

Below:
Former Midland Railway 0-6-0 Class 4F No 44013 heads for Broom Junction, running as engine and brake van on 11 May 1959. The station had been closed for over nine years and the platform was becoming overgrown. The brick building appears to be a toilet, but I am uncertain what the other hut would have been used for. *R. J. Sellick*

Broom Junction

Broom Junction and Joint station was 57 chains south of Wixford. It was the junction of the Midland and Stratford-upon-Avon & Midland Junction railways. At first the line between Studley and Evesham was worked by train staff only, but from 1880 the block telegraph was introduced and on 29 June 1891 the section from Alcester to Evesham North became two staff and ticket sections.

An unadvertised service for passengers commenced on 2 January 1879 but there is some doubt as to the exact date that Broom station was opened for passenger traffic, various sources giving 1 November 1880 or October 1881. At first, Broom was just a passenger station, and goods traffic was not dealt with until February 1882. The signalling arrangements and the number of signalboxes also changed over the years. The method of working, as described by the Board of Trade inspector, appears in Chapter 2, so I will not repeat what I have already said about the primitive methods that were in use for a number of years after the station opened.

Both the North and South signalboxes opened on 2 June 1879 and the method of operating was as described in Chapter 2. The North box was replaced on 3 September 1913 and closed on 6 May 1934. The South Junction signalbox was replaced on 9 October 1892. In 1934 Broom was resignalled and the new signalbox, named Broom Junction, was opened on 6 May. This new box replaced two old ones and enabled the LMS to reduce staff and maintenance costs. There were to be further signalbox changes but first we must return to the 19th century and record other events that took place.

On 9 October 1892 block working commenced between the North and South Junction and in 1896 the station was made joint with the Evesham, Redditch & Stratford Railway,

nominally independent but worked by the East & West Junction Railway. In 1909, the East & West Railway became part of the Stratford-upon-Avon & Midland Junction Railway, usually referred to as the SMJR.

The goods facilities at Broom were basic with two sidings having a capacity to hold 46 wagons provided for local traffic, and other than coal, this would be of an agricultural nature. I suspect that much of this siding capacity was often used for wagons being transferred either to or from the East & West Junction Railway or its successor the SMJR and the Midland Railway. In addition, there were two other sidings that could hold 60 wagons which were specifically for exchange traffic between the Midland and the SMJR. Connected to them was a turntable shown as being 40ft 10in in the SMJR Appendix, and 40ft by the LMS.

During World War 2 the volume of traffic that came off the SMJR line for destinations to the south was considerable and reversing the train at Broom was very time consuming. For example, the 4/15 Avonmouth to St Pancras banana train arrived at Broom at 7/43 and departed at 8/5, 22 minutes being required to reverse the train, that is to place the brakevan on the rear, and to change engines. To overcome this wasteful practice during the

Fig 31. This drawing shows the triangle at Broom that was made when the curve from the Stratford line south towards Evesham was put in during World War 2. This drawing also shows the four signal boxes that were in service at Broom together with the opening and closing dates and change of name where applicable. The individual diagrams for the junctions are reproduced on page 81 Broom North Junction, page 82 Broom West Junction and page 83 Broom East Junction. They are drawn as individual layouts and as a result the bracket signals, which include the distant signals, have been duplicated on each plan and are shown as D on the individual plans.

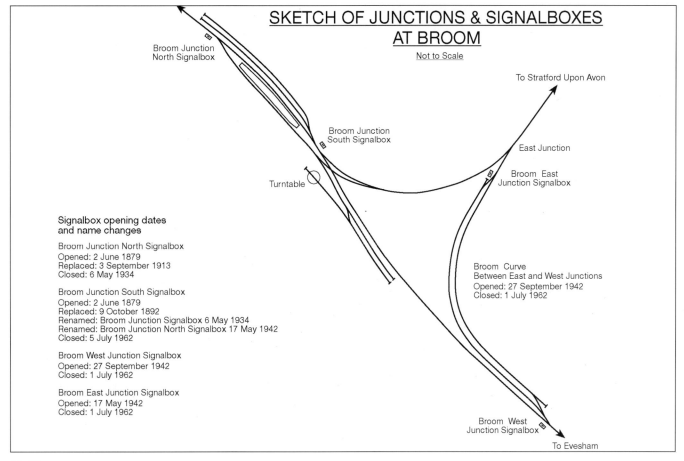

SKETCH OF JUNCTIONS & SIGNALBOXES AT BROOM

Not to Scale

Broom Junction North Signalbox

Broom Junction South Signalbox

Turntable

To Stratford Upon Avon

East Junction

Broom East Junction Signalbox

Broom Curve
Between East and West Junctions
Opened: 27 September 1942
Closed: 1 July 1962

Signalbox opening dates and name changes

Broom Junction North Signalbox
Opened: 2 June 1879
Replaced: 3 September 1913
Closed: 6 May 1934

Broom Junction South Signalbox
Opened: 2 June 1879
Replaced: 9 October 1892
Renamed: Broom Junction Signalbox 6 May 1934
Renamed: Broom Junction North Signalbox 17 May 1942
Closed: 5 July 1962

Broom West Junction Signalbox
Opened: 27 September 1942
Closed: 1 July 1962

Broom East Junction Signalbox
Opened: 17 May 1942
Closed: 1 July 1962

Broom West Junction Signalbox

To Evesham

Fig 31.

These two pictures should be considered together as they were taken from the road bridge, but many years separate them. The first was taken after the box was opened on 6 May 1934, but before it was renamed on 12 May 1942. The other was taken c1955; the most significant difference is the area around the turntable.
Collection R. J. Essery

Fig 32. Chapter 2 outlined what the Board of Trade inspector described as 'a dangerous mode of working' at Broom before the arrangements shown here were brought into use. The drawing shows that Broom was made into a passing loop, with signalboxes at both ends of the station. The North signal cabin was small, containing just six working and two spare levers, while the junction signalbox held 20 working levers and four spare. This layout was to remain unaltered for many years, the first change coming when the station was resignalled in 1934, and the second when the turntable went out of use. The drawing is based on a Midland Railway original that was submitted to the Board of Trade by the company in 1892 and is now held at the PRO Kew. *A. E. Overton*

Fig 33. This undated LMS 40ft to 1in plan shows the arrangements at Broom Junction prior to the 1934 resignalling which saw the closure of Broom North signalbox. The facilities at Broom Junction were basic. On the platform there was a booking office and booking hall, a ladies' waiting room, two water closets, a urinal and a lamp room. The station staff probably used the booking office as a rest room, although there was a mess room in the yard. Broom was an interchange station where most passengers came by train, local passengers approaching the station by walking along the roadway and then going on to the platform by means of the barrow crossing.

busy wartime period a new line was built, creating a triangle, which opened on 27 September 1942 and was to have a life of almost 20 years. This railway had single-line junctions at each end with two running lines between the junctions. Two new signalboxes were required, one at Broom West to the south of the station towards Salford Priors, and the other at Broom East on the Stratford line, to the east of Broom station (see page 75). In keeping with these changes the name of Broom Junction signalbox was altered to Broom North. The station was closed on 1 October 1962, a few months after the line from Broom West to Broom East had closed on 1 July 1962.

There can be little doubt that in an operational sense Broom in its heyday would have been a most interesting place to watch trains: a country junction, which before 1923, had been between

two independent companies where trains were reversed. At times, it was possible to have three passenger trains in the station area at the same time; one was an SMJR, and the others were up and down Midland trains.

The first station was no more than an exchange platform between the Midland Railway and the newly arrived Evesham, Redditch & Stratford-upon-Avon. The line from Stratford, which was really a continuation of the east to west railway, provided a connection to the Midland that was, at Broom, a north to south route. Although strictly speaking the East & West Junction Railway is not part of the story I think readers will have a better understanding of the traffic which flowed through Broom if I pause a while at Broom and explore in some detail certain aspects of this cross-country line.

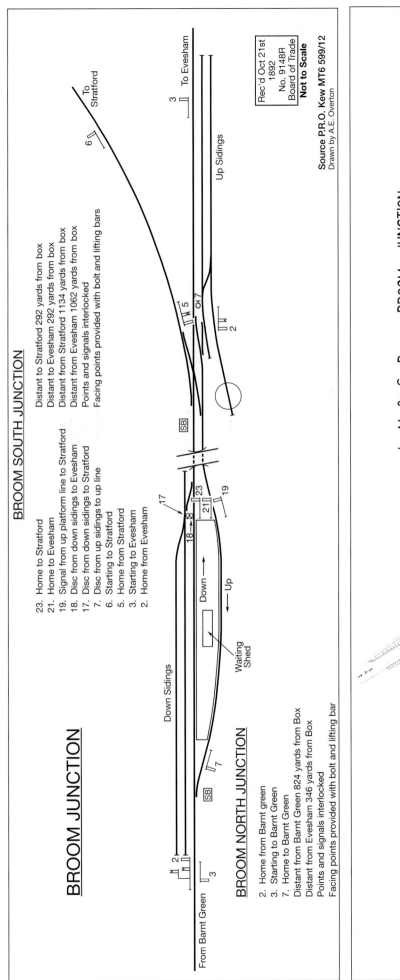

BROOM JUNCTION

BROOM SOUTH JUNCTION

23. Home to Stratford
21. Home to Evesham
19. Signal from up platform line to Stratford
18. Disc from down sidings to Evesham
17. Disc from down sidings to Stratford
7. Disc from up sidings to up line
6. Starting to Stratford
5. Home from Stratford
3. Starting to Evesham
2. Home from Evesham

Distant to Stratford 292 yards from box
Distant to Evesham 292 yards from box
Distant from Stratford 1134 yards from box
Distant from Evesham 1062 yards from box
Points and signals interlocked
Facing points provided with bolt and lifting bars

BROOM NORTH JUNCTION

2. Home from Barnt green
3. Starting to Barnt Green
7. Home to Barnt Green
Distant from Barnt Green 824 yards from Box
Distant from Evesham 346 yards from Box
Points and signals interlocked
Facing points provided with bolt and lifting bar

From Barnt Green

Down Sidings

Down →
← Up

Waiting Shed

To Stratford
To Evesham

Up Sidings

Rec'd Oct 21st
1892
No. 9148R
Board of Trade
Not to Scale

Source P.R.O. Kew MT6 599/12
Drawn by A.E. Overton

Fig 32.

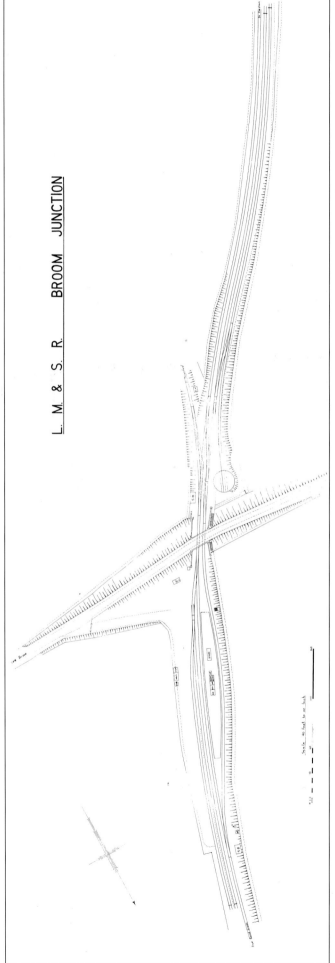

L. M. & S. R.   BROOM   JUNCTION

Fig 33.

Above left:
Broom Junction South signalbox was opened on 9 October 1892, as seen in this undated view, replacing the 1879 box. Another replacement box was opened on 6 May 1934. *Collection R. J. Essery*

Left:
The new signalbox opened on 6 May 1934 was initially known as Broom Junction, but when the new work was completed in 1942 it was renamed Broom North as seen here. The box was built to one of the early LMS designs; the locking frame is at the rear and the nameboard is of the later LMS standard pattern. *Collection R. J. Essery*

Above:
The signalman at Broom North was probably photographed on the same day as the previous view of his box.
Collection R. J. Essery

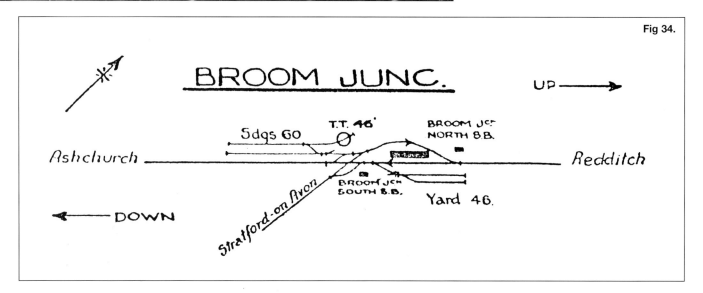

Fig 34. An LMS track diagram of c1932 shows the sidings and the turntable at Broom. Trains from the Stratford line ran on to the up line and goods traffic for the Midland that was to go in the up direction would be set back on to the two sidings to the southwest of the station. Traffic for the down direction would be placed in the yard which held 46 wagons.

Above:
Broom Junction, looking north from the overbridge before the north signalbox was removed in 1934 and probably in the late 1920s. The station nameboard is one of the Midland Railway designs that were introduced in 1895 and described as 'double and angled'. The station name, Broom Junction, faces the up platform only. The small building just beyond the nameboard does not appear in later pictures. There are a number of wagons in the sidings; those close to the signalbox are probably to be despatched over the Stratford line, while the others are mostly coal or empty goods wagons. Traffic to or loading from Broom would have been placed on this siding as it was the only one with road access.
Collection R. J. Essery

Centre left:
Broom Junction, as seen from the north end of the station. The station nameboard is of Midland design and faces the down platform with the legend 'For Stratford Line' placed below the station name. Later two small buildings replaced this nameboard, which appears to have then been moved to the other end of the platform, a smaller board replacing the angled nameboard that was originally at the south end.
Collection Roger Carpenter

Lower left:
A number of changes took place when the north signalbox was closed and some of these can be seen in this picture. New upper quadrant signals have replaced the old Midland signals seen earlier, the second nameboard has gone, the black line in front of the white-painted coach body is the small board that has replaced it. The hut at the far end of the platform is one of the two mentioned in the previous caption, the other is hidden behind the station building.
Collection R. J. Essery

Broom North, in the British Railways period. To the left is a Class 4F 0-6-0 at the head of a stopping freight train that has been held at the home signal to wait for the down passenger train to pass. A Class 4MT Ivatt 2-6-0 heads this train which is probably going to Ashchurch, and there are a number of vans in the sidings awaiting collection by a northbound train. *Collection R. J. Essery*

The story begins in 1864 with Parliamentary sanction for the construction of a railway some 33¼ miles long from Green's Norton Junction, on the Northampton & Banbury Junction Railway to Stratford-upon-Avon. This new line was to be called the East & West Junction Railway. Financial difficulties delayed the start of construction. The line from Fenny Compton, where a junction was made with the GWR, to Kineton was 6¼ miles in length, and was opened on 1 June 1871. Further extensions of the line were west to Stratford-upon-Avon and east to Green's Norton where this railway joined the Northampton & Banbury Junction Railway. The East & West enjoyed running powers through Towcester to Blisworth where a connection was made with the LNWR. The distance between London and Stratford by this route was 101 miles compared with 110¼ miles via Fenny Compton over the GWR. This was helpful in promoting passenger traffic from London to Stratford-upon-Avon using the shorter route. The Evesham, Redditch & Stratford-upon-Avon Junction Railway made further extensions to the west, and although independent it was worked by the East & West Junction Railway. This was the line that made the junction with the Midland Railway at Broom.

There were to be other additions to this small network of railways, the most important being the eastward extension to effect a junction with the Midland Railway's Bedford and Northampton branch at Ravenstone Wood Junction. This final connection gave the East & West Junction a direct east to west route that was 52 miles long. It was connected at each end with the Midland Railway and made a chord which connected with the London to the north main line of the Midland Railway near Bedford and with the Bristol-Birmingham main line via Evesham and Ashchurch, or via Redditch and Barnt Green. Therefore it

will be seen that the junction at Broom was an important part of our story.

Although there was some mineral traffic in the Towcester area, this was a local railway that ran through a mainly agricultural area. Because it did not generate enough revenue the company was in the hands of the Receiver in 1875 and during the period between 1877 and 1885, other than between Broom and Stratford-upon-Avon, passenger traffic was discontinued entirely. From 15 March 1887 arrangements were made with the LNWR that allowed the company to work its goods traffic for destinations in the west over the line from Blisworth to Broom but this traffic was small in volume and these trains ceased on 31 October 1888.

In April 1891, a joint committee under the title of the East & West Junction, Stratford-upon-Avon, Towcester & Midland Junction Railways Joint Committee was set up in order to enable the whole system to be worked as a single undertaking. Following the opening of the final section through Ravenstone Wood Junction the Midland Railway began to run a service of freight trains between London and Bristol. These trains began to run on 13 April 1891 and continued until 8 December 1891. Thereafter locomotives owned by the joint committee worked the trains because the Midland Railway locomotives were too heavy for the light permanent way of the East & West Junction Railway. A thorough reorganisation of the line came in 1908 which included the change of name to the Stratford-upon-Avon & Midland Junction Railway. Thereafter the company entered its most prosperous period before becoming part of the LMS in 1923. The importance of Broom may well have increased considerably if the 14-mile long Worcester & Broom Railway had been built. The line was authorised in 1885, but it was never constructed and, although it was finally abandoned in 1894, attempts to revive the scheme were made as late as 1923.

From the construction of the junction at Broom in 1879 until 1942, all trains joining the Stratford lines going to or coming from the Evesham direction had to reverse at Broom. The existence of an engine turntable, which was in use for many years, greatly assisted matters as far as the locomotive crews were concerned. I have been unable to establish with any degree of certainty when the turntable was installed, or when it was taken out of service. One source gives abandonment as the mid-1930s although it could have been in service until the triangle was created in 1942.

Broom was, for a large part of the line's existence, an important junction. The passenger train service between Broom and Stratford survived for 68 years, being introduced in 1879 and ceasing to operate in 1947. In 1903 there were four trains between Broom and Blisworth each day, departing at 8.17, 11.10, 2/37 and 6/17. By 1915, the service had been reduced to three through trains, at 11.10, 2/42 and 6/20. The early morning service terminated at Kineton, no doubt in connection with the armaments establishment at this location. The only through train in 1921 was the 11.15 which ran from Broom to Blisworth.

In 1903, the Midland Railway service on the Evesham branch included a number of trains which connected with trains that ran over the Stratford lines and these can be summarised as below.

Broom

Arrived	Departed	Train
8.09	8.11 to Ashchurch	6.30 from Birmingham
9.08	9.09 to Birmingham	8.52 from Evesham
10.55	10.58 to Birmingham	10.38 from Evesham
10.58	11.01 to Ashchurch	9.40 from Birmingham
2/29	2/30 to Birmingham	2/10 from Evesham
2/30	2/31 to Ashchurch	1/15 from Birmingham
4/16	4/17 to Birmingham	4/0 from Evesham
6/10	6/12 to Birmingham	5/18 from Ashchurch
6/10	6/11 to Ashchurch	5/0 from Birmingham
8/31	8/32 to Evesham	7/32 from Birmingham

Although some trains were later retired, this was to be the basic service from Birmingham to Evesham and Ashchurch for the next 50 years or so, but at the southern end of the line the passenger trains from Birmingham terminated at Ashchurch rather than Evesham.

Fig 35 The most significant feature of Broom North Junction is the Victorian arrangement for a single line junction. In some respects it is 'over engineered' but the underlying factor was safety. For example, with this arrangement of tracks a Down train that ran past signal 8 would run onto the Stratford line, which carried less traffic, and not possibly run into a n Up direction train. In the Up direction an Up train that ran past signal 30 would be directed onto the correct Up line at the west side of the platform. Finally it should be pointed out that signal 10 was a starting signal for Stratford on Avon trains from this platform as described in the text. The explanation of D duplicated signal will be found on page 75, Fig 31.
Drawing and notes by A. E.Overton

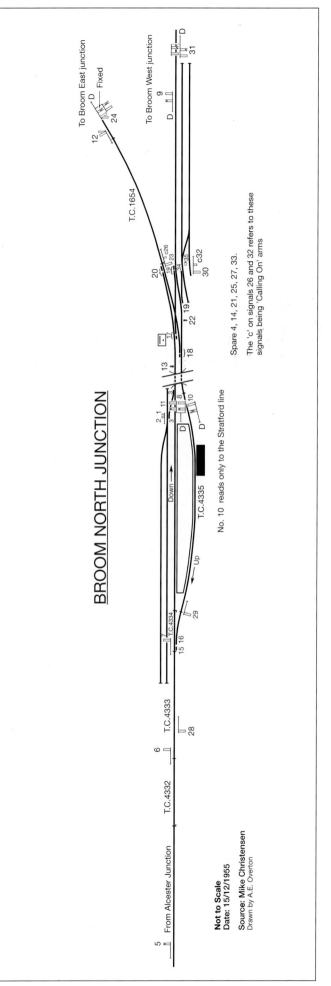

BROOM NORTH JUNCTION

To Broom East junction

To Broom West junction

Spare 4, 14, 21, 25, 27, 33.

The 'c' on signals 26 and 32 refers to these signals being 'Calling On' arms

No. 10 reads only to the Stratford line

Not to Scale
Date: 15/12/1955

Source: Mike Christensen
Drawn by A.E. Overton

From Alcester Junction

Fig 35.

81

Fig 36.

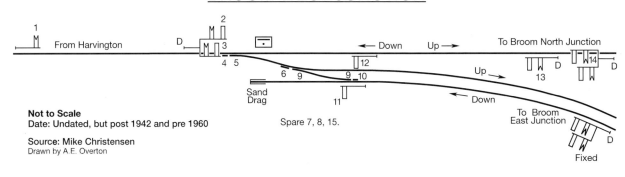

BROOM WEST JUNCTION

From Harvington

To Broom North Junction

← Down   Up →

Up →

← Down

Sand Drag

Not to Scale
Date: Undated, but post 1942 and pre 1960

Spare 7, 8, 15.

Source: Mike Christensen
Drawn by A.E. Overton

To Broom East Junction

Fixed

Fig 36. The arrangements at Broom West with the simplified junction layout were very similar to those at Broom East as described on page 83. The explanation for the duplicated signals, shown as D, will be found in Fig 31, page 75. *Drawing and notes by A. E.Overton*

Broom East signalbox, which opened on 17 May 1942 and was closed on 1 July 1962. During the 1930s the LMS developed the production of wooden signalbox parts that were prefabricated and designed around standard flake lengths. ('Flake lengths' was the term used to describe the prefabricated panels used in the construction of signalboxes.) This flexible system was most useful during World War 2 and this signalbox was built by using these parts. Note the wide tablet exchange platform for the signalman. Train tablets had to be exchanged with the train crews travelling in both directions. *W. Garbett*

Broom West signalbox was unlike the wooden construction employed for Broom East, this box being built to the ARP design introduced prior to the outbreak of war in 1939. The ARP signalboxes were built using 14in thick brickwork walls and a reinforced concrete floor and roof and resembled a blockhouse. They also later proved to be difficult to demolish! West signalbox was opened on 29 September 1942, when the curve between the East and West signalboxes was opened. It closed, together with the East signalbox, on 1 July 1962. *W. Garbett*

Also in 1903, the Stratford line connections at Broom began with the arrival of the 7.40 from Stratford at 8.0 which gave a connection for passengers travelling south, who were able to join the 6.30 from Birmingham that arrived at Broom at 8.09. Passengers from the Birmingham train for the Stratford line joined the 8.17 departure from Broom for Stratford and Blisworth. At 10.48 a through service from Blisworth arrived, this train having left Stratford at 10.25. There were seven minutes to unload any parcels, for the passengers to alight and the train to be shunted clear before the 10.38 from Evesham arrived at 10.55. This train used the same platform as the Stratford line train, while the other platform was for the 9.40 from Birmingham due at 10.58. The passengers changed trains and the Evesham and Birmingham trains departed, this enabling the Stratford line train to return to the platform, and while the passengers rejoined the train, the engine ran round in readiness to depart at 11.10.

Above:
Midland Railway 2-4-0s rarely appear in photographs of the Evesham branch, but one is seen in this c1910 view of Broom Junction. The locomotive is No 168 with a down train and carries an express passenger train headcode. There are quite a number of passengers on the platform, but it is impossible to say if they are waiting for an up Midland train or for the Stratford line train to return to the platform. There is a Midland Railway ventilated goods van in the siding to the right of the engine. *Collection R. J. Essery*

Fig 37. By this date the Ministry of Transport, as successors to the Board of Trade, requirements for junctions had been altered and they now permitted the simplified arrangement as shown on this plan that employed a sand drag on the Up line from Broom West Junction. The only 'passenger trains' to run over this line were troop trains that were worked under different regulations to public passenger trains. An explanation for the duplicated signals, shown as D, will be found in Fig 31, page 75. *Drawing and notes by A. E.Overton*

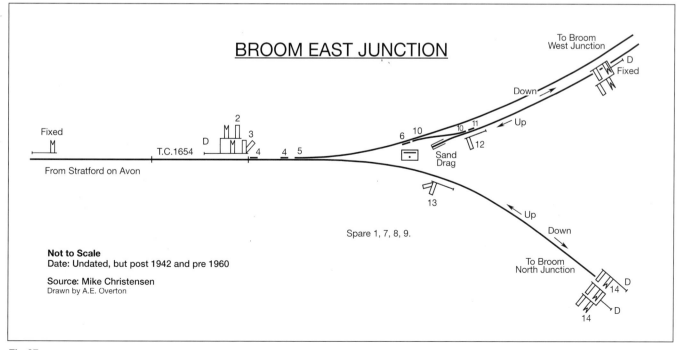

Fig 37.

The principle of connecting trains continued, the times and frequency varying over the years (although there was never a connecting Sunday service). I have summarised four years of weekday services between 1903 and 1934 below.

1903 Public Timetable
Broom

arrive at 8.0	7.40 from Stratford
depart at 8.17	8.38 at Stratford, train goes through to Blisworth
arrive at 10.48	10.25 from Stratford, train started at Blisworth
depart at 11.10	11.21 at Stratford, train goes through to Blisworth
arrive at 2/18	1/55 from Stratford, train started at Blisworth
depart at 2/37	2/58 at Stratford, train goes through to Blisworth
arrive at 5/58	5/35 from Stratford, train started at Blisworth
depart at 6/17	6/38 at Stratford, train goes through to Blisworth

1915 Public Timetable
Broom

arrive at 7.55	7.35 from Stratford
depart at 8.15	8.35 at Stratford, train goes through to Kineton
arrive at 10.52	10.32 from Stratford, train started at Blisworth
depart at 11.10	11.30 at Stratford, train goes through to Blisworth
arrive at 2/20	2/0 from Stratford, train started at Kineton
depart at 2/42	3/2 at Stratford, train goes through to Blisworth
arrive at 6/0	5/40 from Stratford
depart at 6/20	6/40 at Stratford, train goes through to Byfield

1921 Public Timetable
Broom

arrive at 10.52	10.30 from Stratford, train started at Blisworth
depart at 11.15	11.35 at Stratford, train goes through to Blisworth
arrive at 2/30	2/10 from Stratford
depart at 2/50	3/10 at Stratford
arrive at 8/0	7/40 from Stratford
depart at 8/50	9/10 at Stratford

1934 Working Timetable
Broom

arrive at 7.43	7.22 from Stratford
depart at 8.13	8.34 at Stratford, booked to run as a mixed train
arrive at 10.47	10.27 from Stratford, train started at Blisworth
depart at 11.15	11.35 at Stratford, train goes through to Blisworth
arrive at 2/36	2/15 from Stratford
depart at 2/59	3/19 at Stratford
arrive at 5/50	5/30 from Stratford, Saturdays only
depart at 6/30	6/50 at Stratford, Saturdays only
arrive at 8/0	7/40 from Stratford, Saturdays excepted
arrive at 8/36	8/15 from Stratford, Saturdays only
depart at 8/55	9/15 at Stratford

The details of the freight train services will be found in the various timetables set out in Chapter 4; the most interesting were the London to Bristol and Bristol to London express freight trains that carried the banana traffic. Three engines and two brake vans originally handled these trains which were reversed at Broom.

This presumption about the brake van is based upon reports that SMJR brake vans worked through to London. In the pre-1923 period a London train would leave Bristol and work to Broom. Upon arrival at Broom the train would be reversed and another engine would work forward to Olney with the brake van that was attached at Broom. Both the brake van and engine would be SMJR stock. At Olney, a Midland engine would take over and the train, with the SMJR brake, would go through to London, the SMJR brake returning with a Bristol train the following day. After 1923 I expect that Midland engines from London worked through to Broom and the London men lodged at Stratford, returning the following day. This would mean that only two engines would be required for each leg, one from Bristol to Broom and one from Broom to London. At first they may have been Class 3 goods engines but the most likely choice would later be a Class 4F 0-6-0.

Above:
I believe this is the 11.15am from Broom Junction to Stratford on the final day of the connecting service in 1947 with Class 3F 0-6-0 No 3523 and what appear to be two third class brake coaches. *R. J. Essery*

Right:
This is the only picture I have found that shows a banana train at Broom and was taken in 1934. The train is waiting for the engine to be coupled to the front of the train, which is almost under the bridge. *R. E. Lacy*

Below:
Ex-Midland Railway Class 4F No 43979, now running with an LMS old standard tender which has replaced the original Midland tender, heads a northbound freight train at Broom Junction. The train is passing the site of the North signalbox which was removed in 1934, with the buffer stops at the end of the two yard sidings to the right. *M. Mensing*

Salford Priors

Salford Priors was 1 mile 31 chains south of Broom. The station was opened for goods traffic on 16 June 1866 and for passengers on 17 September in the same year. The station area included a goods shed adjacent to the platform and the rail entry to the shed was from a loop off the main line. There was also a siding which served cattle pens with their own road access, and there was a further siding in the yard which was no doubt used by coal merchants for loading direct to their road vehicles.

The goods facilities included a 1½-ton crane and the station was able to handle furniture vans, livestock, horseboxes and prize cattle traffic, while carriages by passenger trains were also catered for. The yard capacity was 35 wagons. The OS map reproduced on page 88 shows the station area before the new connection was put in for the use of Messrs Bromford & Evershed. Fig 39 is taken from the Midland Railway plan that was submitted to the Board of Trade on 23 May 1910 when permission was sought to open the siding for traffic. The Board of Trade appointed Major Pringle RE to conduct the inspection and this is what he had to say in his report dated 21 July 1910:

'I made an inspection yesterday of the new works at Salford Priors on the Evesham-Redditch single-line branch of the Midland Railway. At the north end of this station, a new siding has been laid on the east side of the main line, to which access is provided through a new set of points, which face trains travelling from the north. The points are fitted with a lock and the siding is trapped.

'The new connection is worked from a ground stage, which contains two levers properly interlocked, which is controlled by the tablet for the single-line section. The arrangements are satisfactory and I recommend the Board of Trade to approve the new works.'

There were two ground stages at Salford Priors: one controlled the two connections to the loop and the other, new one, controlled the entrance to the Bromford & Evershed's sidings. This was an engineering company which supplied steam ploughing, dredging and road rolling equipment that was moved by rail. This eventually came to an end and the station was closed to all traffic on the 1 October 1962.

This c1934 picture of Salford Priors should be compared with the next view taken in 1951. The original Midland Railway angled station nameboard can be seen and the ivy on the end of the stationmaster's house will be removed later, and may have been the result of a change of stationmaster. The corrugated iron lean-to will go and in its place there will be a garden shed. The two seats are evident in both pictures, at the far end of the platform in this picture, but one will be moved up to the station building in the later view. *The Roy F. Burrows Midland Collection Trust*

Fig 38

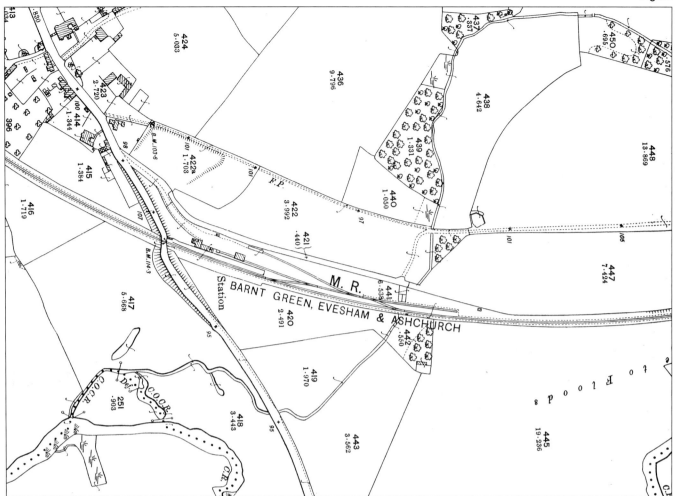

This picture was taken c1962 and is looking towards Evesham. The station has retained the LMS Hawkseye nameboard and the entrance from the road by the steps can be seen. This picture also shows one of the stages, left, that controlled entry to the loop and sidings. *Joe Moss*

Fig 39

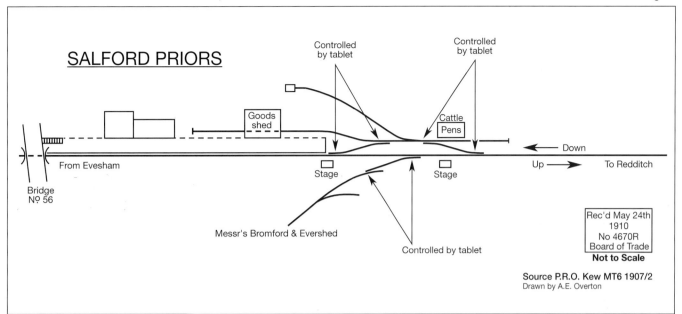

SALFORD PRIORS

Controlled by tablet

Controlled by tablet

Goods shed

Cattle Pens

From Evesham

Down

Stage

Up

To Redditch

Stage

Bridge Nº 56

Messr's Bromford & Evershed

Controlled by tablet

Rec'd May 24th 1910 No 4670R Board of Trade
Not to Scale

Source P.R.O. Kew MT6 1907/2
Drawn by A.E. Overton

Fig 38. (*Above left*) This Ordnance Survey map pre-dates the 1910 alterations when the Midland Railway put in the siding for Messrs Bromford & Evershed. Unlike some of the stations on the line, there were a few houses fairly close to the station, and no doubt fishing in the River Arrow also generated some passenger traffic. The entrance to both the passenger station and the goods yard was along the road that terminated at the cattle pens although there was also an entrance by steps. The small hut that contained the weighbridge controls is the building opposite the station, close to the gated entrance. *Crown Copyright*

Fig 39. (*Above*) This diagram, redrawn from an original Midland Railway plan held at the PRO Kew, shows the new connections that were put in for the use of Messrs Bromford & Evershed. Trains that were either detaching or attaching traffic at Salford Priors did so by using the train tablet to unlock the stages that controlled entry to the sidings on both sides of the single line. This task was usually undertaken by the train guard who, in conjunction with the station staff, would advise the locomotive driver what had to be done in the way of shunting. *A. E. Overton*

Centre right:
A 1951 view of Salford Priors station which shows the station building with the stationmaster's house and the goods shed alongside the station platform. The station nameboard is an LMS Hawkseye design introduced during the 1930s. The loop, with the two stages, can also be seen in the distance to the right of the track. The one nearest the end of the platform is similar to the corrugated iron hut stage at Alvechurch; the other stage is a larger wooden structure. The 'Beware of Trains' notice, seen at the far end of the platform in the previous view is no longer there. *Collection Philip Jarvis*

Lower right:
This undated view provides a close-up of the platform with part of the stationmaster's garden. The sign beyond the nearest oil lamp reads 'Gentlemen' and the two entrances are probably to the booking hall and waiting room. *Collection Philip Jarvis*

Harvington

Harvington was 2 miles 1 chain south from Salford Priors and was the final station on the line before trains arrived at Evesham from the north. Harvington station had just a single-face platform and the goods facilities were a loop and a siding with the capacity to hold 25 wagons. There was a loading gauge about halfway along the loop and a weighing machine near to the entrance of the yard area.

The station opened on 16 June 1866 for passengers and on 17 September for goods. The signalbox was opened on 2 June 1891 and it was to remain in service until 1 March 1964, the station having closed for all traffic on 1 October 1962. Train services at Harvington were somewhat limited and it is surprising that the station remained active for so long. For about half of the distance between Harvington and Evesham the line ran to the west of the River Avon, but as the railway turned due west into Evesham the river looped to the south of the town before passing beneath the line between Evesham and Bengeworth.

Fig 40. Unlike some stations on the line, the one at Harvington was just a short distance from the village and the only entrance was along the road that went past the station and ran alongside the siding. *Crown Copyright*

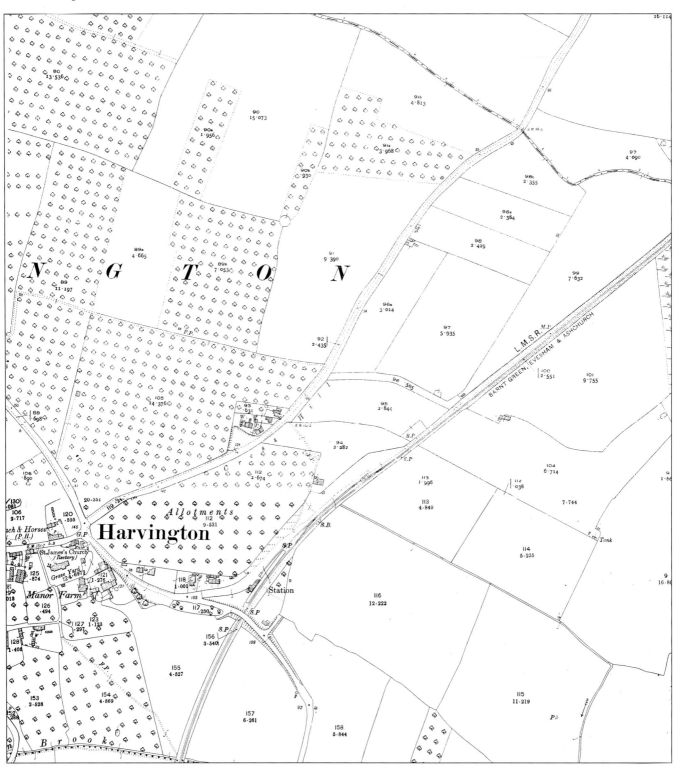

Fig 40

Above:
This idyllic picture shows Harvington station in 1906 with the substantial stationmaster's house and beyond, the booking office, waiting room and toilets. The station comprised a single platform face with one straight station nameboard above the white-painted fence to the right of the picture. The trees obscure any wagons that may be on the loop. *Collection R. J. Essery*

Below:
Harvington was about 3½ miles north of Evesham and was the only block post between Evesham and Broom Junction. The line through the station was single but there was a loop which contained a loading gauge as seen in this undated picture taken looking north. To the right is the signalbox, opened on 2 June 1891 and closed on 1 March 1964. *Collection R. J. Essery*

Fig 41. The layout at Harvington was similar to Wixford but unlike Wixford, Harvington had a signal box. From either direction movements into the siding were handsignalled by the signalman, but the exit from the siding was controlled by signals 11 and 12.
Drawing and notes by A. E.Overton

This is the road approach to the station and the rear of the stationmaster's house with a corrugated iron hut in the garden. This type of building was often used as a lamp room or oil store; I wonder if it was in use for railway or private purposes?
Collection R. J. Essery

When compared with the earlier view of the station, a number of changes can be seen in this undated but post-1948 picture of Harvington. The LMS Hawkseye station nameboard has replaced the Midland board that was at the other end of the platform, the ivy has been removed and while there has been a reduction in trees and bushes, the station has become somewhat overgrown. There has also been a change of lamp design. *Collection David Tee*

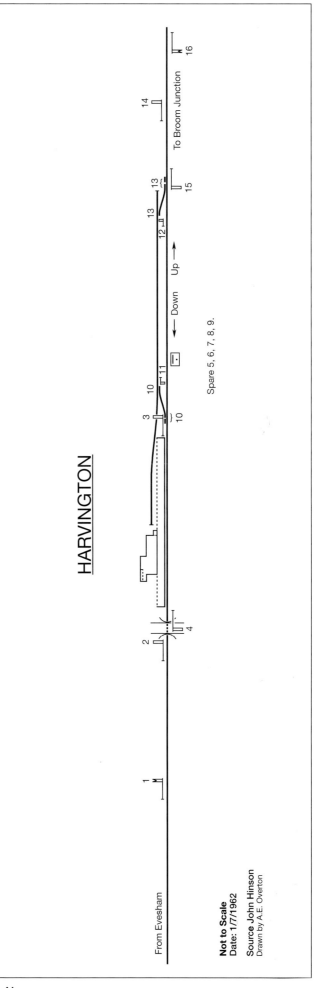

HARVINGTON

From Evesham

To Broom Junction

← Down   Up →

Spare 5, 6, 7, 8, 9.

Not to Scale
Date: 1/7/1962

Source John Hinson
Drawn by A.E. Overton

Fig 41.

The photographer was facing Evesham and this picture shows the loop and the siding which ran back towards the rear of the platform. The weighbridge hut can be seen to the right of the station building, and there was also a small office but this is hidden behind the hut. The weighbridge is shown in Fig 40, but the office was a later addition. The signalman was responsible for all shunting and ground signals, referred to as discs on Midland Railway drawings, controlled the exit from the loop. *R. J. Essery*

Evesham

Evesham was 21 miles 21 chains from Barnt Green and it marked the end of the single-line section from Redditch. Although this old market town's population was less than that of Redditch, it was the most important place on the line. Not a junction in the accepted sense, it did provide a connection with the GWR where a considerable amount of traffic was exchanged. The town was situated on the banks of the River Avon in the rich and beautiful Vale of Evesham, a mainly agricultural district devoted to market gardening and orchards. The coming of the railways enabled the produce to be sold to markets in the developing industrial towns and cities that were too far away to be served by other forms of transport. Other industries included jam making and fruit and vegetable canning.

Inward traffic, in addition to coal for both industrial and domestic use, consisted of fertilisers and similar products for the agricultural community. Messrs Espley's steam saw mills required a steady supply of large tree trunks and the arrival of particularly large trunks was sometimes reported in the local newspaper, the *Evesham Journal*.

The Midland Railway station at Evesham was able to handle goods and passenger traffic together with furniture vans, carriages, portable engines, machines on wheels, livestock, horseboxes and prize cattle vans as well as carriages by passenger trains. A 5-ton crane was provided.

The track plan of the two stations at Evesham was fairly simple. From the north the single Midland Railway line ran to the west of the River Avon and crossed over the GWR's line from Worcester to Oxford, 26 chains to the east of the passenger station. On the approach to the station the Midland line became two tracks and continued as a double line through to Ashchurch, where there was a junction with the Birmingham to Gloucester Railway. All the Midland Railway traffic facilities at Evesham lay to the south of the Midland station. In 1932, the wagon capacity in the marshalling sidings was 97 wagons while the goods yard could hold a further 110 vehicles. One of the Evesham merchants with his own wagons was Richard White & Sons whose wagons were painted black with white lettering. An example painted in lead colour is on page 103.

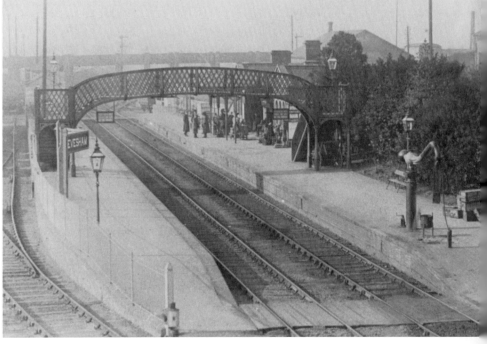

This delightful picture of Evesham was taken after the 1905 alterations were made but probably before the Great War. There are a number of points of interest: the angled station nameboard, the 'Passengers are requested to cross the line by the bridge' sign hanging below the footbridge, the water crane painted in Denby Pottery cream and Venetian red, and the disc signal that controlled the exit from the goods sidings behind the station. This picture should be compared with the one in Chapter 2, taken c1904. *Collection R. J. Essery*

Fig 42.

Fig 42. The Ordnance Survey map dated 1904 features both the Midland and Great Western Railway stations at Evesham. The Midland Railway approached Evesham from almost due north and, after crossing over the Great Western's Oxford, Worcester & Wolverhampton line, turned west into the Midland station. After passing through the station and crossing the River Avon the line swung in a southerly direction towards Bengeworth. The earlier layout of the Midland station is shown in Fig 46 with later alterations in Fig 44. The LMS track layout can be seen in Fig 45. In 1904, there was only one connection between the Midland Railway and the Great Western, this having been opened about the time that the line from Ashchurch came into use but I do not know the date that the second connection was made. Finally, a new junction with the Western Region was opened on 19 March 1957. *Crown Copyright*

A small, two-road locomotive shed, with entry over the 42ft diameter turntable, can be seen on the 1904 OS map. At this time the engine shed was to the west of the sidings but from the later LMS line diagram it is clear that the sidings were extended in the area of the saw mill. The LMS diagram shows there were 50 yards of track outside the shed and space inside for two locomotives.

The GWR station was just to the north of the Midland station, separated by a road area. It possessed similar facilities to those on the Midland, including an engine shed. The interchange between the two railways was made by the two transfer roads that ran from the south side of the GWR dock and trailed into both the up and down Midland Railway main lines.

As noted in the previous chapter, the Midland Railway station at Evesham was opened for goods traffic on 1 July 1864 and to passengers on 1 October. At first, the station was the terminus of the line from Ashchurch, with the section from Ashchurch and Evesham Junction to Beckford worked by telegraph bells and the section from Beckford to Evesham on the time interval system. Later, the block telegraph was introduced. Evesham became a through station when the line to Alcester was opened in 1866.

The first signalbox at Evesham station was opened before 1 November 1875 and was closed on 23 September 1890. On that date two new signalboxes were opened: Evesham South to replace the original box at Evesham station, and one at Evesham North. This enabled block telegraph working between the two signalboxes to be introduced. The new work was inspected by Major Hutchinson RE and the report of his inspection has been reproduced here. 'The siding connections at this station have been partly rearranged and provided with safety points; the signals have been placed in conformity with modern practice and the levers working the points and signals concentrated and interlocked in two cabins and a dwarf frame controlled from one of them containing the following levers.

Fig 42.

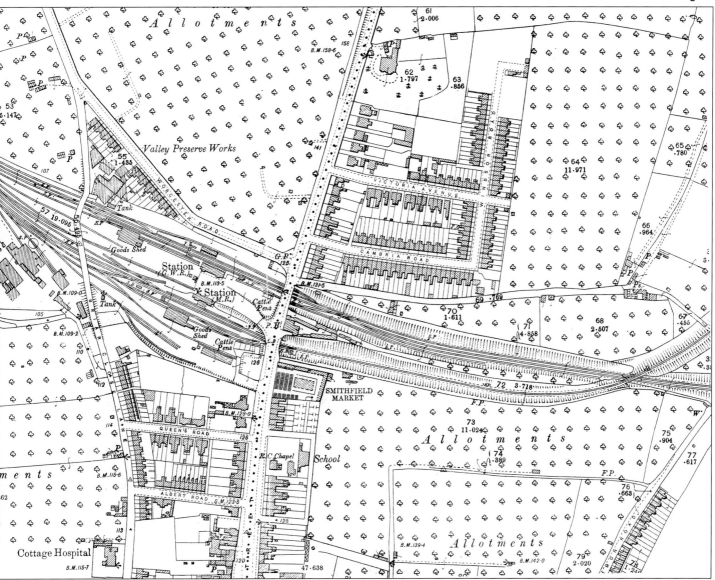

North cabin six working and two spare levers. South cabin 14 working and two spare levers. Dwarf frame three working, no spare levers.'

The inspecting officer continued: 'The arrangements are satisfactory, except that at the South cabin No 17 crossing should be shortened and an intermediate safety point provided in No 14 crossing. Subject to these requirements, to an old siding connection not now required being removed, and to the points being properly connected with the levers that are to work them, I can recommend the Board of Trade to sanction the use of alterations at Evesham.'

Prior to the North box being replaced on 25 June 1905 and the replacement box built seven chains nearer to Alcester, the up line was extended. The inspection by Major Pringle was carried out on 13 September 1904 and this is what he reported to the Board of Trade. 'The up line has been extended eastwards for a distance of about 220yd, and a new up advance starting signal provided. The facing points of the single line towards Redditch have been thereby taken eastwards, and the down home signal has been altered in position accordingly. Evesham North signal cabin, from which the new signals are worked, contains an old frame with eight levers of which one is spare. The necessary interlocking has been correctly supplied and the arrangements being satisfactory I can recommend the Board of Trade to confirm their provisional authority for the new works.' This layout is shown in Fig 44.

Major Pringle made the inspection of the new North signalbox on 30 August 1905; this is the substance of his report. 'The old signalbox at the north end of the station has been replaced by a new box situated about 125yd further east. A new crossover road has been laid between the loop lines at the east end, and a through crossing from the down sidings to the up line has been formed by the addition of slip points to the crossover. These new connections are worked from Evesham North signalbox, which contains a new frame with 16 levers of which three are spare. The interlocking is correct and the arrangements are satisfactory.' Fig 45 shows this arrangement.

The next inspection that Major Pringle made was in connection with the new sidings that were built by the saw mill to the west of the station close to the engine shed. Dated 13 March 1906 his descriptive report said: 'I have made an inspection of the new works near Evesham on the Midland Railway. Additional siding accommodation has been laid on the south of the railway to which access is provided through a new set of trailing points. The connection is worked from an old ground stage containing three levers, which is as formerly bolt locked from Evesham South signalbox. The interlocking and arrangements are satisfactory. There are no additions of any sort in Evesham South signalbox. I recommend the Board of Trade to sanction these new works.' Fig 46 illustrates this new work.

The South signalbox was replaced on 14 October 1934 and this box was renamed Evesham on 20 January 1935. As a result

Above:
This undated but probably c1920 view of Evesham was taken from the south end of the station and shows the old South signalbox which was replaced in 1934. The transfer road to the Great Western can be seen in the bottom left corner as can the scotch blocks that are across the rails. These are an alternative to trap points and prevent rolling stock from running forward and possibly fouling the running lines. The Great Western station is to the left of the picture and the public road between the two stations is clearly visible. The fence on the side of the loading dock marked the boundary between the GWR and the Midland Railway. *Collection R. J. Essery*

Below:
Saltley-based Horwich Mogul, No 42790, is carrying a fitted freight train headcode and an explanation could be that the engine has run forward to take water while the train is being prepared. There are some wagons further along the platform, just visible under the overbridge, and the first vehicle is a vacuum-fitted open goods wagon. When compared with the earlier view from the same direction it can be seen that there have been some further alterations to the track layout. The connection to the running lines seen in Figs 45, 46 and 47 has gone and it has been replaced by buffer stops. This may have been done when Evesham North signalbox was closed. *H. C. Casserley 85297*

Fig 43. This is the earliest file on Evesham to survive at the PRO Kew, which shows signalling alterations that were inspected by the Board of Trade. Dated 1890, this plan was to show the two new signalboxes and the block telegraph working between them that the Midland Railway was about to open. The substance of the inspecting officer's report has been reproduced in the text. The drawing has been marked where the GWR connection was made; it ran to the siding which terminated in the loading dock at the west end of the up platform. Also note that on the original Midland Railway drawing the disc from the siding at the Ashchurch end was not numbered. It was worked from the stage and not the signalbox. *A. E. Overton*

Fig 44. During a relatively short period of time there were a number of changes made at Evesham beginning with the 1904 alterations which increased the length of the loop. A picture in Chapter 2, on page 25, illustrates the layout at the Redditch end of the station post-1903 but before the 1905 changes shown in Fig 45 which included the construction of the footbridge connecting the two platforms. The inspector's report was brief and it has been reproduced in the text. Approval for this work was given by the Board of Trade on 16 September 1904. *A. E. Overton*

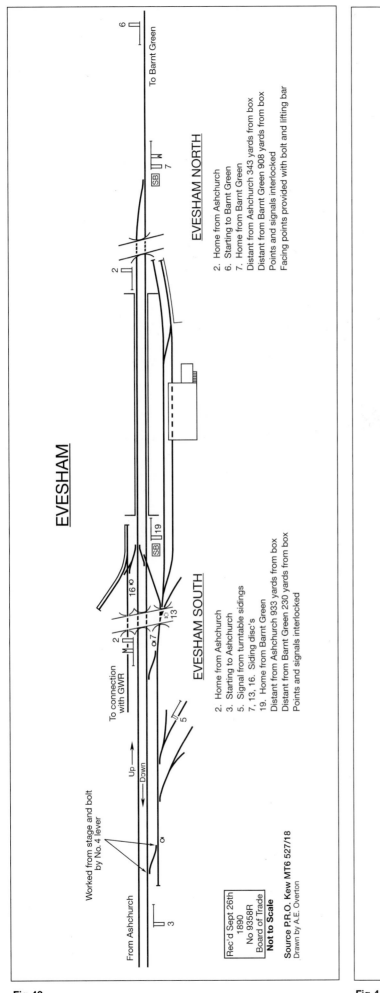

EVESHAM

From Ashchurch

To connection
with GWR

Worked from stage and bolt
by No. 4 lever

Up
Down

To Barnt Green

EVESHAM SOUTH

2. Home from Ashchurch
3. Starting to Ashchurch
5. Signal from turntable sidings
7, 13, 16. Siding disc's
19. Home from Barnt Green
Distant from Ashchurch 933 yards from box
Distant from Barnt Green 230 yards from box
Points and signals interlocked

Rec'd Sept 26th
1890
No 9358R
Board of Trade
Not to Scale

Source P.R.O. Kew MT6 527/18
Drawn by A.E. Overton

EVESHAM NORTH

2. Home from Ashchurch
6. Starting to Barnt Green
7. Home from Barnt Green
Distant from Ashchurch 343 yards from box
Distant from Barnt Green 908 yards from box
Points and signals interlocked
Facing points provided with bolt and lifting bar

Fig 43.

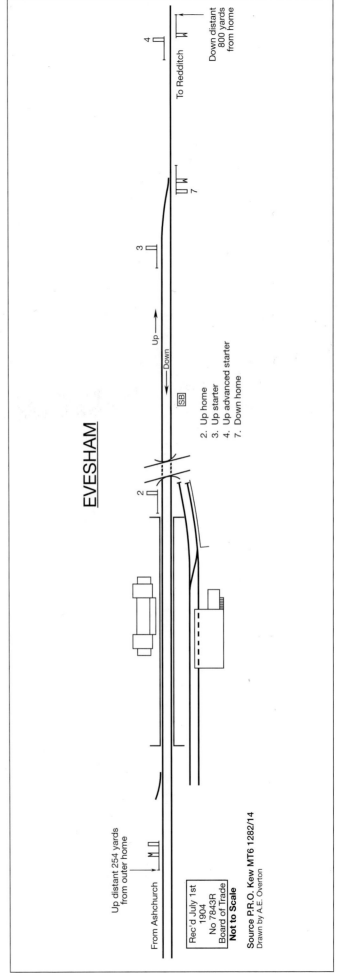

EVESHAM

From Ashchurch

Up distant 254 yards
from outer home

Up
Down

To Redditch

Down distant
800 yards
from home

2. Up home
3. Up starter
4. Up advanced starter
7. Down home

Rec'd July 1st
1904
No 7843R
Board of Trade
Not to Scale

Source P.R.O. Kew MT6 1282/14
Drawn by A.E. Overton

Fig 44.

Fig 45. The 1905 changes shown on the original Midland Railway plan, now at the PRO Kew, were to connect the goods yard at the Redditch end of Evesham to the up loop by a trailing crossover, and to the down main line by a slip point. Safety points protected the passenger lines from the goods sidings. In addition, a new Evesham North signalbox was built and the old box closed. The footbridge, shown on the drawing was also new work and it was mentioned in the inspector's report. Approval for this work was given by the Board of Trade on 1 September 1905. *A. E. Overton*

The LMS Railway sign is still prominent in this 1963 picture which shows GWR 0-6-0PT No 8743 in the Midland station with an ex-LMS third class brake coach. The GWR engine is carrying an ordinary passenger train headcode so it may be working an Evesham to Ashchurch train. *M. Mensing*

of the rationalisation and cost saving that we have previously encountered at Alcester and Broom the signalbox at Evesham North was closed on 20 January 1935.

The Midland Railway engine shed at Evesham was opened c1870, and although it was closed on 14 September 1931, crews were outstationed there for traffic purposes until well into the BR era. They remanned engines that spent time at Evesham between turns and were employed on balanced workings with Saltley men. Amongst the duties carried out by Evesham men over the years were those to work north with stopping freight trains and to change over at Alcester before returning with the southbound train. During the early years of British Railways a certain amount of name changing took place, and in September 1951 the name of the ex-LMS goods depot was altered to Evesham South. Although the Evesham traffic was dominated by agricultural produce, we must not overlook the coal and other inward traffic required by its inhabitants on a daily basis.

The GWR possessed traffic facilities over the Evesham and Redditch line with contingent running powers between Evesham Junction and Redditch, if such facilities were not afforded. A similar arrangement applied over the Evesham and Ashchurch line but as far as I am aware these running powers were not used by the GWR. Finally, it should be noted that a new junction with the Western Region line came into use on 19 March 1957.

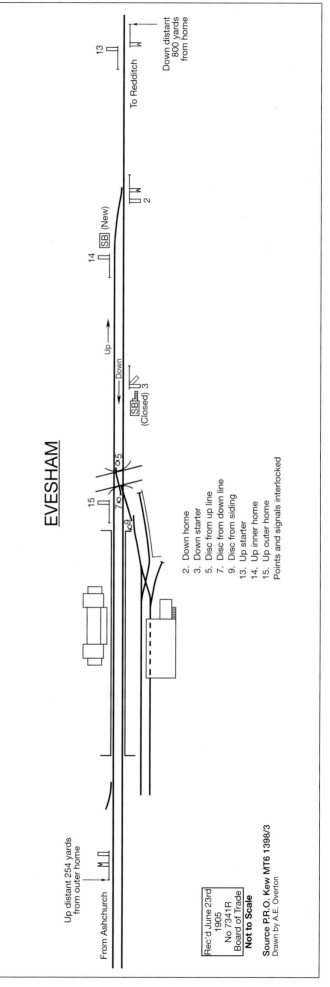

EVESHAM

To Redditch

Down distant 800 yards from home

13

2

14 SB (New)

SB (Closed) 3

Up

Down

15

5

7

9

From Ashchurch

Up distant 254 yards from outer home

2. Down home
3. Down starter
5. Disc from up line
7. Disc from down line
9. Disc from siding
13. Up starter
14. Up inner home
15. Up outer home
Points and signals interlocked

Rec'd June 23rd 1905
No 7341R
Board of Trade
Not to Scale

Source P.R.O. Kew MT6 1398/3
Drawn by A.E. Overton

Fig 45.

There were water cranes at both ends of the station and this picture shows part of the crane on the down platform, right. In addition to the crane, the frost fire can also be seen. These were used in frosty weather to prevent the water from freezing, the fires being maintained by various departments, depending upon the location. Judging by the style of dress this picture was probably taken in the 1950s, and the station nameboard appears to be a British Railways replacement for the previous board. *Collection R. J. Essery*

These two pictures show Saltley's Fowler Class 4MT 2-6-4T No 42416 on passenger train work on 14 April 1962. The first view illustrates the 2.55pm from Redditch to Ashchurch arriving at Evesham station. After working forward to Ashchurch the engine ran round the train of corridor coaches and departed with the 4.30pm from Ashchurch to Redditch and is seen here at Evesham in the second view. This picture also shows the buffer stops that replaced the connection referred to previously. *Both M. Mensing*

Above:
The exterior of Evesham station on
23 August 1964. *Collection R. J. Essery*

Left:
Although the engine shed at Evesham was
closed in 1931, engine crews were
outstationed there until the end of steam
working. This picture was taken in the late
1950s and shows the turntable and the
inspection pit that has been used when
raking out the ashpan of locomotives. As a
result there is a considerable quantity of
clinker at the far end of the pit. This would
be removed from time to time and shovelled
into wagons. The signalbox in the centre of
the picture is on the Western Region.
Collection R. J. Essery

Lower left:
This is another view of the turntable, with
Briar Close Lane in the background.
Collection R. J. Essery

Fig 46. (*Right*) As traffic increased, new
sidings were required and these were built at
the Ashchurch end of the station. Major
Pringle's report has been reproduced in full
on page 95, and approval for this new work
was given by the Board of Trade on 15 March
1906. *A. E. Overton*

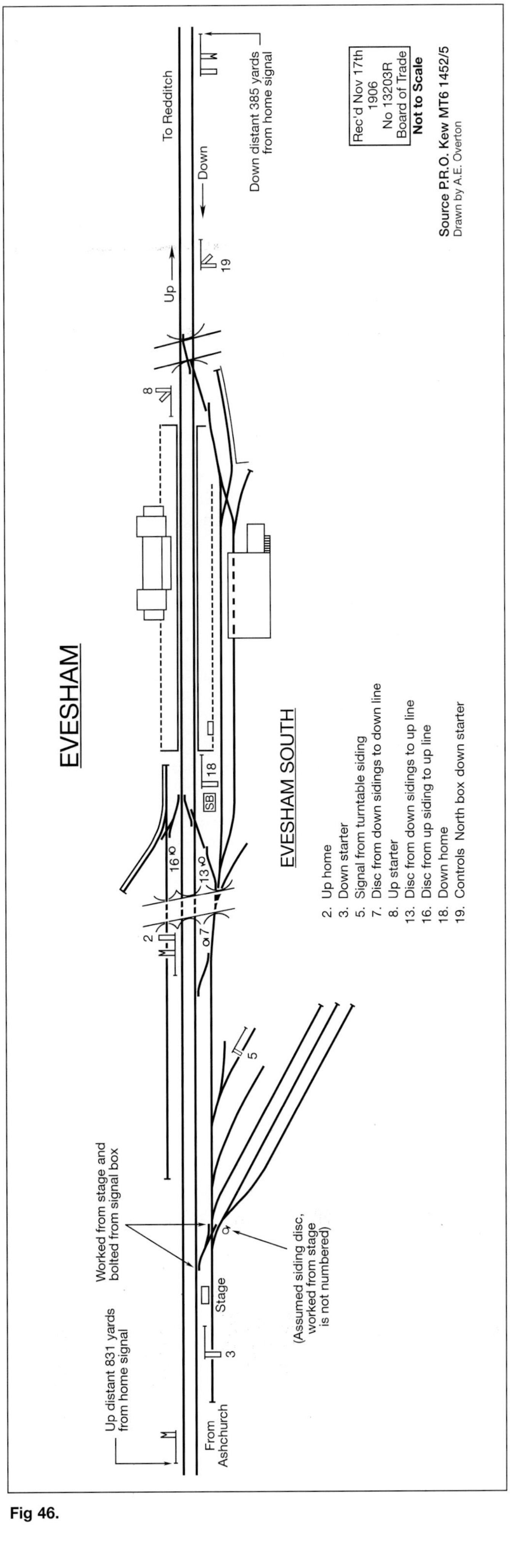

EVESHAM

To Redditch

Down

Up

Down distant 385 yards from home signal

Rec'd Nov 17th 1906
No 13203R
Board of Trade
Not to Scale

Source P.R.O. Kew MT6 1452/5
Drawn by A.E. Overton

19

8

16

13

SB 18

7

2

M

5

EVESHAM SOUTH

2. Up home
3. Down starter
5. Signal from turntable siding
7. Disc from down sidings to down line
8. Up starter
13. Disc from down sidings to up line
16. Disc from up siding to up line
18. Down home
19. Controls North box down starter

Up distant 831 yards from home signal

Worked from stage and bolted from signal box

(Assumed siding disc, worked from stage is not numbered)

Stage

3

From Ashchurch

Fig 46.

Evesham Fruit Traffic

Evesham was the market centre for the area and much of the outward traffic consisted of vegetables and fruit. Although this book describes the old Midland Railway's line from Barnt Green to Ashchurch, at Evesham I cannot ignore the GWR. Both railway companies were in competition for this traffic. Evesham was, and still is, one of the most important centres in Great Britain for fruit and vegetable production and in the years before road transport became a viable alternative the railways were organised to handle the many tons of garden produce grown annually in the area. Sheltered by the Cotswolds and Bredon Hill, the Vale of Evesham is synonymous with the highest quality market garden produce grown and sold in this country. This traffic called for the efficient handling of perishable produce and prompt dispatch, usually made during the late afternoon or early evening, to ensure an overnight delivery at markets many miles away, which required careful planning.

The season commenced in March with early vegetables, and continued through to Christmas, which meant that for almost nine months of the year some special traffic requirements were needed. The first months of the year saw the dispatch of cabbages, brussels sprouts, early onions and spring flowers. Asparagus followed these, until mid-June, and by that date green gooseberries had begun to appear. Strawberries followed in abundance but by far the busiest period of the year began in August and continued through much of September when thousands of tons of red and yellow plums were shipped. It was recorded that during a peak period in the season the Midland Railway could dispatch 1,000 tons of plums per week. If we assume this traffic was equally spread over five days with 200 tons of plums per day, with say 6 tons of fruit per van, then this is around 33 van loads per day to clear this traffic. However, 6 tons may be on the generous side and if this were so then the number of vans required on a daily basis would be even greater. Furthermore, there was a need to work in the daily requirement of empty vehicles. Some of the traffic would go by passenger train in smaller consignments but the bulk went by express goods train.

Other produce from Evesham including damsons, tomatoes, marrows, cucumbers, apples and pears as they were picked throughout the autumn months of the year. The more perishable strawberry traffic was usually dispatched by passenger train and I understand that at the height of the season the Midland was handling about 30 tons of strawberries daily, which required about 19 vans to be attached to various daily passenger trains. I should explain that the cost to the consignee for shipment by the faster passenger train service was more than that charged for despatch by express goods trains. The subject of 'rates' for the various classes of traffic is both fascinating and complex, but I think that the subject of railway rates in general is outside the scope of this book. However, this matter was the subject of an early *Railway Magazine* article and a summary of what was said will provide readers with a flavour of the subject.

It appears that at the time the article was written there was a debate taking place about 'exorbitant rates' being charged to growers, wholesalers and other users of rail transport. The concern was due to the lack of competition. It was suggested that some railway companies were thought to be hampering the development of agricultural and kindred industries by the high rates they charged, a point not made entirely clear in the article. The article said that the Evesham growers were quite happy with both the Midland and Great Western Railway companies' rates but this satisfaction did not apply to one 'British company in the

Fig 47.

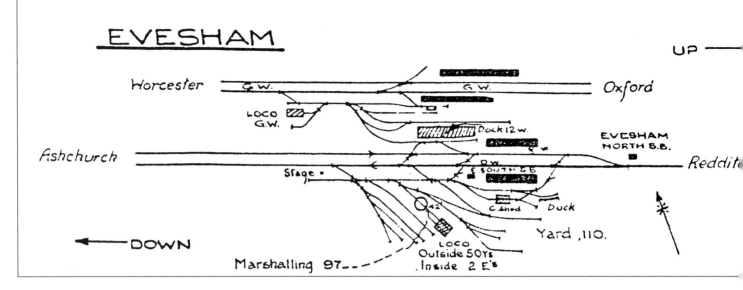

Fig 47. This early LMS 1930s diagram shows the final arrangement at the Midland station, Evesham, prior to the signalbox rationalisation when the North box was closed and the South box was replaced. This new signalbox, Evesham Station, controlled all the signalling, with the stage at the Ashchurch end of the station being retained. The signalbox was closed on 8 March 1964. The diagram also shows the second connection to the GWR which joined the down line with the dock siding and made a crossover between the up and down lines.

north' which refused to grant the 'exceptional' rates for fruit and vegetables conceded by the Midland and Great Western railway companies. I suspect these concessions by both the Midland and GWR were due to the fact that there was a considerable degree of competition for traffic between them for many destinations that could be reached by both companies, either independently or in conjunction with others.

Returning to our unnamed northern British railway company,

it would appear that its charge for fruit and vegetable traffic carried over their lines was about 25% higher per mile than the charge made by the two companies where the traffic originated. The Railway Clearing House apportioned the receipts for all traffic, both passenger and goods, when it crossed company boundaries, and the traffic receipts were divided between the companies that carried it on a mileage basis.

I have mentioned the competition that existed between the Midland and Great Western and it is worth describing some of the traffic which was carried by each company c1910 and the arrangements made to ensure the shipment beyond the territory served by the originating railway. In the case of the Midland Railway the company sent wagons both west towards Ashchurch and north to Birmingham and by use of the company's 1909 timetable we can see how this traffic was dealt with.

Beginning with the 4/45 departure from Evesham, this train reached Ashchurch at 6/30 after collecting traffic en route. A second train to the west was due to leave at 8/25 and this was

The LMS ordered six vans in 1945 that were branded 'Experimental fruit vans return to Evesham'. Normally, ordinary goods vans, either handbrake only or fitted with the automatic vacuum brake, were used for this traffic and this picture shows how it was difficult to obtain a good loading for fruit and vegetables in a vehicle that was rated to carry 12 tons. The experimental van is to Diagram 2112 and the other is to Diagram 2108. The photograph was taken in 1947. *British Railways*

required to stop at Bengeworth, Hinton and Beckford to collect traffic if required. This working was booked as a 'Special fruit train' with an arrival at Ashchurch at 8/52. Some traffic that was due to go north also went by this service and the booked connection was either via a special fruit train (if it was running) or by the 9/20 from Gloucester.

The 4/15 goods train provided direct northbound services to Birmingham and this train was required to leave coal empties at Broom and only work important traffic forward to Birmingham. I expect that this train did not convey 'important' fruit and vegetable traffic from Evesham and the important traffic referred to came off the Stratford-upon-Avon line. It seems likely that the first major fruit and vegetable working from Evesham was the 7/15 (7/0 on Saturday). When required, this train was booked to be worked by two Class 1 engines (almost certainly Kirtley double-frame locomotives) and a maximum of 50 wagons of goods was conveyed. Clearly a train of that weight required two engines and the WTT stipulated that the brake van must be either a 15- or 20-ton rated vehicle.

A further northbound service was available by the 3/50 Class B Goods from Gloucester Barnwood to Birmingham which was due to depart from Evesham at 7/40 with a booked arrival time of 11/15 at Birmingham Lawley Street. The final evening northbound train was the 9/10 which had commenced its journey from Gloucester at 7/45 and was due to arrive at Lawley Street goods station at 2.15. What is not clear from the 1909 timetable is if there were any particular requirements and therefore paths laid down for special trains. It is possible that special traffic notices would cover these workings.

The division of traffic between the GWR and the Midland Railway saw the Midland originating traffic for the West of England which went on the Ashchurch trains noted above and then on to Gloucester. There the wagons were transferred to the GWR and taken forward to destinations such as Plymouth and Barnstaple, as mentioned in the *Railway Magazine* article.

Lawley Street in Birmingham was the destination for the northbound trains, where the traffic was remarshalled before joining other trains bound for Liverpool, Manchester, a number

There were several coal merchants at Evesham and one was Richard White whose wagon No 50 is shown here. This wagon was built in 1898 by the Gloucester Railway Carriage & Wagon Company Ltd and has the brake hand lever on one side of the wagon only. The vehicle measured 14ft 11in x 6ft 11in x 3ft 1in. The body was lead colour with white letters shaded in black .
Collection R. J. Essery

Another coal merchant was H. Burlingham & Co. The Gloucester Railway Carriage & Wagon Company Ltd built this vehicle in 1896; it measured 15ft 6in x 6ft 11in x 2ft 9in. The body colour was described as slate with white letters shaded in black . This wagon had lower sides than Richard White's but it had raised ends, a common feature of coal wagons built during this period. Both wagons were registered by the Great Western Railway.
Collection R. J. Essery

This 8-ton W. H. Wallis & Co wagon was photographed after being rebuilt by the Gloucester Railway Carriage & Wagon Company Ltd. Unfortunately, it is not possible to make out the wording on the board that gives the date and colour of the wagon. *HMRS 24833*

of destinations in Yorkshire, the North East and Scotland. Although it is possible that much of this traffic went by Midland trains, the Great Western provided considerable competition by taking all the South Wales and most of the London traffic. By co-operation with the LNWR and the Caledonian Railway, the Great Western was able to take some of the Scottish traffic and this was achieved by dispatching a train at 1/50, which reached Scotland in the early hours of the following morning. After the Grouping, the LMS retained the traffic and in 1930 this service was provided by the 3/15 from Evesham to Crewe which was booked to run 'when required'. Another post-1923 service was a 4/40 train to Water Orton, which conveyed traffic from Evesham and was known as 'the fruit'. This job was worked by Walsall Ryecroft men, usually with a Class 4F 0-6-0.

Further co-operation with the LNWR enabled the GWR to compete for Manchester and Liverpool traffic while the Midland found it difficult to take much London traffic from the Great Western, whose services were often duplicated, that is two separate train loads being worked forward when the traffic was heavy. Connection with the Great Central Railway at Banbury (I am unsure which route was followed, Kingham and reverse or via Honeybourne, Stratford and Leamington), enabled the Great Western to send traffic to Leicester, Nottingham and Sheffield, all Midland Railway strongholds! Little wonder the rates offered to growers by both companies were competitive! The GWR would despatch loads of more than half a ton direct to the destination but lesser amounts were dealt with by its transhipment station at Worcester, and this may have caused some delays to this perishable traffic.

The produce was packed at the farms using crates, hampers, boxes, tubs and sacks depending upon what was to be carried and, in the days before motor transport, was conveyed to the goods yard by horse and cart. To move this produce by rail, special ventilated vans were built by the Midland Railway and as these vehicles became time expired, LMS standard ventilated vans replaced them.

The important 'direct to user' plum traffic required specially made boxes that held about 20lb of fruit and these usually went direct from the grower to the consumer by passenger train, with the shipper paying passenger train rates. Goods trains included wagons which were loaded with large quantities of plums packed into hampers, these usually being bound for the wholesale markets. The cost of shipment per pound of plums was rather less to the consignee or consignor than plums sent by passenger train.

The Great Western and Midland railways were close to each other at the western end of Evesham before they parted company. This picture shows the old Midland line that curved to the south and crossed the River Avon by the bridge seen on the left of the picture, while the Great Western line curved northwest towards Worcester. The small Great Western Railway engine shed was between the two railways and the new junction between the railways, which was opened in 1957, can be seen. The locomotive is Ivatt 2-6-0 No 43046 and the train is the empty stock which will form the 12.20pm Evesham to Birmingham New Street. *J. M. Tolson*

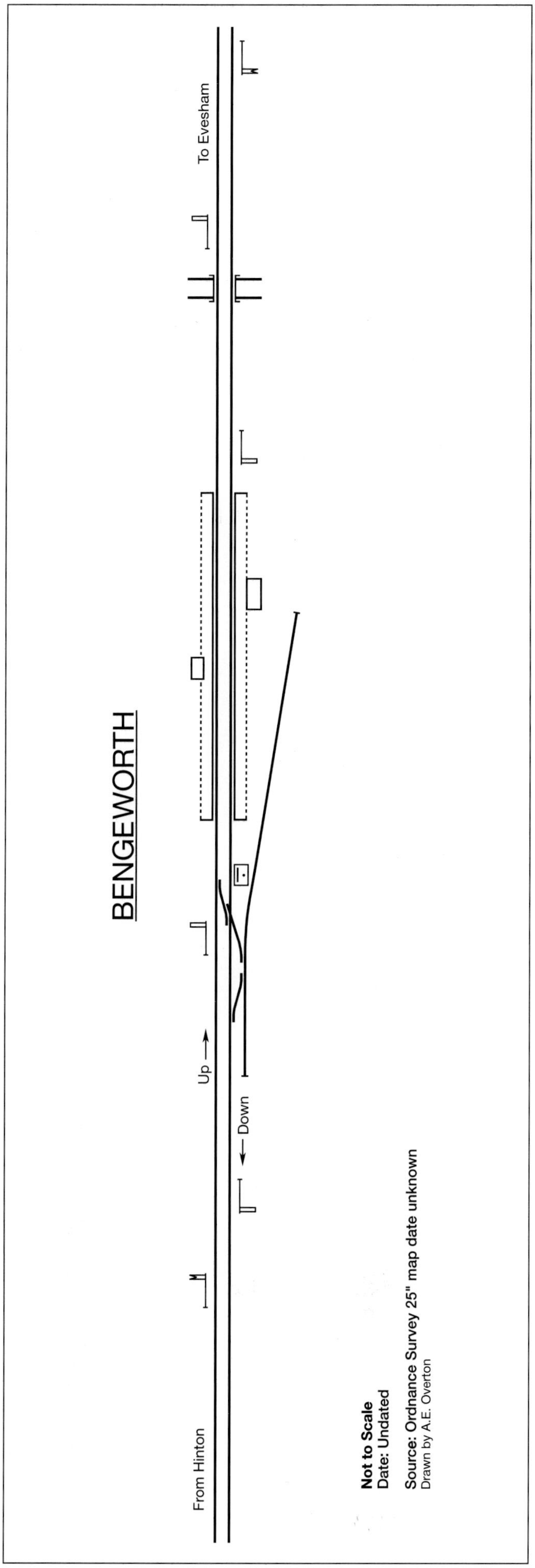

Bengeworth

Bengeworth was 1 mile 41 chains from Evesham and the station opened to passengers on 1 October 1864, but probably due to the fact that it was close to Evesham, it did not open for goods until 1 June 1867. There was a single siding with trailing connections from both the up and down main line but there were no other goods facilities. When the line was opened the time interval system was used; therefore Bengeworth did not receive a signalbox until 19 July 1890. This box was to remain in operation until the station was closed for both passenger and goods traffic on 8 June 1953.

Single-line working was introduced between Bengeworth and Beckford on 31 January 1917 and this arrangement lasted until 22 February 1921 when normal double-line working was restored. The reason for singling the line was to release the track that was lifted for other wartime use. Some was used by the Railway Operating Division on the Western Front during World War 1, while other rails etc remained in England for use in new marshalling yards, ordnance factories and, where suitable, on main lines to release other material for use in France.

The stations on this line varied; those south of Barnt Green and north of Evesham were not built by the Midland Railway. On the other hand the Midland Railway built Bengeworth, Hinton, Ashton-under-Hill and Beckford, and with the exception of Ashton, the track layout was very similar at each. They could be described as 'a typical Midland Railway layout for a country goods station on a double-track main line'. The trailing crossover from both the up and down directions exemplifies this with a single slip connecting the running lines and a loop parallel to them. This arrangement enabled trains to gain access to the yard from either the up or down lines. Although the arrangement varied from station to station across the system, as indeed with the three examples mentioned, this principle applied to the majority of small country stations built by the Midland Railway Company. There were no special facilities at Bengeworth and the station dealt with local traffic as necessary to suit the needs of the community, with fruit and vegetables being the principal outward traffic. The siding capacity was 24 wagons.

I have included an OS map, Fig 49, to show the layout of the station which, apart from the period when the line was singled, did not alter after the station was opened for goods traffic until it was closed.

BENGEWORTH

To Evesham

From Hinton

Up →

← Down

Not to Scale
Date: Undated

Source: Ordnance Survey 25" map date unknown
Drawn by A.E. Overton

Fig 48.

Fig 48. This plan is based upon an undated Ordnance Survey map and does not show the signal and point numbers. Because we are uncertain about any ground signals at Bengeworth they have also been omitted. *Drawing and notes by A. E.Overton*

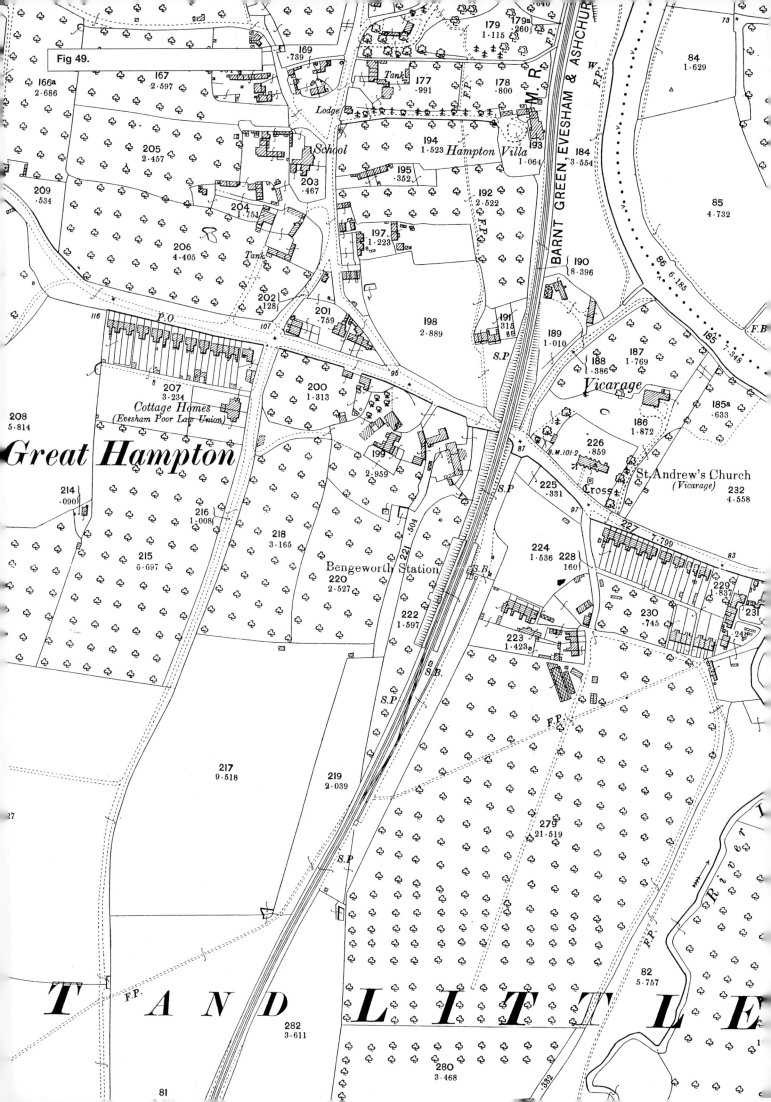

Fig 49.

Fig 49. (*Left*) Bengeworth station was less than two miles from Evesham and the facilities for goods traffic were simple: a loop where down trains could set back through a trailing connection, and a crossover between the up and down lines that enabled up trains to set back on to the loop. There was a short siding off the far end of the loop and a longer siding that ran behind the station platform. There was also a weighbridge on the approach road to the siding. *Crown Copyright*

The nameboard at Bengeworth was still of Midland Railway design in this LMS-period picture and the station was a wooden structure, being little more than a booking office that may have served as a staff office and a small waiting room. The sign over the platform entrance reads 'You may telephone from here'. The signalbox was on the down side of the line and controlled the movements into and from the sidings. It was opened on 27 July 1890 and was closed on 8 June 1953. The weighbridge can be seen behind the station building and there was a small waiting shelter on the up platform. *Lens of Sutton*

This picture was taken on 9 March 1956, almost three years after the station had closed on 8 June 1953, and shows the road entrance to the station and goods sidings. *H. C. Casserley 84520*

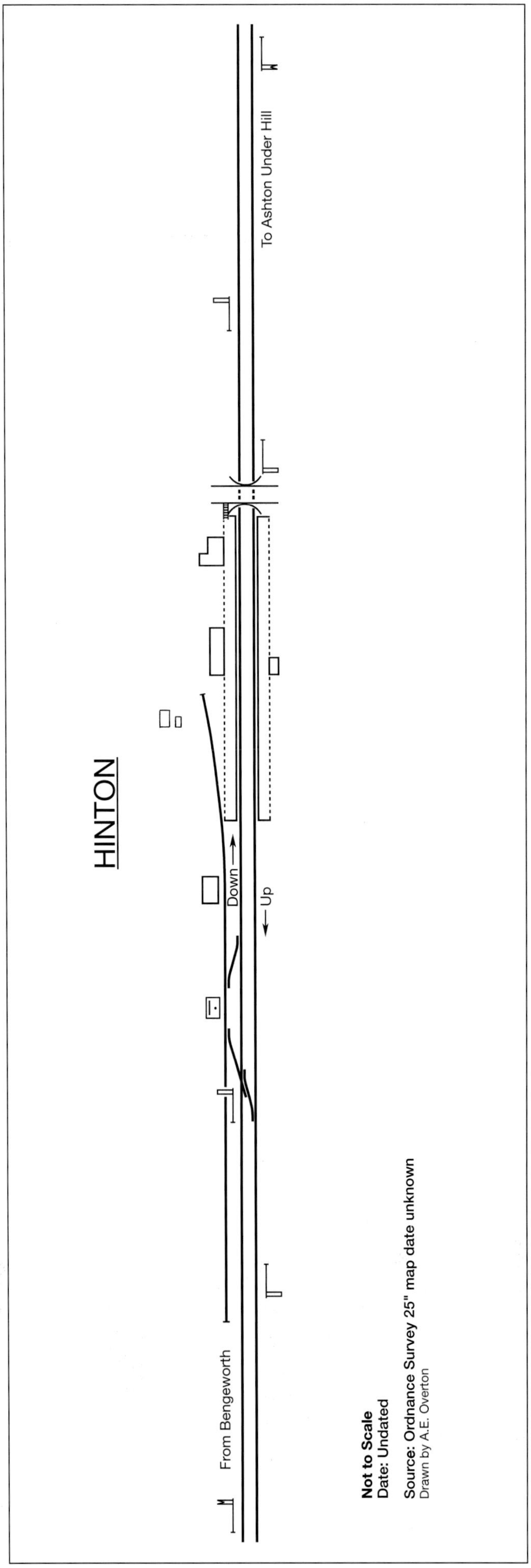

Hinton

Hinton was a passenger and goods station 1 mile 51 chains south of Bengeworth. The siding capacity was 32 wagons and there were facilities for livestock. The principal traffic was coal for domestic users, but during the 1950s the adjacent Midlands Electricity Board depot provided useful revenue from the movement of wooden poles, drums of wire and power distribution equipment.

The station was opened in 1864, on 1 July for goods and 1 October for passengers. Closure came in 1963, to passengers on 17 June and for goods on 1 July. The signalbox was opened on 29 July 1890, a replacement box being opened on 8 January 1924 and closing on 1 March 1964.

Fig 51. (*Right*) Hinton was another rural station with the passenger entrance from the road overbridge. The goods facilities comprised two short sidings with a small wooden goods shed, and there was a weighing machine at the entrance to the yard which appears to have a gated entrance. *Crown Copyright*

Right:
Hinton, looking towards Evesham in June 1934 and providing a good view of the station with the stationmaster's house, booking hall and office, waiting rooms, etc. Both station nameboards are of the double-angled type and placed at the approach end of the platforms. Beyond the end of the down platform there is a small goods shed of wooden construction which is alongside the siding that runs behind the platform. The signalbox is beyond the goods shed. The original box at Hinton was opened on 29 July 1890 and the replacement, seen here, came into service on 1 January 1924, closing on 1 March 1964. There were no passenger facilities on the up platform. *Collection R. J. Essery*

Fig 50. (*Left*) This plan is based upon an undated extract of an Ordnance Survey map and does not show the signal and point numbers. Because we are uncertain about the number and position of ground signals at Hinton these have also been omitted.
Drawing and notes by A. E.Overton

To Ashton Under Hill

HINTON

Down

Up

From Bengeworth

Not to Scale
Date: Undated

Source: Ordnance Survey 25" map date unknown
Drawn by A.E. Overton

Fig 50.

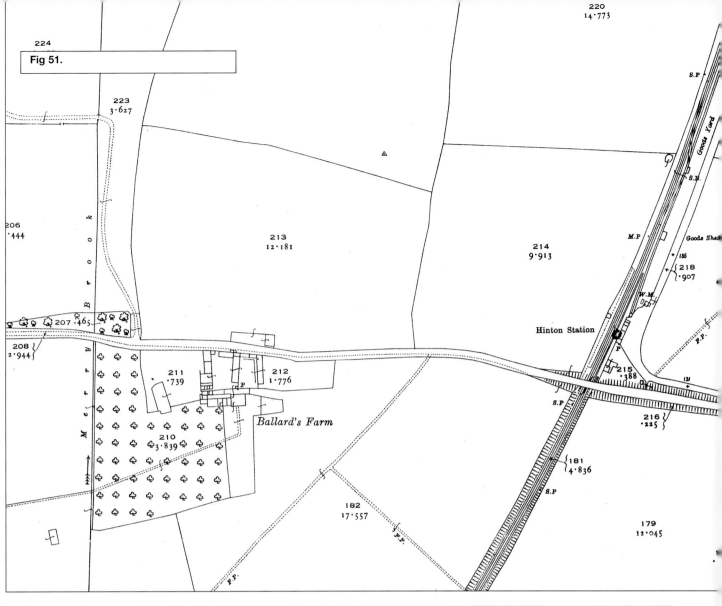

Fig 51.

Above:
The station at Hinton may have been closed when this undated picture was taken, looking towards Ashchurch. An LMS-style Hawkseye nameboard has replaced the original Midland angled board on the down platform but it is not possible to be sure about the board on the up platform. *Collection Philip Jarvis*

This view of the station building is from the Midland period, Edwardian era and shows the earlier condition of the station building. Note the vegetation, absent in the later picture and the number of wagons in the goods yard. *Collection David Tee*

Ashton-under-Hill

Ashton-under-Hill was 1 mile 70 chains from Hinton and was a small station with a single siding, the capacity, according to the LMS line diagram, being 38 wagons. The station opened on 1 July for goods and 1 October 1864 for passenger traffic. For a number of years the line between Evesham and Beckford was worked on the time interval system but when the block telegraph was installed a new signalbox was opened on 12 August 1890.

In 1910, the Midland Railway made some changes to the layout at Ashton and these are summarised in the Board of Trade inspection report by Major Pringle, dated 12 February 1910.

'I made an inspection on the 10th inst., of the works at Ashton-under-Hill on the Evesham branch of the Midland Railway. A through crossing from the down main line to the up siding has been removed together with the trailing points leading thereto. The trailing connection on the up line remains in position.

'In place of the former ground signalbox, from which the points and the distant and home signals on each line were controlled, a stage has been provided on each platform at the station. In the case of the down line stage, it contains two levers which work the down distant and home signals respectively. The normal position of these, as well as the up line signals is 'clear', and they will be placed at danger behind a train at the down platform. The up line stage contains four working levers and, in addition to controlling the up distant and home signals, works the siding points and exit signal.

'The arrangements are satisfactory, and I can recommend the Board of Trade to approve these new works.'

The original hand-written report contains a note from Major Pringle, which said: 'It is necessary at this place, in working to and from the dead end siding, to make use of a tow rope. I understand that, on account of the very considerable expense that would be involved to determine this method of working, the Board has assented to this method of working.' This note was not included in the report which was sent to the Midland Railway when the new work was sanctioned; however the internal Board of Trade note is rather revealing. Dated 14 February it said: 'Agreed to strike out the note from the report on the grounds that Ashton-under-Hill was included in a list furnished by the MR (1904) of places where the tow rope was used. We have raised no objection to the continuance of this practice, but do not appear to have given any direct assent to the arrangement.'

There was a further internal Board of Trade note dated 17 February. 'Can you kindly say if the question of tow roping at Ashton-under-Hill came up in an accident?' The answer to that question was, 'Not in last six years.'

Tow roping was a rather dangerous method of shunting and I have touched upon the practice in the section about Alvechurch. The method of undertaking tow roping was covered by rule 113 in the Midland Railway rulebook and was the movement of vehicles by towing with a rope attached to a locomotive or vehicles moving on an adjacent line and it was permitted only at specific places. The Railway Employment (Prevention of Accidents) Act 1900 and the Prevention of Accidents Rules 1902 sought to reduce the number of places on railways were this method of shunting was undertaken. The Board of Trade gave the various British railway companies until 8 August 1903 to provide a list of those places where tow roping would be discontinued except where no other reasonably practicable means could be

Ashton-under-Hill station was opened in 1864 and the signalbox, which opened in 1890, was taken out of service in 1910, when replaced by two stages. Unfortunately, I have not been able to find any pictures of this station showing the signalbox that was on the down side of the line. However, this undated picture was taken by the photographer facing towards Ashchurch, and the trailing connection to the siding from the up line can be seen. One of the stages that replaced the signalbox is visible on the up platform. It was in the open and exposed to the elements, and can be seen just beyond the end of the station buildings. *Collection R. J. Essery*

Fig 52.

provided for dealing with the traffic. The Board of Trade pressed the Midland Railway for an answer, and on 5 October the company replied stating that at 130 places the practice had been stopped, but at several places it was still in use.

The Board of Trade was not impressed with this evasive reply and requested a list and the Midland stalled on the basis that it was still investigating the matter. Several letters were exchanged, and finally on 21 May 1905, a list was provided giving 74 locations. By 10 April 1907 the total had been reduced to 66 places and this number was included in the Midland Railway Appendix No 24 dated June 1911. In addition to Ashton-under-Hill and Alvechurch on the Evesham branch, the practice of tow roping was employed at Redditch, to and from the goods shed and dock sidings, and at Alcester, to move wagons clear of main line connections.

Ashton-under-Hill was the scene of a tragic accident that took place on 25 February 1935 when an 0-6-4T engine was derailed, leading to the death of the driver, Alfred Woolley aged 60, from Cotteridge, Birmingham. The accident report, written by Lt-Col A. H. L. Mount, appears in Volume 3 of *An Illustrated Review of Midland Locomotives* by R. J. Essery and D. Jenkinson, published by Wild Swan in 1988, and the recollections of a Midland Railway engineman who worked with these engines appeared in *Midland Record 11* by the same publisher. The inquest was reported in the *Evesham Journal* and *Four Shires Advertiser*, on Saturday, 20 April 1935, the jury returning a verdict of accidental death, adding that in their opinion there had not been adequate supervision of the permanent way.

Fig 52. (*Right*) The signalbox at Ashton-under-Hill did not enjoy a long life: installed in 1890, it was removed in 1910 when the track layout at this station was simplified. The report, reproduced in full in the text, does not make clear which siding was the subject of tow roping. I would imagine that all traffic to and from Ashton-under-Hill was dealt with by up direction trains and that it was the siding behind the platform which was the problem. Wagons would be set back into the siding then tow roped forward into the platform end of the siding, with the reverse applying when wagons had to be removed. The signals were not numbered and were normally in the 'off' position. The original Midland Railway plan that was used to make this drawing was sent to the Board of Trade by the company on 4 February 1910 and approval was granted on the 19th.
A. E. Overton

Fig 53. (*Above right*) By 1910 there was no requirement for a signal box and although still shown on the plan it had been taken out of service. The new arrangements at Ashton-under-Hill are described in the text and shown here. Two stages, mounted on the platform, controlled a distant and home signal in both directions. In addition the Up platform stage also controlled the connection from the Up line to the Up siding where tow roping was permitted.
Drawing and notes by A. E.Overton

Bottom right:
Ashton-under-Hill before the signalbox was closed in 1910, probably c1905. When compared with the 1958 view on page 114, a number of other changes can be seen: the up starting signal and down home signals are in place, the trees and bushes were not there 50 years later and the telegraph pole on the up platform has been replaced. The six fire buckets, visible in both pictures, are unusual; they were normally in threes. The angled station nameboard with the hyphenated station name can be seen on the down platform and there would have been a similar sign at the approach end of the up platform. *The Roy F. Burrows Midland Collection Trust*

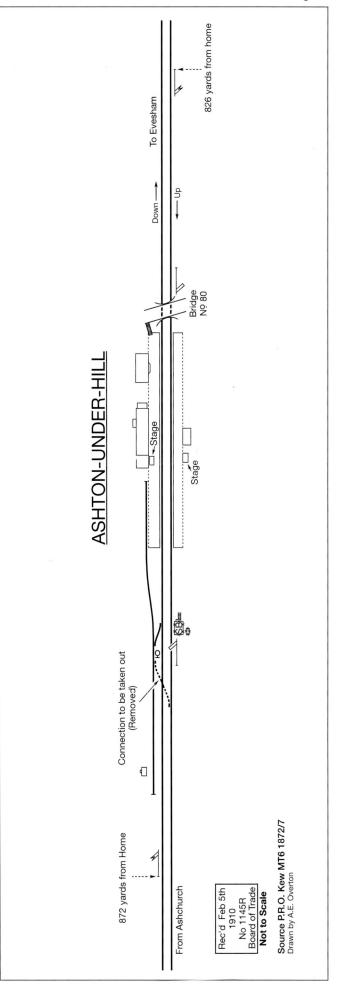

ASHTON-UNDER-HILL

826 yards from home

To Evesham

Down →
← Up

Bridge Nº 80

Stage

Stage

Connection to be taken out (Removed)

872 yards from Home

From Ashchurch

Rec'd Feb 5th 1910 No 1145R Board of Trade **Not to Scale**

Source P.R.O. Kew MT6 1872/7
Drawn by A.E. Overton

Fig 53.

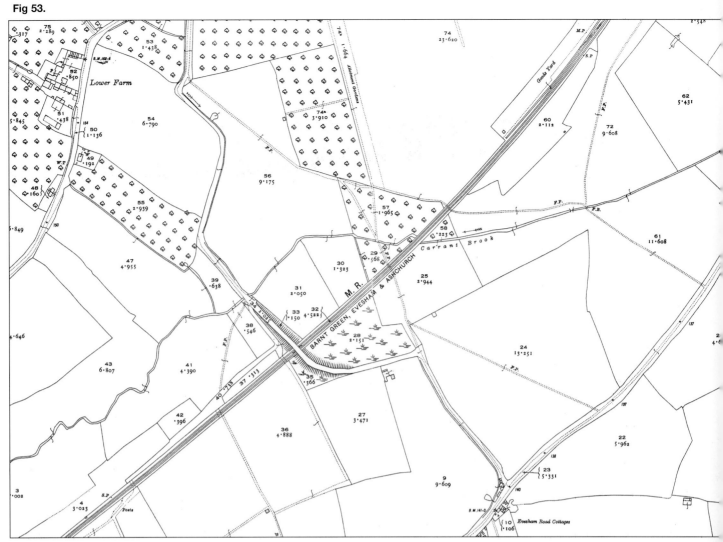

Above:
Saltley's Ivatt Class 4MT No 43049, at the head of an Ashchurch to Birmingham New Street passenger train, runs into Ashton-under-Hill station on 24 April 1958. The steps from the road overbridge, together with the well-constructed stationmaster's house, are in the middle of the picture. The young man could be a passenger who is waiting to cross the line to join the train, or he could be accompanying the photographer. *H. C. Casserley 93228*

Below:
This picture of Ashton-under-Hill, facing the down direction, was taken on 24 April 1958. Two replacement LMS Hawkseye nameboards are on the down platform and the lever frame (stage) can just be seen by the side of the lamp and telegraph pole at the end of the building. Passengers could enter the station on the down side by the steps which led from the road, but it would appear that passengers for the up side crossed the line by the barrow crossing. *H. C. Casserley 92227*

Beckford

The distance from Ashton-under-Hill to Beckford was 1 mile 71 chains. In the up direction Beckford was 3 miles 48 chains from Ashchurch, greater than that between any other two stations on the Evesham branch. It was the largest station between Evesham and Ashchurch. The opening dates were 1 July for goods and 1 October 1864 for passenger traffic. When the section to Evesham was changed from the time interval system to the block telegraph system on 12 August 1890 a new signalbox was opened. This was replaced on 18 December 1923 and the replacement box closed on 1 March 1964. The closure dates for the station were, for passenger traffic, 17 June, and goods, 1 July 1963.

Beckford was well served and dealt with both goods and passenger traffic, furniture vans, livestock, horseboxes and prize cattle and carriages by rail. Lifting power was a 1½-ton crane. Prior to the opening of the GWR line throughout from Honeybourne to Cheltenham in 1906 this station was the railhead for Winchcombe, and considerable traffic was handled here. The goods warehouse with its wooden crane dealt with heavy loads while the loading of fruit, flowers and vegetables into either open goods wagons, which were sheeted over or into covered goods vans, was dealt with in the yard. This method of loading was a regular feature with fruit traffic which required speedy transit once it had been picked. Beckford was the originating point for at least one express goods train that conveyed fruit and vegetable traffic, and I have described my own experiences when working this train with my Driver Charles Reay in Chapter 1.

Beckford had also a major cattle market which was close to the station and the cattle pens. In 1925, George Hone was the auctioneer and he dealt with the sale of fat and store sheep, ewes, store lambs, oxen, pigs and heifers. In later years the market was seasonal, being held three times a year: spring, mid-year and October. I expect that most of the animals would have been transported by rail if they were to travel any distance. The only private wagon owner that I can trace at Beckford was a James Taylor & Co, coal and brick merchant. Their wagons were painted purple brown with white-shaded black letters.

Judging by the style of dress this appears to be an Edwardian period picture of Beckford. The rear of the print is annotated 'Auntie May off to Cheltenham'. Unfortunately, no date is given. The Midland angled station nameboards are at the entry end of both platforms and the station awning is complete; compare with other pictures reproduced here. The train is quite short and is probably from Evesham to Ashchurch. The engine, running tender-first, appears to be a single-frame goods engine whose tender has been well coaled. The milk churns on the up platform have been placed close to where the passenger brakevan, or other vehicle into which they will be loaded, is expected to stop. Trains ran more or less in set formations and drivers generally stopped at the same place at the platform each day. This enabled the station staff to place traffic that was to be loaded close to where it should be to ensure trains were not held while station staff pulled the loaded trolley along the platform to the point of loading. *The Roy F. Burrows Midland Collection Trust*

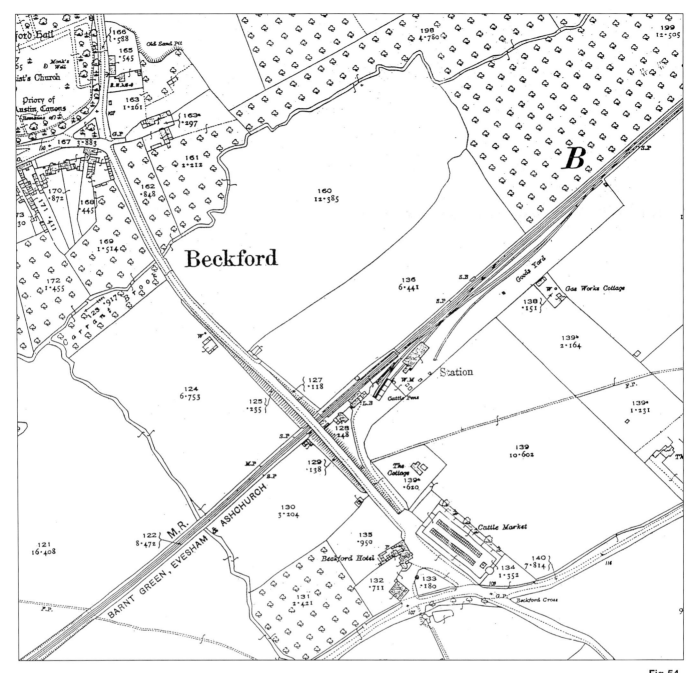

Fig 54.

This undated picture illustrates the change to the station awning that has been made. The trailing connection from the down line can be seen, together with the two crossovers between the main lines, and this is a good view of the up line waiting shelter. The up home signal has been replaced and has a shorter post than the one seen in the earlier view. *Collection R. J. Essery*

Fig 54. *(Left)* In addition to fruit and vegetable traffic Beckford was an important centre for cattle, with the cattle market only a short distance from the railway. This Ordnance Survey map shows the yard which was on the down side of the line, with the goods shed, cattle docks and weighing machine. One source states that the long siding, which curved away from the main line to end at buffer stops close to the goods shed, was made into a loop and this was added by the Midland Railway and installed by 1917. All movements into and out of the goods yard were controlled by the signalbox at Beckford. Shunting could be undertaken in a number of ways: down trains, unless they were only attaching wagons that were in the loops, would need to place the engine at the Evesham end of the train before the yard could be shunted. The train would be set back on to the loop next to the main line and the engine would run round the train using the up main line. The shunting neck was quite short so it is possible that at times the main line would be used when shunting.

The traffic on this line was light and this work was within station limits, so it was perfectly safe. The signalman would control all the moves that took place on the main line; up trains would set back into the goods yard by using one of the two crossovers, the one by the signalbox giving access to the goods shed and cattle pens, the other into the loops and long siding. Trains which were inside the goods yard would depart in either direction from the loops. With the 'Beckford' I recall that we placed the brakevan on either the loading dock or cattle dock road and picked up our train which had been loaded from road vehicles that had backed up against the empty vans. These had been set in readiness for loading on the long siding. *Crown Copyright*

Fig 55. *(Right)* As described elsewhere the heavy fruit and vegetable traffic that originated at Beckford helps to explain the more generous arrangement of sidings that were to be found here when compared with most other stations on the line. In many respects Beckford is a classic example of a Midland Railway country station with the goods and mineral facilities on the one side of the line where trains travelling in either direction could shunt the entire yard without too many problems. *Drawing and notes by A. E.Overton*

Further changes to the station can be seen in this undated picture. The awning has now been removed and the replacement LMS Hawkseye station nameboards are evident, two on each platform. The trackwork in the goods yard remains, but the only wagons are for coal traffic. *Collection R. J. Essery*

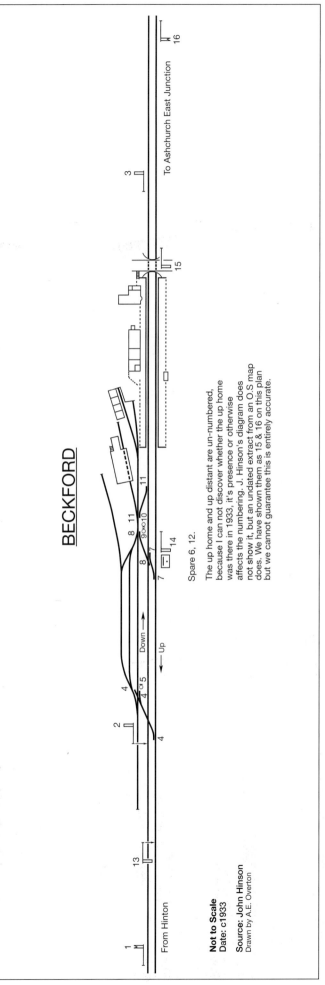

BECKFORD

To Ashchurch East Junction

From Hinton

Down →

← Up

Spare 6, 12.

The up home and up distant are un-numbered, because I can not discover whether the up home was there in 1933, it's presence or otherwise affects the numbering. J. Hinson's diagram does not show it, but an undated extract from an O.S map does. We have shown them as 15 & 16 on this plan but we cannot guarantee this is entirely accurate.

Not to Scale
Date: c1933

Source: John Hinson
Drawn by A.E. Overton

Fig 55.

117

Ashchurch

Ashchurch was a remarkable layout. The main line, Gloucester to Bristol, was double tracked with two platform faces, while the branches to Malvern to the west and Evesham to the east each had a single platform face, as should be clear from the OS map reproduced on page 120. There was a small goods yard with a capacity for 100 wagons to the south of Ashchurch Junction. A major feature at Ashchurch was the provender stores that were to the west of the Birmingham & Gloucester main line and as such not really part of our story. Ashchurch was a goods and passenger station able to deal with furniture vans, portable engines, machines on wheels, livestock, horses and prize cattle, and carriages by passenger trains. Crane power was of 1½ tons capacity. There was also a private siding for the use of the Cotswold Packing Company.

The branch to the west to Tewkesbury was opened in 1840 and to Malvern in 1862. As stated, the line to Evesham was opened two years later, to goods in July and to passengers in October. The line from Evesham Junction on the Evesham branch to Tewkesbury Junction on the Tewkesbury and Malvern line crossed the main Birmingham & Gloucester line at almost

right angles, just to the north of Ashchurch station. Although unusual, this arrangement was not unique in British railway practice. The line was originally double but by 1927 it had been made a single line and was taken out of service in 1957. During World War 2 new sidings were opened at Ashchurch East in connection with War Department traffic and in due course these were lifted.

It has been recorded that there was an engine shed at Ashchurch that was probably opened when the line to Evesham was built, although some sources give 1863. Unfortunately I know no further details, and no picture has been found. Hawkins and Reeve in *LMS Engine Sheds Volume 2* (Wild Swan Publications) suggest that the shed may have gone out of use before 1914, but this cannot be confirmed. It is possible this was a small wooden shed able to hold an 0-6-0 tender engine. An engine pit and siding survived for many years. There was a small engine shed at Tewkesbury which remained in use until August 1961 and this provided the necessary servicing facilities for the Birmingham to Ashchurch passenger trains, as described in the next chapter. Although much of Ashchurch was not part of

Ashchurch Junction, as seen from the overbridge to the south of the station when looking north. The Malvern branch, with a two-coach train in the platform, is to the left of the picture and the Evesham branch is to the right. The siding in the centre was added in 1904. On the Ordnance Survey map the siding stops to the south of the bridge, but after the bridge was rebuilt there was room for it to be extended further north. The first signalbox at Ashchurch Junction was opened before 1877 and the replacement box seen here opened on 16 December 1900. To the right of the signalbox is a swan-neck water crane and in front of this there are three revolving discs, or ground signals, side by side. Two discs side by side were not uncommon, but three was unusual. *Collection R. J. Essery*

the Evesham branch, I have included a number of pictures of the area in order to show the extent of the railway that was once to be found there.

The closure of the branch south of Redditch was a protracted affair. Traffic on the section between Alcester and Evesham was suspended on 1 October 1962 for all traffic, due to the condition of the track and this posed some operating problems. Western Region engines from Cheltenham and Gloucester engine sheds replaced those from Saltley motive power depot, which had provided the majority of the locomotives working along the line. John M. Tolson, writing in the December 1964 edition of *The Railway Magazine*, describes his final journey along the line. It began at Birmingham New Street with a two-car diesel unit to Redditch, between Redditch and Evesham it was by Midland Red bus that stopped only at the railway stations, and from Evesham to Ashchurch he travelled in a Scottish Region passenger brake second class coach hauled by Western Region pannier tank No 4614. The Midland Red bus service between Redditch and Evesham which called only at the railway stations, ran between 1 October 1962 and 15 June 1963.

The official closure of the line between Redditch and Evesham, and Evesham and Ashchurch for passenger traffic, came on 17 June 1963 and, according to the weekly engineering notices, the life of the Evesham branch south of Redditch came to an end on 8 March 1964 when all the Evesham branch connections at Ashchurch were taken out of use. Access to the MoD depot remained, the connection being maintained via the existing sidings at Ashchurch.

This 1958 picture was also taken from the overbridge and some changes from the previous view can be seen. The most obvious is the new signalbox, which was to have a short life, built on the site of the box that was closed following the 1900 alterations. Although the nameboard reads Ashchurch Junction, it was later renamed Ashchurch. This signalbox opened on 27 July 1958 and was closed on 16 February 1969. The three revolving disc signals referred to earlier are now LMS standard ground signals that are usually called 'dummies' by railwaymen. These replacement signals have been mounted vertically, while two Midland Railway semaphore arms have replaced the two revolving discs by the side-loading dock in the earlier picture. There is also a passenger footbridge at the far south end of the station in addition to the one shown later.
G. Braithwaite

Believed to have been taken in 1883, this photograph contains many items of interest. The photographer was facing north, towards Birmingham. Ashchurch Level Crossing signalbox, opened before 1877, is at the north end of the up platform; this box was closed and the replacement opened on 16 September 1900. The line between Evesham Junction and Tewkesbury that crosses the Birmingham & Gloucester line can also be seen. The exit from the lie-by on the down side was controlled by a disc signal; the tall signal is the down home and all the signals are most interesting, They are slotted posts with the lamp and spectacle mounted lower down the post. In addition to the main line signal two others can be seen to the right of the picture: one is Evesham Junction signalbox home signal from Malvern, the other is the starting signal for Evesham from the branch platform where the six-wheel carriages are standing. The track on the main line is made from 81lb to the yard rail in 24ft lengths with nine sleepers per rail length. The cast iron chairs weighed 40lb each. The 'Refreshment Rooms' sign on the left of the picture is worthy of note as the shaded lettering is rather unusual. The rooms were probably privately managed and leased from the Midland Railway.
NRM Derby Collection DY 4142

Fig 56

Fig 56. (*Left*) This Ordnance Survey map illustrates the complex nature of the railways at Ashchurch in 1903, as described in the text. In many respects, much of Ashchurch was independent of the Evesham branch but in order to provide a picture of the railway facilities built by the Midland Railway I have included some additional pictures and plans which show other parts of the station. The Evesham branch entered Ashchurch from an easterly direction and the extract from the Midland Railway 1913 Distance Diagram should be of assistance. *Crown Copyright*

Fig 57. (*Right*) Extract from the Midland Railway Distance diagram, 1913.

Below left & right:
These two views were taken in 1904 by a department of the Midland Railway and illustrate the new overbridge that had just been built to the south of the station. The first, north-facing picture, shows how the siding could now be extended under the bridge. The vehicles on the dock siding to the left of the picture are horseboxes; cattle were also dealt with in the same dock. *Collection V. R. Anderson*

The second photograph was taken looking south and beneath the bridge, the three signals that controlled the exit from the goods yard can be seen. From right to left they are: for the Malvern branch, the main line to the north, and the Evesham branch. The goods wagons to the left are two Diagram 299s, with a Diagram 305 between them. *Collection V. R. Anderson*

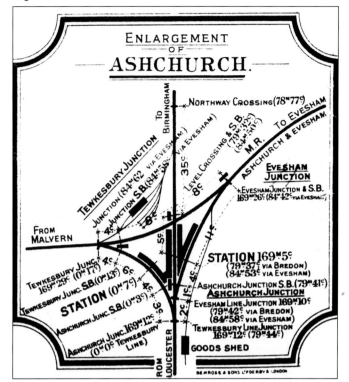

Fig 57.

LMS Standard Compound No 41061 approaches Ashchurch with an ordinary passenger train for Gloucester, seen on 9 September 1949. The down lie-by was converted into a goods loop on 28 September 1941 and the signalling changed accordingly. There are now distant signals beneath the home signals for both the main and goods loop. The crossing is now a single line but the old Midland signal that protects the crossing in the up direction remains. To the right is the signalbox that replaced Ashchurch Level Crossing box shown in the previous view. The new box opened on 16 October 1927 and, in addition to the work on the main line, it took over the functions of the smaller boxes at Evesham Junction and Tewkesbury Junction which were then closed. *H. C. Casserley 58561*

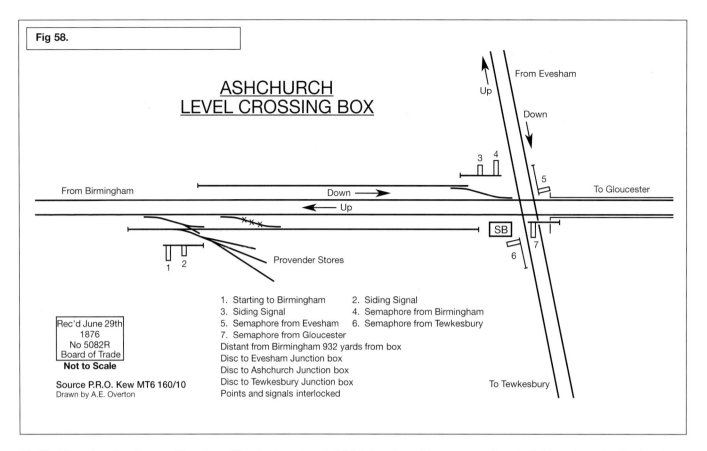

Fig 58.

ASHCHURCH
LEVEL CROSSING BOX

From Evesham

Up

Down

From Birmingham

Down →

← Up

To Gloucester

3 4

5

SB

6 7

Provender Stores

1 2

1. Starting to Birmingham   2. Siding Signal
3. Siding Signal   4. Semaphore from Birmingham
5. Semaphore from Evesham   6. Semaphore from Tewkesbury
7. Semaphore from Gloucester
Distant from Birmingham 932 yards from box
Disc to Evesham Junction box
Disc to Ashchurch Junction box
Disc to Tewkesbury Junction box
Points and signals interlocked

Rec'd June 29th
1876
No 5082R
Board of Trade
Not to Scale

Source P.R.O. Kew MT6 160/10
Drawn by A.E. Overton

To Tewkesbury

Fig 58. Although not really part of the story of the Evesham branch, I felt I should provide a cross-section of photographs and a drawing of this one-time important railway centre. The Midland Railway established one of its provender stores at Ashchurch to the west of the main line. Although there was not direct access to the stores from the Evesham branch, no doubt traffic to and from the stores went over the branch. This drawing is taken from an original Midland Railway plan which was sent to the Board of Trade on 28 June 1876, and is now at the PRO Kew. The purpose was to obtain approval for the new connections with the main line at Ashchurch.

Colonel Yolland was appointed to undertake the inspection and his report was brief and to the point: 'I have inspected the new connections which have been made by the Midland Railway Company between their main lines and the Provender Stores sidings at Ashchurch. There are no additional facing points. The requirements of the Board of Trade have been complied with, and I therefore recommend that its sanction may be given for the use of these new connections.' The Board of Trade wrote to the Midland Railway on 10 July 1876 and confirmed they had no objections to the use of these new connections. The drawing shows how the existing lie-by siding on the up line to the north of the station was used to provide one of the connections to the provender stores. *A. E. Overton*

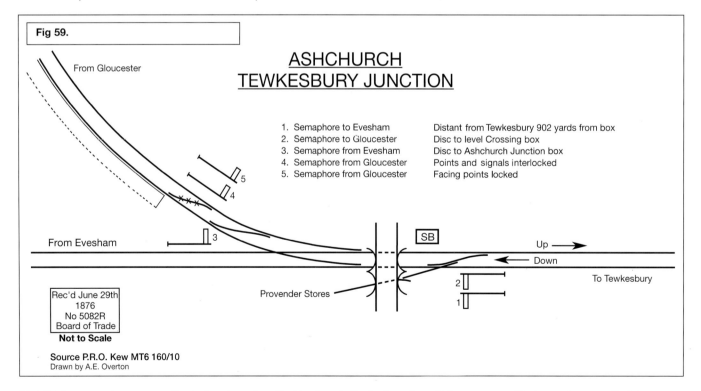

Fig 59.

ASHCHURCH
TEWKESBURY JUNCTION

From Gloucester

1. Semaphore to Evesham   Distant from Tewkesbury 902 yards from box
2. Semaphore to Gloucester   Disc to level Crossing box
3. Semaphore from Evesham   Disc to Ashchurch Junction box
4. Semaphore from Gloucester   Points and signals interlocked
5. Semaphore from Gloucester   Facing points locked

5

4

From Evesham

3

SB

Up →

← Down

2

1

To Tewkesbury

Provender Stores

Rec'd June 29th
1876
No 5082R
Board of Trade
Not to Scale

Source P.R.O. Kew MT6 160/10
Drawn by A.E. Overton

Fig 59. There was also a connection to the stores from the Evesham to Tewkesbury line which was covered in the same report. Both junctions were on the same plan but it was more convenient to make two separate drawings for the purpose of this book. *A. E. Overton*

Right:
It was always an impressive sight to see a locomotive running over the branch across the main line at Ashchurch Level Crossing. This picture, taken on 21 March 1957, shows Saltley's Ivatt Class 4MT No 43046, with the ordinary passenger train headcode in position in readiness to work a train from Ashchurch to Birmingham. A modern tubular post with an upper quadrant signal has replaced the old Midland signal seen before. *T. J. Edgington*

Right:
This picture was taken after the line from Evesham Junction to Tewkesbury Junction was singled, the work being undertaken by 1927. To the right, the line curves round to the Malvern branch platform at Ashchurch, while ahead the single line joins the Evesham branch at Evesham Junction. The new signalbox at Ashchurch Level Crossing, which opened on 16 October 1927, taking over the functions of both Evesham and Tewkesbury Junction signalboxes, as well as that of the 1900 Ashchurch Level Crossing signalbox, can be seen on the left. *NRM Derby Collection DY 14235*

Below:
This rather impressive picture was taken from the footbridge at the south end of Ashchurch station and shows Class 5MT 4-6-0 No 44963 on the 12.20pm passenger train from Worcester Shrub Hill to Gloucester Eastgate on 8 September 1962. The train on the left is the 11.38am from Redditch headed by Class 3F 0-6-0T No 47276. *J. M. Tolson*

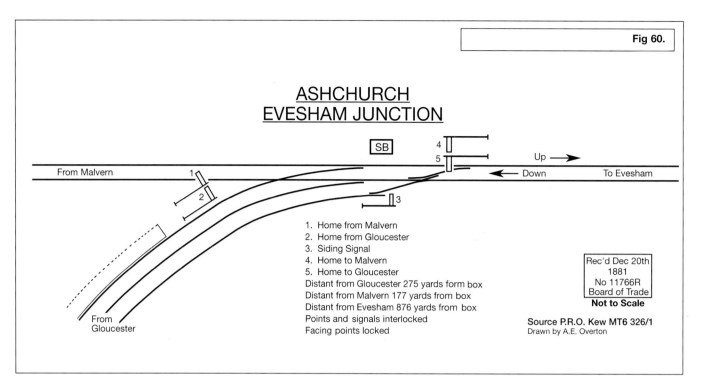

Fig 60.

ASHCHURCH
EVESHAM JUNCTION

1. Home from Malvern
2. Home from Gloucester
3. Siding Signal
4. Home to Malvern
5. Home to Gloucester
Distant from Gloucester 275 yards form box
Distant from Malvern 177 yards from box
Distant from Evesham 876 yards from box
Points and signals interlocked
Facing points locked

Rec'd Dec 20th
1881
No 11766R
Board of Trade
Not to Scale

Source P.R.O. Kew MT6 326/1
Drawn by A.E. Overton

Fig 60. Evesham Junction, Ashchurch.
The cabin at Evesham Junction had 13 working and three spare levers. The requirements of the Government Inspector before the Board of Trade would sanction this layout are given on page 125.

Fig 61, 62 and 63. Ashchurch.
With Fig 60 these three plans can be considered together as they formed part of a large application that was made by the Midland Railway to the Board of Trade on 19 December 1881. The work at Ashchurch was described as 'Rearrangement of connection'. Major Marindin made the inspection and his report, dated 31 December 1881, covered a total of 19 locations spread throughout the Midland Railway. At Ashchurch he said: 'The crossing cabin contains 16 levers of which one is spare (Fig 62). Evesham Junction cabin contains 16 levers of which three are spare (Fig 60). Ashchurch Junction cabin contains 28 levers of which four are spare (Fig 61). Tewkesbury Junction cabin contains 16 levers (Fig 63).

'Requirements. At Evesham Junction there are no means of bringing trains from Evesham to the platform except by running them across the main line to Tewkesbury Junction then backing them into the Tewkesbury platform. A separate platform on the down side from Evesham should be provided, or a facing point connection which has been taken out should be restored, so that trains from Evesham for which Ashchurch is a terminal station, may be brought up to the outside of the down main line platform, in the same manner as Tewkesbury trains are brought to the Tewkesbury platform. A longer locking bar to be fitted to the facing points. No 1, the down distant signal to be proceeded by either No 7 or No 8 home signals.' The plan that was proposed by the company is shown in Fig 60.

There were no requirements for Ashchurch Junction and the track layout is shown in Fig 61. This drawing also includes the coal stage where there may have been a small engine shed.

The requirements for Tewkesbury Junction, shown in Fig 62, were that safety points should be provided on the goods line. Major Marindin said: 'It appears that trains from Gloucester instead of

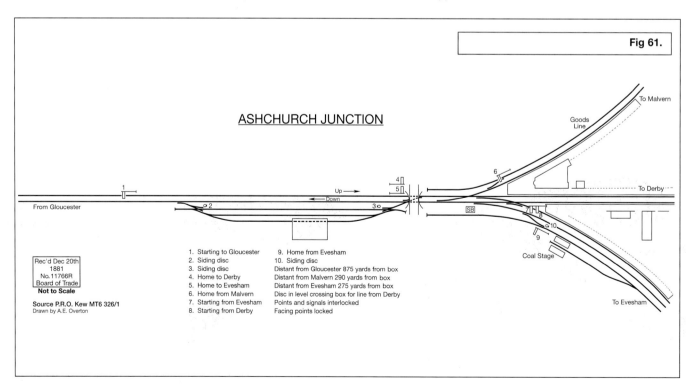

Fig 61.

ASHCHURCH JUNCTION

1. Starting to Gloucester
2. Siding disc
3. Siding disc
4. Home to Derby
5. Home to Evesham
6. Home from Malvern
7. Starting from Evesham
8. Starting from Derby
9. Home from Evesham
10. Siding disc
Distant from Gloucester 875 yards from box
Distant from Malvern 290 yards from box
Distant from Evesham 275 yards from box
Disc in level crossing box for line from Derby
Points and signals interlocked
Facing points locked

Rec'd Dec 20th
1881
No. 11766R
Board of Trade
Not to Scale

Source P.R.O. Kew MT6 326/1
Drawn by A.E. Overton

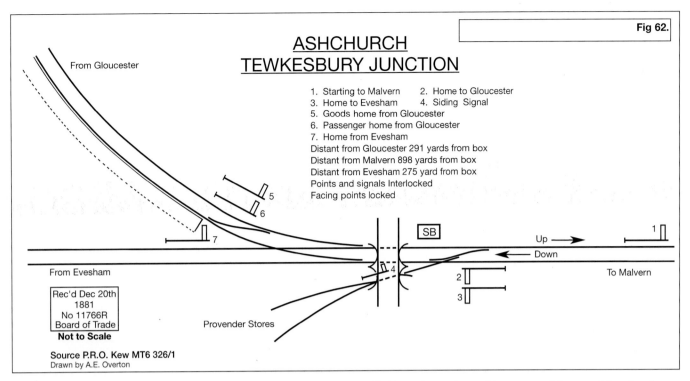

Fig 62.

ASHCHURCH
TEWKESBURY JUNCTION

1. Starting to Malvern   2. Home to Gloucester
3. Home to Evesham   4. Siding Signal
5. Goods home from Gloucester
6. Passenger home from Gloucester
7. Home from Evesham
Distant from Gloucester 291 yards from box
Distant from Malvern 898 yards from box
Distant from Evesham 275 yard from box
Points and signals Interlocked
Facing points locked

From Gloucester

From Evesham

To Malvern

Up →
← Down

SB

Provender Stores

Rec'd Dec 20th
1881
No 11766R
Board of Trade
Not to Scale

Source P.R.O. Kew MT6 326/1
Drawn by A.E. Overton

running directly up to the Tewkesbury platform like the Tewkesbury trains, are run across the main line to Evesham Junction and then backed into the Evesham platform. After being emptied they are taken into the Tewkesbury platform from which they start. The only object for this is to keep the engine in its right position for starting away, but this practice of backing the trains, when they are loaded, should be discontinued. A bridge or subway between the platforms should be provided.'

He continued that subject to the satisfaction of the requirements

detailed in each case he could recommend the use of the alterations be sanctioned.

Fig 62 shows Ashchurch, Tewkesbury Junction. The original method used by the Midland Railway to terminate passenger trains from Gloucester did not meet with the Government Inspector's approval and his requirements are given above.

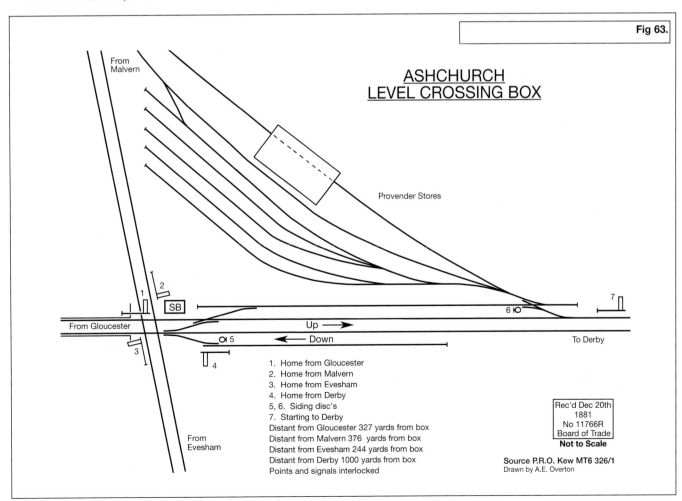

Fig 63.

ASHCHURCH
LEVEL CROSSING BOX

From Malvern

Provender Stores

From Gloucester

Up →
← Down

To Derby

From Evesham

SB

1. Home from Gloucester
2. Home from Malvern
3. Home from Evesham
4. Home from Derby
5, 6. Siding disc's
7. Starting to Derby
Distant from Gloucester 327 yards from box
Distant from Malvern 376 yards from box
Distant from Evesham 244 yards from box
Distant from Derby 1000 yards from box
Points and signals interlocked

Rec'd Dec 20th
1881
No 11766R
Board of Trade
Not to Scale

Source P.R.O. Kew MT6 326/1
Drawn by A.E. Overton

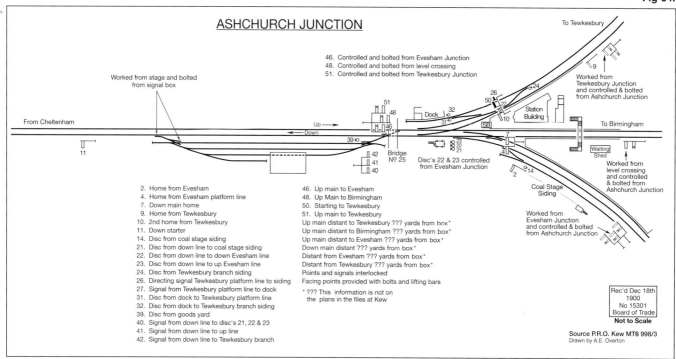

Fig 64.

ASHCHURCH JUNCTION

To Tewkesbury

46. Controlled and bolted from Evesham Junction
48. Controlled and bolted from level crossing
51. Controlled and bolted from Tewkesbury Junction

Worked from stage and bolted
from signal box

Worked from
Tewkesbury Junction
and controlled & bolted
from Ashchurch Junction

From Cheltenham

Up →
← Down

Dock

Station
Building

To Birmingham

Waiting
Shed

Worked from
level crossing
and controlled
& bolted from
Ashchurch Junction

Bridge
No 25

Disc's 22 & 23 controlled
from Evesham Junction

Coal Stage
Siding

Worked from
Evesham Junction
and controlled & bolted
from Ashchurch Junction

Rec'd Dec 18th
1900
No 15301
Board of Trade
Not to Scale

Source P.R.O. Kew MT6 998/3
Drawn by A.E. Overton

2. Home from Evesham
4. Home from Evesham platform line
7. Down main home
9. Home from Tewkesbury
10. 2nd home from Tewkesbury
11. Down starter
14. Disc from coal stage siding
21. Disc from down line to coal stage siding
22. Disc from down line to down Evesham line
23. Disc from down line to up Evesham line
24. Disc from Tewkesbury branch siding
26. Directing signal Tewkesbury platform line to siding
27. Signal from Tewkesbury platform line to dock
31. Disc from dock to Tewkesbury platform line
32. Disc from dock to Tewkesbury branch siding
39. Disc from goods yard
40. Signal from down line to disc's 21, 22 & 23
41. Signal from down line to up line
42. Signal from down line to Tewkesbury branch

46. Up main to Evesham
48. Up Main to Birmingham
50. Starting to Tewkesbury
51. Up main to Tewkesbury
Up main distant to Tewkesbury ??? yards from box*
Up main distant to Birmingham ??? yards from box*
Up main distant to Evesham ??? yards from box*
Down main distant ??? yards from box*
Distant from Evesham ??? yards from box*
Distant from Tewkesbury ??? yards from box*
Points and signals interlocked
Facing points provided with bolts and lifting bars

* ??? This information is not on
the plans in the files at Kew

Fig 64. On 26 September 1899 there was an accident to a passenger train at Ashchurch and this was to have far-reaching consequences beginning with the submission of a plan by the Midland Railway Company to the Board of Trade. Dated 28 March 1900, the plan was to show proposed alterations that would meet the requirements made by the inspecting officer, Lt-Col G. Von Donop. The Board of Trade wrote to the company on 3 April giving approval on condition that the work was submitted for inspection when complete. On 17 December the Midland Railway advised that the work would be complete by the 24th and the Board of Trade appointed Major Pringle to undertake the inspection 'as soon as he conveniently can'.

Major Pringle's report was dated 15 January 1901 and stated:

'I made an inspection of the new works at Ashchurch on the Midland Railway. Ashchurch Junction is the point where the double-line Evesham branch and the single-line Tewkesbury branch both join the main line from Birmingham to Cheltenham. The alterations referred to have been carried out partly in consequence of the accident that occurred to a passenger train at this place in September 1899, and mainly concern the junction of the Tewkesbury line: the other additions have been made in the signalling to bring the arrangements up to date. The old single-line junction has been converted into a double-line junction by a short loop line, and a new connection with

this new up loop line has been made to an engine siding on the up side. There are two new facing points introduced and these together with an old facing point are now provided with all the necessary safety appliances. A new signalbox and frame in a more commanding position have been erected, and some additional signals besides those necessitated by the new work.

'The frame contains 52 levers of which eight are spare and two work gongs. Three of the working levers control the down home signals respectively from Tewkesbury Junction, Ashchurch Level Crossing (main line) and Evesham Junction, and one lever bolts a siding connection to the down main line.

'The only requirements that I noted were:
1. Signal No 26 requires to be led by No 29.
2. No 28 should lock No 50.

'Subject to the fulfilment of these requirements and the submission of a report on their completion I can recommend the Board of Trade to sanction the alterations and works at Ashchurch.'

The Midland Railway wrote to the Board of Trade on 13 March 1901 and confirmed that these requirements had been complied with. This drawing, based upon a Midland Railway original plan at the PRO Kew, shows the arrangements that were the subject of Major Pringle's inspection. *A. E. Overton*

Left:
Another scene, believed to be from 1883, taken to record the new footbridge that connected the two platforms at Ashchurch. Seen from the Evesham branch area of the station, the single platform face was used by both arriving and departing trains. Understandably, the track is older than that on the main line, and I am not entirely sure what weight rail it is. The 1869 Midland Railway standard introduced by Barlow was 20ft rail lengths weighing 80lb and 83lb to the yard with seven sleepers to the rail length. It is possible that this track was laid with earlier second-hand rails; generally there were seven sleepers to the length but one section of track at the platform has only six sleepers in the length. (However, it *could* be 1869 83lb rail.) Of particular interest is the joint chair that can just be seen in the bottom right-hand corner of the picture. One reason for including this view is to show the provender stores which dominate the area on the left, beyond the bridge. The Midland Railway used an attractive painting style for most of its structures, Denby Pottery cream and Venetian red that was close to chocolate in colour, although in this instance on the panels of the water tower three colours have been used. *NRM Derby Collection DY 4143*

4
Train Working Over the Evesham Branch

The Evesham branch, from the Birmingham & Gloucester Railway at Barnt Green Main Line signalbox to Ashchurch Junction, where it rejoined the Birmingham & Gloucester Railway, was built in three separate sections as previously described. During its lifetime this line was not always worked as a single unified route, and in many respects it was operated as two separate branches. Some trains only worked over the original line between Redditch and Barnt Green or beyond and other trains only ran over the Midland branch from Ashchurch to Evesham. A number of trains ran through from end to end, while finally some joined or left the line at Broom Junction. When I worked in the Evesham Link I did not know either the origin or the history of this railway, but even as a young railwayman I was conscious of the fact that it was somewhat haphazard as far as the workings were concerned. Later, when undertaking research for this book, it became clear that in some respects the railway never really overcame its fragmented heritage, and this is most evident when the passenger services are considered.

At the northern end of the line there was the Birmingham to Redditch service, the oldest and the only part still operating. Today, this is really the southern end of a Lichfield to Redditch service or 'Cross City Link' as railway operators now describe it. This is a most sensible arrangement but the route was never used as such during the steam era. The Birmingham to Evesham service was also important and was to survive until the line closed, while some passenger trains started or terminated their journeys at Ashchurch. The service over the southern end of the railway from Ashchurch to Evesham also lasted until the line was

finally closed, although the traffic over this section was less intense. There were also some services that, from an operational point of view, were designed to place engines and coaches where they were needed at the start of the day, and I will draw attention to these services later.

The Passenger Train Service 1869-1964

Although only a few trains per day were involved, the junction of the Midland Railway with the East & West Junction Railway, later the Stratford-upon-Avon & Midland Junction Railway, at Broom was most important in an operational sense, and the withdrawal of these passenger services in 1947 marked the end of a useful connection for a few travellers. Less important was the cessation of the GWR's passenger train service from its branch into the old Midland Railway station at Alcester. As we have seen, this was a local service for travellers from stations served by the Great Western who wished to go to Alcester rather than one for travellers who needed a forward connection.

On the other hand, the freight services show a steady development which began as a line serving the local communities but ended with the railway fulfilling a most important service as a relief or avoiding line for trains running in either direction between Birmingham and the West of England. This enabled some through trains to bypass the bottleneck of the Lickey Incline. As the freight traffic using the Birmingham & Gloucester line increased, the Midland and then

Although the 2-4-0s worked over the line, there are very few pictures of them on the branch. This c1920 scene of No 176 shows an up passenger train at Barnt Green with a Clayton four-wheel passenger brake van followed by a third brake carriage.
W. L. Good

Above:
The Johnson 0-4-4Ts were regular engines on the Evesham branch, working from Birmingham to Redditch via both the Camp Hill line and the Birmingham West Suburban. This August 1921 picture shows No 1386 on a Birmingham to Redditch train approaching Kings Norton. *W. L. Good*

Centre left:
At one time many of the passenger trains that ran to and from Redditch from Birmingham New Street did so over the Camp Hill line. With the closure of the remaining stations between King's Norton and Camp Hill on 27 January 1941 the only passenger trains to use this route were for operational reasons. I recall that c1950 there were one, perhaps two, passenger trains per day over this line. This picture, taken on 1 August 1959, shows the 2.35pm from Redditch, hauled by Ivatt Class 4MT 2-6-0 No 43103, arriving at the east end of Birmingham New Street Platform 10 after having run over the Camp Hill line.
M. Mensing

Lower left:
It is not possible to say if this up train started from Redditch, Evesham or Ashchurch. The photograph was taken near Northfield in 1937 and shows Stanier 2-6-2T No 92 at the head of a seven-coach passenger train made up of two ex-Midland and five LMS-built coaches. *W. L. Good*

Although Stanier 2-6-2T No 113 is not on the 1937-8 list of engines known to have worked on the line (Appendix 2), it is seen at Evesham on 13 September 1935, confirming it made at least one visit to the branch. The Railway Hotel overlooked both the GWR and the LMS stations and proclaimed the merits of Stratford-upon-Avon's Flower & Sons brewery. *Collection R. J. Essery*

the LMS improved the railway at the approaches to both the southern and northern end of the Lickey Incline. This was done by building additional goods or slow lines and making some signalling improvements, but the problem of the Lickey remained. The 2 miles 5 chains of the Lickey Incline, between Bromsgrove and Blackwell stations, meant there was a physical limit to the number of trains that could be worked over this section of double line. Therefore any trains originating north of Barnt Green and heading for destinations south of Ashchurch, or running in the reverse direction, which could be diverted over the Evesham branch and therefore away from the Lickey were of immense operational benefit to those responsible for managing the movement of trains. Over the years, and in particular during the World War 2 period, there was increasing use made of the line as an alternative route for this traffic.

Wartime needs for the movement of trains from the East Midland to South Wales, and in the reverse direction, generated a traffic flow that the promoters of the original railways never foresaw. This traffic further altered the local character of the railway by making it even more of a through route. The one development that would have been of immense benefit would have been the doubling of the line from Barnt Green to Evesham, so that more trains could have avoided the bottleneck of the Lickey Incline, but as far as I am aware, this was never considered.

Appendix II provides details of locomotives known to have worked over the line in the later years, from which it will be seen that there were some quite large locomotives involved. The British Railways, London Midland Operating Area book, 'Routes over which engines may run', dated March 1958, details the engines that were permitted to travel over the branch. Only one steam engine was banned, this was the single 'Royal Scot' No 46170 *British Legion*. I believe the Garratts were allowed on the line but at the date the document was published the class was virtually extinct and so was not included. Although permitted on the line, a number of classes were restricted to 25mph throughout. These were LMS Standard Class 5, both the taper and parallel boiler LMS mixed traffic 2-6-0s, the Rebuilt 'Royal Scots' Nos 46100-46169 and the British Railways Standard Class 5 4-6-0s. Other classes permitted on the line, provided they did not exceed 25mph, included the British Railways 'Clan' Pacifics and No 71000 *Duke of Gloucester,* the British Railways Class 9F 2-10-0s, the LMS '8F'

class and ex-WD 2-8-0s, ex-LMS and LNWR 0-8-0s, ex-S&D 2-8-0s, the BR 'Britannia' 4-6-2s and the LMS 'Jubilee' and 'Patriot' 4-6-0s. The only main line diesel that was not restricted was No 10800. Nos 10000 and 10001 and 10201-10203 were all banned as either single or double units, together with the Fell diesel No 10100. The 'not to exceed 25mph' rule also applied to a number of diesels, these being given as Type 2 Nos D5700-D5719, Type 4 Nos D600-D604, the 350hp ex-LMS and BR standard diesel-electrics and the 500hp EE diesel-electric and diesel-hydraulic.

The Midland Railway also restricted certain locomotives. The Midland Railway book I have, dated January 1910, and corrected on 4 June 1910, gives the following info/rmation.

Between Barnt Green and Redditch the 4-2-2 engines, Nos 600-694, together with the 4-4-0s Nos 700-779 and the 0-6-4 tank engines, Nos 2000-2039, were permitted. There was a general restriction over the line from Barnt Green to Ashchurch south of Redditch. The only engines that were permitted at this time were the No 1 Class Passenger engines (Nos 600-684 excepted) and Nos 1 and 2 class goods engines (American engines excepted). At this time the passenger tank engines were not subject to the recently introduced power classification system so this Midland Railway document has to be interpreted. With the exception of the Compounds and the '990' class 4-4-0s all Midland classes were permitted to run between Barnt Green and Redditch but over the rest of the line the classes that could run were the 2-4-0s and those 4-4-0s that were in power class 1, all the 0-4-4 tank engines and the power class 1 and 2 goods engines other than the American 2-6-0s. The H boiler Class 3 goods engines were not permitted; I am unsure about the '2000' class 0-6-4 tank engines. I have never seen an LMS document of this nature so am unable to say when the severe restrictions of the Midland era were raised to permit the larger locomotives listed in the 1958 document to travel over the line.

The Train Services Analysed

For most of the Midland Railway period the company produced a single working timetable that covered both the passenger and freight trains. In this review I propose, where possible, to describe all services at a given date. When we arrive at the end of the Midland Railway period it will be found more convenient to examine the passenger and freight train services separately. This

is because the timetables available to me have various dates and it has not been possible to match the passenger and freight services at a given time. I hope this approach is acceptable.

The line from Barnt Green to Redditch opened in September 1859 and although I do not have a copy of the working timetable I do have a typed copy of the passenger timetable from 1 June 1860. The train times were very similar to the 1 July 1861 service shown on page 131, but there were some differences. The running time from Redditch to Barnt Green was also 15 minutes and the service to and from Birmingham was over the original Birmingham & Gloucester Railway via Camp Hill and what became St Andrews Junction to Birmingham New Street. The Birmingham West Suburban Railway that enabled trains to run over the shorter route from New Street to King's Norton did not open fully until 1885.

In 1860, the weekday departures from Redditch were at 8.25, arrive Birmingham at 9.25, then at 10.10 arriving 11.0, 1/40 arriving 2/35, 2/30 arriving 3/25, 4/55 arriving 5/55 and 7/25 arriving 8/35. The departures from Birmingham to Redditch were at 7.5, arriving 8.5, 10.0 arriving 10.55, 1/35 arriving 2/20, 4/50 arriving 5/45, and 7/10 arriving 8/15. There was also a service from Barnt Green to Redditch which departed at 2/55 and arrived at Redditch at 3/10.

The Sunday service comprised trains from Redditch at 7.0 to Barnt Green arriving at 7.15, at 10.10 to Birmingham, arriving at 11.15, 5/10 to Barnt Green arriving at 5/25 and at 8/40 to Birmingham arriving at 9/45. The down direction trains began with the 6.45 from Birmingham arriving at Redditch at 7.40 and then one at 5/0 arriving at 5/55. There were two Barnt Green to Redditch services, the first departed at 10.40 and the second at 9/10, both trains taking 15 minutes for the journey.

The 1 July 1861 public timetable was presented with the *Redditch Indicator* on that date and this has been reproduced at Table 1. This shows the Birmingham to Redditch service some

two years after the line was opened and provides details of connecting omnibus services. Note that whereas the 1860 timetable allowed Government class passengers on all trains, in 1861 there were some restrictions.

The earliest working timetable I have for the Evesham branch is for December 1869. Unfortunately I do not have all the arrival and departure times for trains starting and terminating off the branch but I expect that the passenger times would be similar to those described above. I have set out these details, separating the passenger trains from the goods trains and showing the workings as either up or down trains.

The goods train service in 1869 was not fully balanced, but was nearly so. In effect there was one up and one down train between Birmingham to Gloucester, but it involved more than one numbered train in each direction with variations on certain

days. What probably happened was that the trains, e.g. down trains 2 and 6 or 2 and 7 were worked by the same engine and men throughout the week. There was also a Birmingham-Redditch-Birmingham daily service although in the up direction it was part of the through Gloucester working involving up trains 20 or 21 and 22 and 23. Table 2 illustrates this early rather basic goods train service.

The 1 October 1872 Appendix to the working timetable gives Loads for Engines between Barnt Green and Redditch. Between Evesham and Barnt Green, 30 loaded goods, 25 loaded minerals and 40 empties were permitted, while between Ashchurch and Evesham the trainloads were 40 loaded goods, 35 loaded minerals and 50 empties. There was also a note to the effect that 35 loads of grain and timber constituted a load for an engine between Gloucester, Evesham and Birmingham. At this date the standard goods engine was the Kirtley double-frame locomotive.

The line was opened throughout in 1868 and the December 1869 timetable is probably very similar to the train service that was worked over the Evesham branch during the first year. At this date the Birmingham West Suburban Railway had not been built. All the passenger services to and from Birmingham to the West of England ran via the Camp Hill line to King's Norton

Table 1
This timetable was presented with each copy of the 1 July 1861 *Redditch Indicator*, the local newspaper. Courtesy Hereford and Worcester County Record Office.

Presented with the "REDDITCH INDICATOR," July 1st, 1861.

REDDITCH RAILWAY.
TIME TABLE FROM JULY THE FIRST UNTIL FURTHER NOTICE.

Trains leave	WEEK DAYS.						SUNDAYS.			
	1 2 and GOV. A.M.	1 and 2 CLASS A.M.	1 and 2 CLASS P.M.	1 and 2 CLASS P.M.	1 and 2 CLASS P.M.	1 2 and GOV. P.M.	1 2 and GOV. A.M.	1 2 and GOV. A.M.	1 2 and GOV. P.M.	1 2 and GOV P.M.
REDDITCH	8, 20	10,* 0	1, 25	2, 30	5, 0	7, 25	7, 0	10, 10	5, 10	8, 40
Alvechurch ...	8, 29	10, 9	1, 34	2, 39	5, 9	7, 34	7, 9	10, 19	5, 19	8, 49
Barnt Green, arr.	8, 35	10, 15	1, 40	2, 45	5, 15	7, 40	7, 15	10, 25	5, 25	8, 55
Arrive at Bham.	9, 20	10, 50	2, 35	3, 25	6, 0	8, 35	...	11, 15	...	9, 45
„ Worcester	...	11, 30	2, 35	...	6, 17	8, 48	8, 15	...	6, 25	...

Trains leave	WEEK DAYS.						SUNDAYS.			
	1 2 and GOV. A.M.	1 and 2 CLASS A.M.	1 and 2 CLASS P.M.	1 and 2 CLASS P.M.	1 and 2 CLASS P.M.	1 2 and GOV. P.M.	1 2 and GOV. A.M.	1 2 and GOV. A.M.	1 2 and GOV. P.M.	1 2 and GOV. P.M.
Birmingham	7, 5	10, 5	§1, 20	...	5, 15	7, 10	6. 45	...	5, 0	...
Worcester ...	7, 44	9, 28	...	2, 5	4, 40	7, 10	...	9, 50	...	8, 20
Barnt Green ...	8, 45	10, 40	1, 50	2, 55	5, 45	8, 0	7, 25	10, 40	5, 40	9, 10
Alvechurch ...	8, 51	10, 46	1, 56	3, 1	5, 51	8, 6	7, 31	10, 46	5, 46	9, 16
Arrive at Redditch	9, 0	10, 55	‡2, 5	3, 10	6, 0	8, 15	7, 40	10, 55	5, 55	9, 25

ALCESTER & STUDLEY.—An Omnibus leaves Alcester calling at Studley every Week-day in time to meet the Trains leaving Redditch at 10,0 a.m. and 5,0 p m, and returns from Redditch after the arrival of Trains leaving Birmingham at 10.5 a.m., and 5,15 p.m.

Third Class with all trains between Redditch and Birmingham.

§A Train leaves Birmingham for Barnt Green at 1.0 p.m., but does not go on to Redditch until the next, arriving 2,5 p.m

*These two carry mails out. ‡ This one brings a mail in.

131

1869 Working Timetable

Down Direction Passenger Weekdays only

STATIONS

Train Number	Description	Birmingham	Barnt Green	Alvechurch	Redditch Arr	Redditch Dept	Studley & Astwood BK	Coughton	Alcester Arr	Wixford Dept	Priors	Salford Harvington	Evesham Arr	Evesham Dept	Bengeworth	Hinton	under-Hill	Ashton-Beckford	Ashchurch	Ashchurch Arr
1	Pass									6.30	6.36	6.41	6.47	6.55						
3	Pass		7.40	7.46	7.53	7.55	8.2	8.8		8.14	8.20	8.25	8.31	8.38	8.40	8.45	8.50	8.56	9.1	9.10
5	Pass	9.40	10.22	10.28		10.37	10.44	10.50	10.55	10.56	11.2	11.7	11.13	11.20	11.22	11.27	11.32	11.38	11.43	11.52
8	Pass	1/0	1/37	1/43	1/50	1/51	1/58	2/4		2/10	2/16	2/21	2/27	2/34	2/36	2/41	2/46	2/52	2/57	3/6
11	Pass	3/50																		5/50
12½	Pass	5/10	5/52	5/58		6/7	6/14	6/20	6/25	6/27	6/33	6/38	6/44	6/51	6/56	7/1	7/6	7/12	7/17	7/26
13	Pass	6/30	7/12	7/18	7/27															
14	Pass		9/2	9/8	9/15															
15	Pass	10/0	10/36		10/50															
15½	Pass															5/20	5/25	5/30	5/36	5/41

RUNS ON MONDAY ONLY (train 11)

Must take cattle from Barnt Green to Redditch when required (trains 14, 15)

Down Direction Goods Weekdays only

Train Number	Description	Birmingham	Barnt Green	Alvechurch	Redditch Arr	Redditch Dept	Studley & Astwood BK	Coughton	Alcester Arr	Wixford Dept	Priors	Salford Harvington	Evesham Arr	Evesham Dept	Bengeworth	Hinton	under-Hill	Ashton-Beckford	Ashchurch	Ashchurch Arr
2	Goods	6.0	7.30	7.37	7.43	8.25	8.40	9.0	9.6	9.17	9.29	9.52	10.6	10.20						
6	Goods													11.40	11.50	12/0	12/10	12/20	12/30	
7	Goods etc													12/30	12/40	12/50	1/0	1/10	1/20	
9	Goods etc	10.40	11.50	12/0	12/15	1/56	2/12	2/25	2/25	2/45	2/51±	2/55±	3/2±	3/15	3/50	3/59	4/5	4/13	4/21	4/30
10	Goods														3/50	3/59	4/5	4/13	4/10	4/25
11	Goods																		4/21	4/30
12	Goods etc																			
31	Goods etc																			

Runs Tuesday, Thursday & Saturday only
Runs Monday, Wednesday & Friday only
Runs on Monday, Wednesday, Friday and Saturday only
Runs on Monday, Wednesday & Friday only
Runs on Tuesday, Thursday & Saturday only
Runs to Gloucester arrives 6/5
±Passing Times

Up Direction Passenger Weekdays only

STATIONS

Train Number	Description	Evesham Dept	Salford Harvington Priors	Wixford	Priors	Alcester Arr	Studley & Coughton Dept	Astwood BK	Redditch Arr	Birming Alvechurch Dept	Barnt Green	Birmingham
16	Pass	7.10	7.17	7.23	7.29		7.36	7.41	7.47 / 7.53	7.55	8.3	8.45
17	Pas										7.18	7.25
18	Pass									8.50	8.58	9.40
19	Pass	10.30	10.37	10.43	10.49	10.55	10.56	11.1	11.7 / 11.15	11.15	11.23	12/10
24	Pass	1/6	1/13	1/19	1/25		1/32	1/37	1/43 / 1/51	1/56	2/4	2/55
24½	Pass											
26	Pass	5/59	6/6	6/12	6/18	6/24	6/26	6/31	6/37 / 6/44	5/0	5/8	5/50
29	Pass									6/50	6/58	7/5
30	Pass	8/11	8/18	8/24	8/30	8/36				8/20	8/29	8/35

Departs from Gloucester at 1/15 runs on Monday only
Runs on Monday only at 1/15
Birmingham

Up Direction Goods Weekdays only

Train Number	Description	Evesham Dept	Salford Harvington Priors	Wixford	Priors	Alcester Arr	Studley & Coughton Dept	Astwood BK	Redditch Arr	Alvechurch Dept	Barnt Green	Birmingham
20	Goods etc	11.49	11.55	12/5	12/15	12/21	12/35	12/46	12/57 / 1/7	2/45	2/20	2/0
21	Goods etc									10.35	10.35	10.20
22	Goods etc									10.50		
23	Goods etc	11.0										
25	Goods etc								2/5	2/45	2/20	2/0
26	Goods	11.15							5/5	5/14	3/45	3/30
27	Goods						12/57		1/7	5/20±	3/55	3/55

Departs from Gloucester at 8.20 Runs on Tuesday, Thursday & Saturday only
Departs from Gloucester at 9.17 Runs on Monday, Wednesday & Friday only
Runs on Monday, Wednesday & Friday only
Runs on Monday, Wednesday, Friday & Saturday
Runs on Monday, Wednesday & Friday only
Runs on Tuesday, Thursday & Saturday only

±Passing times

and Barnt Green, with most through trains to and from the north reversing at New Street station. Those that did not reverse at Birmingham detached/attached coaches to and from New Street at Saltley and King's Norton.

The down direction daily passenger service was made up of three through trains from Birmingham to Ashchurch. In addition, there were two trains that ran from Barnt Green to Ashchurch which connected with trains from Birmingham that were going forward to Bristol and three trains per day that ran from Birmingham to Redditch. The Ashchurch trains took about 2 hours 15 minutes from Birmingham or about 1 hour 30 minutes for a journey of 33 miles from Barnt Green. From the opening of the line the Birmingham to Redditch service was established as a separate working and probably reflected the need for more frequent communication between these two manufacturing centres, rather than a service from either of them to the primarily agricultural centres to be found between Redditch and Ashchurch. It should also be noted that this timetable pre-dated the junction with the East & West Junction Railway at Broom Junction and with the GWR at Alcester.

I have never found any locomotive or carriage diagrams that confirmed how the stock was utilised on this branch. I expect

that the through trains between Birmingham and Ashchurch, and Birmingham and Redditch, were worked on the out-and-back principle, referred to in later LMS documents as turnback trains. However, the presence of a turntable at Barnt Green is explained by the need to turn the locomotive that worked the Barnt Green to Ashchurch service. It is possible that train No 1 became train No 17 in the up direction, while train No 16 became train No 3 on the down line.

The next public timetable that is available to me shows services over the branch for the period 1 May to 30 June 1879. This indicates only the passenger trains, as details of goods trains would be shown only in the appropriate working timetable. The passenger trains for 1879 are given below. Compared with 1869 it is less complex, but the timings of the trains are similar. Unfortunately, I do not have details of either the times of arrival or departure at New Street.

			MO	TSO	MO	
Barnt Green dep	7.30	10.21				5/45
Redditch dep	7.46	10.34	2/5	2/5		5/58
Alcester dep	8.9	10.55	2/25	2/32		6/20
Evesham arr	8.33	11.19	3/0			6/43
Evesham dep	8.35	11.22			5/10	6/50
Ashchurch arr	9.5	11.53			5/39	7/20

			TO	MO		
Ashchurch dep		9.52		1/55	5/20	7/45
Evesham arr		10.21		2/55	5/47	8/15
Evesham dep	7.0	10.32	1/0		5/56	
Alcester dep	7.23	10.55	1/45		6/20	
Redditch dep	7.48	11.20			6/45	
Barnt Green arr	8.1	11.33			6/58	

All trains called at all stations except the 2/5 Monday Tuesday and Saturday only from Redditch which did not stop at Coughton. These 'selected days trains' were run in connection with various market days.

I have chosen 1909 for the next date to be examined in detail and the April working timetable has been set out at Table 3 together with some explanatory notes. There was no Sunday service on the line, but when compared with the 1869 service, it will be seen that there was a considerable increase in traffic over the line. In this timetable we can see that at least one train which used the line could have gone via the Lickey, namely Down Train 3. The practice of using the Evesham branch as an avoiding line was to become more widespread in later years.

A brief summary of the 1915 public timetable is included here in order to show the early wartime period passenger service on the line that was very similar to the service operated in 1914.

Table 2 (page 132)
The Midland Railway December 1869 Working Timetable.
This table has been prepared from the working timetable and some explanations are called for. Pass — passenger train. Goods — goods train; the significance of etc is not clear. Arr — arrival time. Dept — Departure time. + — passing time, Birmingham. Passenger trains ran to and from the west via the Camp Hill line to New Street station. Goods trains ran from Lawley Street Goods station.

At this date Washwood Heath was not open and these sidings do not appear in the working timetable.

am time is shown as 01.0; pm is shown as 01/0. Unless an arrival time is shown, all times are either passing or departure times.

E&B — engine and brakevan.

Notes on the original 1869 timetables.
2 Train shunts at Redditch for No 3 Passenger Train. Must not leave Barnt Green until the arrival of 16 Up Train.
2 and 3 Down Trains must pass No 17 Up Train at Redditch.
5 Down Train must not leave Alcester until the arrival of No 19 Up Train.
8 Down Train must not leave Redditch until the arrival of No 24 Up Train.
13 Down Train must pass No 29 Up Train at Alcester.
10 Train from Barnt Green must stop at Gas Co's Siding, Redditch.
11 Train from Evesham runs on Mondays, Wednesdays and Fridays.
19 Up Train must not leave Evesham until the arrival of No 2 Down Train.
22 Up Train must not leave Evesham until the arrival of No 5 Down Train.
23 Train must stop at Dixon's Wharf, Redditch.
25 Train from Ashchurch runs on Mondays, Wednesdays and Fridays.

Down Direction Weekday Service

6.45 dep Redditch	7.0 Alcester arr
6.25 dep Birmingham	9.1 Ashchurch arr
9.55 dep Birmingham	11.55 Ashchurch arr
1/5 dep Evesham	1/32 Ashchurch arr
1/12 dep Birmingham	3/40 Ashchurch arr
4/50 dep Evesham	5/15 Ashchurch arr Monday only service
5/0 dep Birmingham	7/17 Ashchurch arr
7/35 dep Birmingham	8/53 Evesham arr
11/30 dep Birmingham	12.55 Evesham arr Saturday only service

Sunday Service

9.0	dep Birmingham	10.32	Evesham arr
5/50	dep Birmingham	7/22	Evesham arr

Up Direction Weekday Service

7.11	dep Alcester	8.28	Birmingham arr
7.45	dep Evesham	9.16	Birmingham arr
9.42	dep Ashchurch	12/20	Birmingham arr
12/21	dep Ashchurch	12/43	Evesham arr
1/47	dep Ashchurch	3/42	Birmingham arr
4/0	dep Evesham	5/23	Birmingham arr
4/12	dep Ashchurch	4/38	Evesham arr Monday only service
5/22	dep Ashchurch	7/58	Birmingham arr
7/50	dep Ashchurch	8/14	Evesham arr
9/48	dep Evesham	11/25	Birmingham arr Saturday only service

Sunday Service

10.45	dep Evesham	12/30	Birmingham arr
7/35	dep Evesham	9/20	Birmingham arr

In 1909, there was no Sunday service, but by 1915 the pattern of two trains each way between Birmingham and Evesham had been established. In the 1915 timetable there was a separate section that dealt with the Birmingham-King's Norton-Redditch service that was intense. Some trains ran via the Camp Hill line while others went via the Birmingham West Suburban Railway. Some trains, for example the 8.33 arrival from Birmingham, terminated at Barnt Green. This train ran only during July and August and carried passengers bound for the Lickey Hills, a popular beauty spot favoured by day-trippers.

Timetable 3 (page 135)
The Midland Railway April 1909 Working Timetable

Down direction trains
Notes on the original timetables.
1 Train 10.35 Class 'B' Goods from Lawley Street to Bath. Attaches vegetables at Evesham, but when there is nothing for train to attach at that place, wagons for Evesham are put off at Broom Junc. and sent on by the 12.5 ex Washwood Heath. Passes train 44 at Redditch.
3 Train 11/45 Class 'B' Goods from Birmingham Central to Gloucester. Arrives 2.55.
5 Train 12.5 Goods from Washwood Heath. At Camp Hill attaches traffic for the S&M Junction line only. Stops at Alcester to attach or detach traffic as required.
7 Train Class 'B' Goods to Gloucester, arrives 6.10.
8 Train 1.30 Class 'B' Goods from Lawley Street to Bristol. Attaches at King's Norton when required. Arrives at Broom 4.53. When cannot clear Broom will convey maximum loading and carry Class 'B' lights, running at 25 miles per hour.
10 Train 6.58 Passenger from Redditch to Evesham. Passes Up Train 6 at Alcester.
12 Train 3.50 Goods from Lawley Street to Evesham. Detaches at Salford Priors and Harvington. Marshals its wagons at Redditch. Passes Up 6 and 9 trains at Redditch, 11 at Alcester and 10 and 12 at Broom.
13 Train 7.18 Passenger from Barnt Green to Ashchurch. Passes Up Train 6 at Redditch and Up Train 9 at Broom.
14 Train 8.2 Passenger from Birmingham to Redditch. Runs via the Camp Hill line.

16 Train 6.50 Goods from Washwood Heath to Evesham. Detaches important traffic at King's Norton.
17 Train 9.56 Passenger from Birmingham to Ashchurch. Runs via the Birmingham West Suburban line.
19 Train 11.40 Class 'B' Goods from Evesham to Lawley Street. This Saturday-only train runs south to Ashchurch, arriving at 12/40. The train is reversed and departs at 1/0 arriving at Lawley Street at 4/35.
20 Train 8.20 Goods from Washwood Heath to Evesham. Guard informs the signalman at Barnt Green Main Line Junction what traffic (including Tariff) on train for Alvechurch.
21 Train 12/5 Passenger to Redditch. Runs via the Camp Hill line.
22 Train 12/33 Express passenger from Birmingham to Evesham. Runs nonstop to Barnt Green via the West Birmingham Suburban line. Stops at Broom for tablet purposes only. Passes Up Train 18 at Alcester.
24 Train 12/48 Passenger from Birmingham to Evesham. Runs via the Camp Hill line. Arrives at Broom at 2/30. Passes Up Train 18 at Alcester and Up Train 23 at Broom.
28 Train 4/45 Goods to Ashchurch. Leaves at 4/55 on Mondays, Hinton depart as other days. Arrives at Ashchurch at 6/30 and departs light engine to Tewkesbury engine shed at 6/35 arriving at 6/40.
29 Train 5/0 Passenger from Birmingham to Ashchurch. Runs via the Birmingham West Suburban line. Calls at Bournville Mondays to Fridays to take up passengers.
31 Train 6/40 Passenger from Birmingham to Redditch. Runs via the Birmingham West Suburban line.
32 Train 8/25 Fruit to Ashchurch to connect with Special Fruit train from the west, or 9/20 from Gloucester. Stops at Bengeworth, Hinton and Beckford when required to take up fruit traffic.
33 Train 7/35 Passenger from Birmingham to Evesham. Runs via the West Birmingham Suburban line. Passes Up Train 36 at Redditch and Up Train 39 at Broom.
36 Train 10/15 Passenger from Birmingham to Redditch. Stops at Alvechurch on Thursdays and Saturdays.
37 Train 11/20 Passenger from Birmingham to Redditch. Thursdays and Saturdays only. Runs via the Camp Hill line and between Redditch and Evesham on Sunday morning only. Passes Up Train 44 at Redditch.

Sundays
40 Train. 12.5 Goods from Birmingham to Evesham. Attaches traffic at Barnt Green and Harvington when required.
42 Train 2.15 Goods from Birmingham Central Goods Station to Bristol. Arrives 10.45. When cannot clear Broom Junction will detach its wagons at Ashchurch and return special to Broom Junction. (This means that if the wagons to be attached at Broom would increase the train over the loading allowed, the train would be worked to Ashchurch, the train detached and the engine and brake would return to Broom. The timetable does not say that when this took place the train was terminated at Ashchurch or if the journey was resumed and a late arrival at Bristol was acceptable. During the period that I describe in Chapter 1 trains would often finish their journeys on Sunday afternoon. This was particularly true in the winter months, so I expect that the reception siding at Bristol would remain open until the train arrived.) Bristol men returning home from a lodging turn to Birmingham probably worked the train.

Table Three

April 1909 Working Timetable

Down Direction Passenger   No Sunday Service

STATIONS

Train No.	Description	Birmingham	Barnt Green	Alvechurch	Gas Works Sidings	Redditch Arr	Redditch Dept	Studley & Astwood Bk	Coughton	Alcester Arr	Alcester Dept	Wixford	Broom	Salford Priors	Harvington	Evesham Arr	Evesham Dept	Bengeworth	Hinton	Ashton-under-Hill	Beckford	Ashchurch
10	Pass						6.58	7.5		7.13	7.15		7.21			7.33						
13	Pass		7.18	7.23		7.31	7.43	7.50	7.56	8.0	8.1	8.6	8.11	8.15	8.21	8.28	8.34	8.39	8.43	8.48	8.54	9.1
14	Pass	8.2	8.50	8.55		9.2		Runs via Camp Hill Line		9.18≠				S&M Pass 8.17 To Stratford								
15	GWR Pass															Pass	9.46				9.59±	10.6
17	Pass	9.56	10.19	10.24		10.31	10.34	10.41	10.47	10.51	10.52	10.57	11.1	11.5	11.11	11.18	11.28	11.33	11.37	11.42	11.48±	11.55
18	GWR Pass							Runs via Camp Hill Line		11.3≠			S&M Pass 11.10 To Stratford≠									
21	GWR Pass	12/5	12/44			12/56		Runs via Camp Hill Line		1/22	1/23			1/31	1/37		1/5	1/10	1/14	1/19	1/25±	1/32
22	Express	12/33	12/54			1/4	1/7	1/14		1/25≠						1/44						
23	GWR Pass							Runs via Camp Hill Line														
24	S&M Pass	12/48	1/42	1/47		1/54	2/2	2/9	2/15	2/19	2/22	2/27	2/34	2/38	2/44	2/51	3/13	3/18	3/22	3/27	3/33±	3/40
25	S&M Pass							2/41 To Stratford														
26	Pass		2/33	2/38		2/45		Passenger Monday only														
27	GWR Pass							Runs via Camp Hill Line	GWR Pass	5/17≠							4/53	5/0	5/0	5/5	5/11±	5/18
28	Pass	4/5	4/32	4/37		4/44				5/17≠												
29	Pass	5/0	5/27	5/32		5/39	5/44	5/51		6/1	6/2	6/7	6/11	6/15	6/21	6/28	6/44	6/49	6/53	6/58	7/4±	7/11
30	Pass		6/25	6/30		6/37≠		S&M Pass 6/20 To Stratford (shown as train 14)		7/7≠												
31	Pass	6/40	7/7	7/12		7/20																
33	Pass	7/35	7/58	8/3		8/10	8/13	8/20		8/28	8/29		8/35	8/39	8/45	8/52						
35	Pass	9/8	9/45	9/50		9/57																
36	Pass	10/15	10/52			11/5		Runs via Camp Hill Line														
37	Pass	11/20	11/56			12/6	12.10	12.17		12.25	12.26		12.32				12.44 Thursdays & Saturdays only					

± Arrives Beckford 2min earlier

Down Direction Goods   w Booked stop for water

Train No.	Description	Birmingham	Barnt Green	Alvechurch	Gas Works Sidings	Redditch Arr	Redditch Dept	Studley & Astwood Bk	Coughton	Alcester Arr	Alcester Dept	Wixford	Broom	Salford Priors	Harvington	Evesham Arr	Evesham Dept	Bengeworth	Hinton	Ashton-under-Hill	Beckford	Ashchurch
1	Goods	10/35	12.3		12.6	12.18w	12.29	12.37		12.49			12.57		1.7	1.17	1.17	Mondays excepted				1.42
3	Goods	11/45	12.17		12.30	12.32w	12.39	12.48		1.0	1.20		1.17		1.26	1.36	1.44	Mondays excepted				2.8
4	Goods etc					1.0		1.8		1.20	1.22		1.30 Mondays excepted. Q Runs when required									
5	Goods	12.5	1.21		1.34	1.36	1.38	2.0		2.10	2.20		3.5					3.25 Monday & Tuesday excepted				
6	S&M Goods												3.30 To Stratford Monday excepted									
7	Goods	1.30	3.30		3.43	3.45w	3.50	3.59		4.12	4.43		4.45			5.4	5.9w	Monday excepted				
8	S&M Goods												5.5			5.24	5.30	Monday excepted				5.33
9	Goods	3.50	5.22		5.35	5.37w	8.35	9.0	Mondays excepted	9.10	9.20		9.45			10.0						5.52
12	Goods	6.50	9.5		9.16	9.18	10.15	10.23					9.31 To Stratford									
15	Goods																					
16	Goods							10.23	10.35 10.36	10.35	10.36		12/20 12/30			12/55		Saturdays excepted				
18	Goods																	Saturdays only			12/10 12/30	12/20 12/40
19	Goods													3/0	3/20	3/30						
20	Goods	8.20	11.3	11.17	11.25	11.27	12.10	12/45		12/55	1/30	1/45	2/45									
26	GWR Ballast							4/25≠		4/25≠			4/10≠		Goods	5/0	4/45	5/32 5/0	5/5 5/0		5/45 5/5	
28	S&M Goods							Saturdays excepted, runs when required									4/45*			6/20 5/11	6/30 5/18	
32	Fruit Train												9/40			8/25						
35	S&M Goods												11/45									
36	S&M Goods												11.5 on Mondays									8/52

Notes (goods): (9/45 on Saturday) Saturdays excepted

*Departs 4/55 on Mondays

≠ Division between two or more trains that share the same train number

135

Table Three

April 1909 Working Timetable

Up Direction Passenger   No Sunday Service

STATIONS

Train Number	Description	Ashchurch	Beckford	Ashton-under-Hill	Hinton	Bengeworth	Evesham Arr	Evesham Dept	Harvington	Salford Priors	Broom	Wixford	Alcester Arr	Alcester Dept	Coughton	Studley & Astwood Bk	Redditch Arr	Redditch Dept	Gas Works Sidings	Alvechurch	Barnt Green	Birmingham
3	Pass							6.50										6.43		6.52	6.57	7.31
6	Pass								6.58 (From Stratford)	7.3		7.8	7.13	7.14	7.20	7.26	7.33	7.38		7.47	7.52	8.27
8	S&M Pass							7.52	8.0 (From Stratford)	8.5	8.9		8.15	8.16 (GW Pass 8.22≠)		8.25	8.32	8.35		8.44	8.49	9.15
9	Pass								9.0	9.5	9.9	9.9	9.15	9.16		9.25	9.32	9.36		9.45	9.50	10.18
9A	GWR Pass												9.33	9.16								
11	Pass							8.52						11.18				10.49		10.58	11.3	11.25
15	Pass	8.45	8.53				9.5 ≠															
16	S&M Pass	9.40	9.48	9.53	9.58		10.6	10.42	10.50	11.0	11.0	11.3	11.8	11.9	11.15	11.21	11.28	11.35		11.44	11.49	12/13
17	Pass	12/22	12/30			10.2	12/42															
19	Pass																					
20	Pass							2/18			2/20≠							1/13		1/22	1/27	2/13
22	Pass	1/47	1/55	2/0	2/5	2/9	2/13		2/26	2/31	2/35	2/38	2/43	2/44 (2/9≠)	2/50	2/56	Pass	2/8		2/17	2/22	
23	Pass																3/3	3/5 (3/13)		3/21	3/26	3/32
28	Pass																					4/3
30	Pass							4/0	4/8	4/13	4/17	4/20	4/25	4/26	4/32	4/38	4/45	4/46		4/55	5/0	5/22
31	Pass																	5/0			5/11	5/50
32	Pass	4/0	4/8	4/13	4/18	4/22	4/26 (Mondays only ≠)					6/5≠		6/5≠	Pass	Pass		5/57		6/6	6/11	
35A	S&M Pass										6/0 from Stratford											
35	Pass	5/18	5/27	5/32	5/37	5/41	5/45	5/55	6/3	6/8	6/12	6/15	6/20	6/23	6/29	6/35	6/42	6/52		7/1	7/6	7/52±
37	Pass																	8/38		8/47	8/52	9/26
40	Pass	7/44	7/52	7/57	8/2		8/8	9/40	9/48	9/53	9/57		10/4	10/5		10/14	10/22	10/31	On Saturday works train 40	10/40	10/45	11/15
42	Pass																					

Notes within Passenger table: "Runs via Camp Hill Line" (train 3); "Runs via the Camp Hill Line" (trains 20, 30, 31); "GWR Pass" / "GW Pass"; "S&M Pass from Stratford" (train 22); "From Stratford"; "Saturday only" (train 40 Beckford); "Thursday & Saturday only" (Coughton); "Mondays only" (train 32 Evesham).

Up Direction Goods   w Booked stop for water

Train Number	Description	Ashchurch	Beckford	Ashton-under-Hill	Hinton	Bengeworth	Evesham Arr	Evesham Dept	Harvington	Salford Priors	Broom	Wixford	Alcester Arr	Alcester Dept	Coughton	Studley & Astwood Bk	Redditch Arr	Redditch Dept	Gas Works Sidings	Alvechurch	Barnt Green	Birmingham
1	E&B									12.5	12.5		12.11	12.12	Mineral empties	12.21	12.28	1.35			1.48	3.35
2	S&M Goods								From Stratford		3.12											
3	S&M Goods								To Stratford		4.25				Mondays excepted							
4	Goods	5.45	6.10	Mondays excepted							8.30		8.36	9.30	9.55	9.55	10.5	11.50		12/10	12/15	1/25
9A	S&M Goods									9.33	9.33											
10	Goods etc	6.40	7.10	Mondays only			6.25	7.0			9.30		9.36	9.50	10.5	10.5	10.15	12/0		12/20	12/27	1/50
18	Goods	Saturdays excepted					7.30	8.30	11.45	12/5	12/20	12/35	12/40	2/55	3/5	3/15	3/25	3/40		4/10	4/17	5/20
20	Goods etc	12/30	1/30	2/4	2/25	2/50	2/55	3/27			3/46											
28	Goods etc	2/35	2/4	2/25	2/25	2/50	4/10		Saturdays only ≠	Saturdays only ≠	3/46		4/11 Q runs when required	4/35≠								
29	Goods	2/56	3/10	3/30	3/44	4/5	3/26	3/27	S&M Goods when required	Q Runs when required	4/3	To Stratford			4/22	4/22	4/31	5/3			5/21	6/15
31	GWR Ballast			Saturdays only																		
34	Goods	4/35					4/15	4/15		4/55	5/30	5/35	5/50	6/37	7/0	7/0	7/39	7/9	7/35	7/49	7/49	8/35
36	Goods		5/37	5/50			7/15	7/15	7/55	8/5	7/33	5/35	7/39	7/41	7/50	7/50	7/59	8/10			8/24	8/52
39	Goods				6/10	6/25	6/30	7/40	8/50	8/50	8/50		8/56	9/1	9/10	9/10	9/19	9/57		10/11	10/11	11/15
40	S&M Goods								11/30		9/5	From Stratford							Sats Excepted			
44	S&M Goods	8/35					8/57	9/10	10/6		10/0		10/6	10/10	11/30		11/40	12/50			1.4	2.15
45	Goods	10/24					10/45	10/46	Saturdays excepted		11/0											
46	S&M Goods								Saturdays excepted		11/15											

Notes within Goods table: "Mondays excepted Q Runs when required" (train 1); "Mineral empties"; "Mondays excepted"; "From Stratford"; "To Stratford"; "Saturdays only"; "Saturdays excepted"; "Q Runs when required"; "S&M Goods when required"; "Sats Excepted".

=Train no 35 runs via the Camp Hill Line

≠Termination of train where another train is on the same line of the timetable

Up direction trains (Timetable 3 [page 135])

1 Train. Engine & Brake. Runs when required and it was worked by the 9/55 ex Barnwood.

2 Train. 1.35 Mineral empties to Birmingham Lawley Street, arrives 3.35.

3 Train. 6.43 Passenger to Birmingham. Runs via the Camp Hill line.

4 Train. 4.10 Goods from Barnwood to Birmingham Lawley Street, to arrive at 1/25. Leaves Barnwood with all wagons for Broom and via Broom marshalled against the brake and attaches traffic for same district at Ashchurch together. From Tuesdays to Fridays detaches wagons for Harvington and Salford Priors at Evesham. On Saturdays works wagons for Harvington and Salford Priors through to Broom to be returned by 3.30 Birmingham to Evesham. Passes Down Trains 16, 17 and 20 at Redditch. Stops at Coughton to detach and for tariff purposes on Saturdays and on Alcester cattle days. Tariff for Wixford is put out at Alcester and tariff for Coughton at Studley except on Saturdays and Alcester cattle sale days.

6 Train. 6.50 Passenger Evesham to Birmingham New Street. Arrives at 8.27. Runs via the West Birmingham Suburban line. Passes Down Train 10 at Alcester.

9 Train. 7.52 Passenger to Birmingham New Street. Arrives at 9.15. Runs via the West Birmingham Suburban line. Passes Down Train 13 at Broom and Down Train 12 at Redditch.

10 Train. 5.30 Goods from Gloucester to Birmingham Lawley Street. Arrives 1/50. Detaches rough traffic for Alcester, (rough traffic is wagons that require shunting into station order, that is not all intermixed). Stops at Alvechurch for traffic purposes on Evesham cattle days, Evesham advising Redditch and Alvechurch on cattle days, on other Mondays stops for tariff purposes only.
Stops at Wixford and Coughton to attach or detach traffic as required.

11 Train. 8.52 Passenger from Evesham to Birmingham New Street. Arrives at 10.18. Passes Down Train 12 at Alcester and Down Train 16 at Redditch.

16 Train. 10.49 Passenger to Birmingham New Street. Arrives 11.25, runs via the West Birmingham Suburban line.

17 Train. 9.40 Passenger to Birmingham New Street. Arrives at 12/13. (The train arrives at King's Norton at 12/0 where the train terminated on Saturday.) Shown in the timetable as 'Sats excepted King's Norton to Birmingham where it arrives at 12/0.' Arrives Broom 10.58 Passes Up Trains 16 and 17 at Broom and Up Train 20 at Redditch.

18 Train. 11.25 Goods to Birmingham Lawley Street. Arrives at 5/20. Passes Up Trains 16 at Broom and 20, 22 and 24 at Alcester. The timetable shows an engine departure at 8.10 (but does not show if it is from Gloucester or Tewkesbury; probably the latter.) Other notes in the timetable are: On Evesham cattle days, runs as far as Broom or Alcester as required, returning E&B to Evesham to work cattle special to Birmingham, stopping where required to detach livestock. To shunt where required on single line for 7/15 from Evesham. On Alcester cattle days engine leaves shed at 10.30 and train runs to Alcester as booked then works as cattle special to Birmingham, stopping where required to detach livestock and shunting when necessary for 7/15 from Evesham.

20 Train. 12/30 Goods from Ashchurch to Evesham. Runs forward to Broom when required. On Saturdays runs to Beckford only returning E&B at 1/30 Beckford to Ashchurch and works 2/11 passenger Ashchurch to Tewkesbury commencing 1 May.

20 Train. 1/13 Passenger to Birmingham New Street arrives at 2/13. Runs via the Camp Hill line.

23 Train. 2/18 Passenger from Evesham to Birmingham New Street arrives at 3/32. Runs via the West Birmingham Suburban line.

28 Train. 3/13 Passenger from Redditch to Birmingham New Street arrives at 4/3. Runs via the Camp Hill line.

29 Train. 1/35 Goods from Gloucester to Birmingham Lawley Street arrives at 6/15.

30 Train. 4/0 Passenger from Evesham to Birmingham New Street arrives at 5/22. Runs via the Camp Hill line.

31 Train. 5/0 Passenger from Redditch to Birmingham New Street arrives at 5/50. Runs via the Camp Hill line.

34 Train. 4/15 Goods from Evesham to Birmingham Lawley Street arrives at 8/35. Detaches traffic for Studley (cattle excepted) at Broom Junction. Loaded equal to 15 loaded wagons on leaving Broom. Passes Up Train 29 at Alcester. Detaches cattle at King's Norton, also cattle for Leicester line and London Goods at Duddeston. Conveys maximum loading from Camp Hill when required. Runs as Through Goods on Saturdays.

35 Train. 5/18 Passenger from Ashchurch to Birmingham New Street arrives at 7/52. Runs via the Camp Hill line. Passes Up Train 29 at Broom. Runs four minutes later on Mondays from Ashchurch to Evesham.

36 Train. 7/15 Class 'B' Goods from Evesham to Birmingham Duddeston Sidings arrives at 8/52. When required is worked by two No 1 Class engines in front and a 15 or 20-ton brake and conveys 50 wagons of goods to Barnt Green. On Saturdays leaves at 7/0, attaches at Broom, thence as other days.

37 Train. 8/38 Passenger to Birmingham New Street arrives 9/26. Runs via the West Birmingham Suburban line.

39 Train. 3/50 Class 'B' Goods Barnwood to Birmingham Lawley Street arrives 11/15. Wagons for the 7/15 from Evesham marshalled next to engine. Detaches wagons for Hereford and beyond at Barnt Green. On Beckford cattle sale days starts from Barnwood at 2/10 and runs earlier to Beckford, thence as booked. Beckford advises Gloucester dates.

40 Train. S&M Goods. Arrives at 9/20 on Saturdays.

40 Train. 10/31 Passenger from Redditch to Birmingham New Street arrives at 11/15. Runs via the West Birmingham Suburban line.

44 Train. 7/45 Class 'B' Goods Gloucester to Birmingham Lawley Street arrives 2.15. When not conveying Camp Hill market traffic runs as a Through Goods train from Broom Junction. Attaches only at Evesham. Arrives Broom 9/30, shunts Studley daily. Passes Down Train 1 at Redditch. On Saturdays leaves Broom at 10/20, Alcester 10/30 Studley dept. 11/40, Redditch 12 .7 Passes Up Train 37), Barnt Green arrives 12.22.

45 Train. 9/55 Class 'A' Goods from Gloucester to Broom. Places wagons at Broom for 10/35 from Birmingham. Works 12.5 Broom to Redditch and 1.0 return when required.

Sundays (Timetable 3, page 138)

49 Train. 1.35 Mineral empties to Birmingham Lawley Street arrives at 3.35. Detaches at Barnt Green when required.

On the working timetable it is clear that some trains had been added to the existing timetable. These are shown as ½ while others no longer run and these gaps are apparent in the train numbers shown in the table.

Cont. p138

Cont. from p137

Table Three

April 1909 Working Timetable

Down Direction Sunday Service Goods Trains

Train Number	Description	Birmingham	Barnt Green	Alvechurch	Gas Works Sidings	Redditch Arr	Redditch Dept	Studley & Astwood BK Coughton	Alcester Arr	Alcester Dept	Wixford	Broom	Salford Priors	Harvington	Evesham Arr	Evesham Dept	Bengeworth Hinton	Ashton-under-Hill	Beckford	Ashchurch
40	Goods	12.5	1.20			1.35	1.36	2.0	2.10	2.20		3.10			3.30					
42	Goods	2.15	3.6			3.19	3.31	3.41	3.51	4.1		4.40			4.55	5.0			5.25	
43	S&M Goods											5.15 To Stratford								

Up Direction Sunday Service Goods Trains

Train Number	Description	Ashchurch	Beckford	Ashton-under-Hill	Hinton	Bengeworth Evesham Arr	Evesham Dept	Harvington	Salford Priors	Broom	Wixford	Alcester Arr	Alcester Dept	Coughton	Studley & Astwood BK Redditch Arr	Redditch Dept	Gas Works Sidings	Alvechurch	Barnt Green	Birmingham
48	S&M Goods									4.55 From Stratford						1.35			1.48	
49	Mineral empties																		3.35	

For some reason the working timetable shows a passing time for all trains at the Gas Works Siding at Redditch. In the down direction this time was two minutes before the station arrival time and in the up direction two minutes after the departure time. Passenger trains arrive at Beckford two minutes before the time for departure, presumably to allow time to load passenger rated traffic, probably fruit.

At this date the Up sidings at Washwood had not been opened, meaning that up goods trains terminated at Lawley Street or Duddeston Sidings. Although opened in 1892, there is no reference to any up trains terminating at Water Orton Sidings.

The LMS in the 1930s

I have chosen 1930 for the LMS freight timetable and 1934 for the passenger services. Like the Midland Railway after 1917, the LMS used separate working timetables for passenger and freight trains but I have never been fortunate enough to obtain timetables for matching periods. However, for the purpose of this survey, where there was little crossover between passenger and goods work, these years will provide a good picture of the train services provided by the LMS. Whereas in 1909, mechanical road transport was not a competitive factor to be considered by the railway companies, by the 1930s the competition was beginning to bite. Unlike 1909 where, as far as I can see, any excursion trains would be operated in accordance with special traffic notices, in 1934 some regular ones appeared in the working timetable.

Another feature that had appeared on the railway was the motor train. This was designed as a cost-saving exercise for short branch lines. While different names were used, for example push-and-pull, 'reversible' trains and auto trains being three, the LMS referred to them as rail motor or motor trains. A rail motor was a vehicle with a self-contained non-detachable engine. The LMS instructions stated that normally two men, a driver and guard or driver and fireman, as may be specially authorised would work a rail motor. No additional vehicle was to be attached except where shown in the instructions. For example, one horsebox, cattle wagon or other four-wheeled vehicle could be attached to LNWR-type of rail motor No 29988 and to all LYR-type rail motors.

A motor train was a train consisting of a detachable engine with specially fitted coaches capable of being driven from either end of the train. The crew would be a driver and fireman. The fireman remained on the engine at all times, but the driver used the driving compartment of the leading coach when the locomotive was propelling. Motor trains first appeared on the Midland Railway in 1908, being employed on a few branches on a trial basis, but by the 1930s they were commonplace and were authorised for use on the Evesham branch between Ashchurch and Barnt Green. Although the LMS used a variety of locomotives for this work across the system, on the Evesham branch the Johnson 0-4-4T was the preferred class.

The early 1930s were years of depression and this was reflected in the freight timetable where a number of trains were shown as 'suspended'. There was a path in the timetable but insufficient traffic to warrant the train being run. From Table 4 it is clear that there were a number of trains using the Evesham branch as an avoiding line: although mostly Washwood Heath to Gloucester workings, there was also a Burton to Gloucester and a Birmingham Central Goods to Bath train. Now that the

Stratford-upon-Avon & Midland Junction Railway was part of the LMS the Bristol to London service via Broom Junction (mostly banana trains and the returning empties) is evident.

The 1934 passenger service, shown in Table 5, is probably the most comprehensive of the years that have been featured in this chapter. In the down direction all the trains terminated at stations on the Evesham branch but there is an interesting working that is worth highlighting. Down train 49 was the 5/2 passenger train from Peterborough that terminated at Redditch at 9/50. The engine and empty stock ran to Alcester as down train 1 and formed up passenger train 3 from Alcester to Leicester. The

Sunday service was only between Birmingham and Evesham, no trains stopping at Coughton, and comprised a morning and afternoon/evening service of two trains per day in each direction, run mainly for fishermen.

The Birmingham to Redditch passenger service was important, the regular practice of terminating trains at Barnt Green having ceased. Although more trains ran between Birmingham and Redditch than between Birmingham and Evesham, and more between Birmingham and Evesham than between Birmingham and Ashchurch, the latter station also being served by the Birmingham to Gloucester trains.

Johnson 0-4-4Ts were used on freight train work, in particular on the southern end of the line. No 1338 is near Bengeworth with an Evesham to Ashchurch freight train on 26 August 1947.
W. A. Camwell

Timetable 4 (pages 140-141)
LMS working timetable of freight trains 7 July to 21 September 1930
Notes on the original timetables.

Down direction trains
11 Train, the 2.35 Through Freight from Burton to Gloucester is shown as suspended.
16 Train. This light engine was to work the 3/15 to Crewe after coupling to the 12/12 Passenger train ex Birmingham New Street. In 1934 this Passenger train was timed to leave Birmingham at 12/14. The locomotive and men would be from the Midland Division, but which shed is impossible to say, Saltley or Bournville. If Saltley then the engine could be coupled as the pilot engine to the passenger train at New Street or work as pilot from the carriage sidings at Saltley. The locomotive would then run to Redditch where it was uncoupled. The engine then ran forward to Evesham where it would be turned prior to working 10 Up Train to Crewe. This train was due to pass Barnt Green at 4/16 and to arrive at Duddeston Road at 4/57 where the engine and men were changed, and to depart at 5/6 with a Western Division engine and men. Water Orton Junction was passed at 5/15

and at Lichfield Road Junction in Walsall it joined the LMS Western Division line for the run to Crewe.
20 Train. Stops at Ashton-under-Hill for tariff purposes only.

Up direction trains
5 Train. On Saturdays leaves Beckford 6/10, Evesham arrives at 6/28, departs at 6/45, Harvington at 6/54, Broom Junction arrives at 7/4 and departs as at other days.
8 Train was a Saturday-only light engine movement at 2/40 from Studley & Astwood Bank to Redditch and it was the return working of Down Train 17 from Redditch to Studley & Astwood Bank that arrived at 1/45. I expect that the 55 minutes were spent in shunting the small yard, although no trains were shown to call at the station until the 8.50 Stopping freight train from Washwood that arrived at 11.45 on Monday.
22 Train. The instructions for this train were complicated. The printed instructions in the working timetable were, M (Monday excepted), Q MO (Q Runs when required, MO Monday only). The times given in the working timetable and reproduced here were for a weekday; a footnote said, 'On Saturdays leaves Evesham 9.13, Harvington, 9.21, Broom Junction arrives at 9.28, departs as other days.

LMS Working Timetable of Freight Trains. July 7th to September 21st 1930

Down Trains

WEEKDAY TRAINS

Train No.	Description	Originating Point	Barnet Green Dep	Alvechurch Arr	Alvechurch Dep	Redditch Arr	Redditch Dep	Studley & Astwood Bk Arr	Studley & Astwood Bk Dep	Coughton Arr	Coughton Dep	Alcester Arr	Alcester Dep	Wixford Arr	Wixford Dep	Broom Arr	Broom Dep	Salford Priors Arr	Salford Priors Dep	Harvington Arr	Harvington Dep	Evesham Arr	Evesham Dep	Bengeworth Arr	Bengeworth Dep	Hinton Arr	Hinton Dep	Ashton under Hill Arr	Ashton under Hill Dep	Beckford Arr	Beckford Dep	Ashchurch Arr	Ashchurch Dep	Terminating Point
2	Mondays excepted — 11/25 Through freight	Washwood Heath	12.5			12.21	12.26	12.35				12.45	12.50			1.0	1.20				1.27	1.37	1.50											2.25	Gloucester
3	Mondays excepted — 11/40 Mineral	Washwood Heath	12.35				12.52	1.4	1.14			1.27	1.30				1.40					2.2													Evesham
4 ‡	Mondays excepted — 11/50 Express freight	Birmingham Central Goods Station	1.55				2.10	2.19				2.29					2.37				2.46	2.56w	3.1											3.25	Bath
6	Mondays excepted — 2.5 Through freight	Washwood Heath	3.2			3.16	3.17		3.26			3.36				3.43	3.45				3.54	4.3w	4.8										4.35		Gloucester
8	Mondays excepted — Express freight	Broom															5.5						5.24										5.48		Bristol
9	Mondays excepted — 2.50 Through freight	Washwood Heath	3.39			3.55w	4.10	4.19				4.29				4.35	5.35				5.44	5.55w	6.5										6.33		Bristol
11	Mondays excepted — 2.35 Through freight	Burton	5.21			5.38w	5.45	5.54				6.4					6.13				6.22	6.32w	6.40										7.7		Gloucester
13	7.15 Mineral	Washwood Heath	8.7			8.25	8.55		9.6			9.18				9.29	11.30	11.35	11.45	11.52	12/2	12/15													Evesham
14	Saturday only — Stopping freight	Alcester											12/0	12/7																					Evesham
15	8.50 Stopping freight	Washwood Heath	10.35	10.42	11.5	11.15	11.35	11.45	11.53			12/5	12/30	12/37		12/52	12/55	1/5		1/10	1/27	1/50													Evesham
16	Q runs when required Saturday excepted	Redditch					1/17	1/25				1/35				1/42		1/58																		Salford Prior
17	Saturday only — Light engine	Redditch					1/36	1/45																											Redditch
18	Saturday only — Light engine	Washwood Heath	4/1			4/20																													Ashchurch
20	2/55 Mineral	Evesham																					5/0	5/5	5/20	5/25	5/37	5/45	5/57	6/5	6/30	6/40		Ashchurch
21	Saturday only — Stopping freight	Washwood Heath	9/0			9/18	9/35		9/46			9/59				10/10																			Broom
22	Saturday excepted — 7/48 Mineral	Washwood Heath	9/10			9/28																													Redditch
23	Saturday only — 7/48 Mineral	Broom																																	Redditch
24	Mineral	Broom															10/30				10/42	10/53w	10/58										11/35		Gloucester
25	Saturday only — 9/5 Mineral	Washwood Heath	10/24			10/40	11/20		11/31			11/46				11/56	12/6				12.16	12/27w	12/32										1.5		Gloucester
	Saturday excepted — 9/5 Mineral	Washwood Heath	10/27			10/43	11/7		11/18			11/33	12.2			12.12	12/27w				12.37	12/48w	12/53										1.27		Gloucester

SUNDAY TRAINS

Train No.	Description	Originating Point	Barnet Green Dep	Alvechurch Arr	Alvechurch Dep	Redditch Arr	Redditch Dep	Studley & Astwood Bk Arr	Studley & Astwood Bk Dep	Coughton Arr	Coughton Dep	Alcester Arr	Alcester Dep	Wixford Arr	Wixford Dep	Broom Arr	Broom Dep	Salford Priors Arr	Salford Priors Dep	Harvington Arr	Harvington Dep	Evesham Arr	Evesham Dep	Bengeworth Arr	Bengeworth Dep	Hinton Arr	Hinton Dep	Ashton under Hill Arr	Ashton under Hill Dep	Beckford Arr	Beckford Dep	Ashchurch Arr	Ashchurch Dep	Terminating Point
27	11/40 Saturday only — Mineral	Washwood Heath	12.37			12.34	12.54	1.5	1.15			1.28	1.48			1.58	2.28					2.39	2.50												Evesham
28	2.50 Through freight	Washwood Heath	3.29			3.45w	3.50		3.59			4.9				4.15	5.10				5.19	5.30w	5.35										6.3		Gloucester

‡ On Saturdays leaves Ashchurch 3.37, does not stop at Cheltenham High St, pass there 3.54, Tramway/June 4.13, Gloucester arr 4.15 Departs Gloucester Daily (inc. Sat) as through freight at 5.35

w Stops for water

Table Four

LMS Working Timetable of Freight Trains July 7th to September 21st 1930

Weekday Up Trains

Times shown as arr/dep where both appear. "w" = Stops For Water.

Train No & Description	Originating Point	Ashchurch	Beckford	Ashton under Hill	Hinton	Bengeworth	Evesham	Harvington	Salford Priors	Broom	Wixford	Alcester	Coughton	Studley & Astwood Bk	Redditch	Alvechurch	Barnt Green	Terminating Point
3 Mondays excepted; 1.15 Through freight	Gloucester (Barnwood)	1.57					2.24/3.0	/3.10		3.20								Broom
5 4.20 (4.25 Monday) Stopping freight	Gloucester (Barnwood)	5.35	5.45/6.15				6.33/6.55	/7.4		7.16/7.28		7.38/8.29		/8.42	8.52w/9.30		9.50	Birmingham
6 Saturday excepted Stopping freight	Evesham						/8.25	8.35/8.50	8.55/9.10	9.15/9.56	10.1/10.26	10.31/12.15	/12.23	12.45/1.45	1.55w/2.15	2.30/2.43	2.50	Lawley Street
7 Saturday only Stopping freight	Evesham						/8.25	8.35/8.50	8.55/9.10	9.15/9.56	10.1/10.26	10.31/12.38						Alcester
8 Saturday only; Light engine; Q runs when required	Studley & Astwood Bank													/2.40	2.50			Redditch
9 Sats excepted; Express freight	Evesham						/2/5	/2/14		/2/22		2/29/2/32		/2/44	/2/53		3/9	Birmingham
10 Q runs when required; Sats excepted; Express freight	Evesham																	Lawley Street
12 Express freight	Evesham						/3/15	/3/24		/3/34		3/41		/3/54	/4/2		4/16	Crewe
13 Stopping freight	Ashchurch	1/15	1/25/2/24	2/30/2/47	2/52/3/12	3/17/3/45	3/50											Evesham
— Fri and Sat excepted; Fitted freight No. 2	Avonmouth Depts 12/30						/3/26	/3/35		3/44/4/13								London St Pancras Go
14 Saturday only; Empties	Redditch														6/10		6/30/6/47	Washwood He. Up Sidings
15 Through freight	Evesham						4/0	4/10/4/20	4/28/4/45	4/50/5/35	5/40/5/50	5/55/6/25		6/40/6/57	7/6/7/30			Birmingham
17 Saturday excepted; Through freight	Evesham						7/15	/7/25		7/32/7/33		7/39/7/41		7/50/8/0	7/59/8/0		8/26	Lawley Street
18 Saturday only; Through freight	Evesham						7/0	/7/10		7/22/7/33		7/39/7/41		7/50/8/26	7/59/8/26		8/42	Lawley Street
19 Q runs when required; Sats excepted	Evesham																	Birmingham
— 4/15 Fitted freight No. 2	Avonmouth	6/50					7/12w/7/27			7/43/8/5								London St Pancras Go
20 Saturdays excepted; 4/32 Through freight	Gloucester (Barnwood)	5/48	5/58/6/10	6/15/6/25	6/30/6/42	6/47/6/58	7/3/8/10	/8/21		8/30/9/0		9/9		9/22/9/32	9/42/10/10		10/26	Birmingham
21 Saturdays excepted; Empties	Redditch														10/45		11/3	Lawley Street
22 Mondays excepted & Q; Runs when required. Monday only.	Gloucester (Barnwood)	8/27					8/55/9/5	/9/13		9/20/10/30		10/40		10/55/11/30	11/5/11/30		11/48	Birmingham (Sats excepted) / Broom (Sats on)
23 Saturday only empties; 7/30 Through freight	Broom							/11/35	11/35	/11/35		/11/45		12.1	12.12		12.31	Birmingham / Lawley Street
24 Saturday excepted; 10/5 Through freight	Gloucester (Barnwood)	10/47					11/15w/11/20	/11/28		11/35/1.20		1.30/1.37		1.53	2.3w/2.42		3.3	Birmingham / Washwood He. up sidings

There was no up direction Sunday Service

w Stops For Water

LMS Working Timetable of Passenger Trains. 9th July to 30th September 1934

Up Direction Trains

Train No. & Description	Originating Point	Ashchurch	Beckford	Ashton under Hill	Hinton	Bengeworth	Evesham Arr	Evesham Dept	Harvington	Salford Priors	Broom Arr	Broom Dept	Wixford	Alcester	Coughton	Studley & Astwood Bk	Redditch Arr	Redditch Dept	Alvechurch	Barnt Green	Terminating Point
1 Passenger	Redditch																	6.40	6.49	6.55	Birmingham New St
2 Passenger (Workmans)	Redditch																	7.15	7.24	7.30	Birmingham New St
3 Passenger	Alcester													7.10		7.19	7.26	7.29	7.38	7.44	Leicester
4 7.22 Passenger	Stratford										7.43										Broom
5 GWR Auto car	Alcester													8.0							Bearley
6 Passenger	Redditch																	8.0		8.13	Birmingham New St
8 Passenger	Ashchurch	7.10	7.17	7.22		7.32	7.36	7.42	7.50	7.56	7.59	8.1	8.5	8.11	8.17	8.23	8.30	8.32	8.41	8.47	Birmingham New St
9 Passenger	Ashchurch	8.40	8.48	8.53	8.58	9.3	9.7														Evesham
10 Passenger	Evesham							9.16	9.24	9.30	9.33	9.34	9.38	9.44	9.50	9.56	10.3	10.4	10.13	10.19	Birmingham New St
12 Motor train	Ashchurch	9.25	9.34	9.40	9.45	9.50	9.54														Evesham
13 GWR Auto car	Alcester													10.39							Stratford
14 8.55 Passenger	Blisworth										10.47										Broom
15 Passenger	Evesham							10.44	10.53	10.59	11.2	11.5	11.9	11.15	11.21	11.27	11.34	11.35	11.44	11.50	Birmingham New St
16 Passenger Saturday Only	Redditch																	12/27	12/36	12/42	Birmingham New St
18 Motor Train	Ashchurch	12/5	12/13	12/18	12/23	12/28	12/32														Evesham
19 GWR Auto Car Saturday only	Alcester													12/43							Bearley
20 Passenger Saturday only	Alcester													12/47	12/53	12/59	1/6	1/12	1/20	1/26	Birmingham New St
21 Passenger Saturday excepted	Redditch																	1/12	1/21	1/27	Birmingham New St
22 Passenger Saturday excepted	Redditch																	1/52		2/4	Birmingham New St
23 Passenger Saturday only	Redditch																	1/58		2/11	Birmingham New St
24 GWR Mixed train Saturdays excepted	Alcester													2/2							Bearley
25 GWR Auto Car Saturday only	Alcester													2/5							Bearley
26 2/15 Passenger	Stratford										2/36										Broom
27 Passenger	Ashchurch	2/7	2/14	2/19		2/26	2/30	2/34	2/42	2/47	2/50	2/52		2/59	3/5	3/11	3/18	3/20	3/29	3/35	Birmingham New St
28 Motor train	Ashchurch	2/45	2/52	2/57		3/5	3/9														Evesham
29 GWR Auto Car	Alcester													4/2							Bearley
30 Passenger	Evesham							3/50	3/58	4/4	4/7	4/8	4/12	4/18	4/24	4/30	4/37	4/40	4/49	4/55	Birmingham New St
31 GWR Auto Car Saturday only	Alcester													5/29							Stratford
32 Passenger	Alcester													5/35		5/44	5/51	5/53	6/2	6/8	Birmingham New St
34 GWR Mixed train	Broom											5/50		5/40							Bearley
36 Passenger Saturday only	Ashchurch	5/8	5/16	5/21	5/26	5/32	5/36	5/43	5/51	5/57	6/0	6/1	6/5	6/11							Stratford
37 Motor Train	Redditch														6/17	6/23	6/30				Redditch
38 Passenger	Evesham																	6/55	7/4	7/10	Birmingham New St
40 Passenger Saturday only	Evesham							7/25	7/33	7/40	7/43	7/45	7/49	7/55		8/4	8/11	8/14	8/23	8/29	Birmingham New St
41 7/40 Passenger Saturday excepted	Stratford										8/0										Broom
42 Passenger	Ashchurch	7/25	7/33	7/38	7/43	7/48	7/52														Evesham
43 Passenger Saturday excepted	Evesham							7/57	8/8	8/18	8/21	8/25		8/33		8/42	8/49	8/52	9/0	9/6	Birmingham New St
44 8/15 Passenger Saturdays only	Evesham										8/36										Broom
46 Passenger Saturday only	Evesham							9/2	9/10	9/16	9/19	9/20	9/24	9/30		9/39	9/46	9/50		10/1	Birmingham New St
47 Passenger Saturday excepted	Redditch																	10/2	10/11	10/13	Birmingham New St
48 Passenger Saturday only	Redditch																	10/2	10/11	10/17	Birmingham New St
49 Passenger Saturday only	Ashchurch	9/30	9/37	9/42	9/47	9/52	9/56	9/57	10/5	10/11	10/14	10/15		10/23		10/32	10/39	10/40	10/50	10/56	Birmingham New St
50 Motor train Saturday only	Alcester													10/30		10/39	10/46				Redditch

LMS Working Timetable of Passenger Trains. 9 July to 30 September 1934

Down Direction Trains

Train Number & Description	Originating Point	Barnt Green Dept	Alvechurch	Redditch Arr	Redditch Dept	Studley & Astwood Bk	Coughton	Alcester	Wixford	Broom Arr	Broom Dept	Salford Priors	Harvington	Evesham Arr	Evesham Dept	Bengeworth	Hinton	Ashton under Hill	Beckford Arr	Beckford Dept	Ashchurch Arr	Terminating Point
1 Empty Carriages	Redditch				6.40	6.49		6.50														Alcester
2 Empty Carriages to Alvechurch Season day excursion then runs as passenger Saturday only	Barnt Green	6.24	6.33	6.40	6.42	6.49		7.0		7.5	7.6	7.10	7.16	7.22	7.23	7.28	7.33	7.38	7.42	7.44	7.55	Ashchurch
3 Motor train	Evesham														7.55	8.0	8.5	8.10	8.14	8.16	8.23	Ashchurch
4 Motor train	Redditch				6.55	7.1		7.9		7.14	7.15		7.21	7.27								Evesham
5 6.32 Passenger	Birmingham New St	7.3	7.8	7.15	7.27	7.34		7.43	7.48	7.51	8.1	8.5	8.11	8.19								Evesham
6 Passenger from Barnt Green Empty Carrs.	Kings Norton	7.44		7.53																		Redditch
7 Passenger (Mixed train)	Broom										8.13											Stratford
8 Light engine	Evesham														9.20				9.35	9.40	9.48	Ashchurch
9 8.35 Passenger	Birmingham New St	9.3	9.8	9.15	9.25	9.31	9.36	9.44	9.49	9.52	9.53	9.57	10.2	10.8								Evesham
10 Motor train	Evesham														10.13	10.18	10.23	10.28	10.32	10.34	10.40	Ashchurch
11 GWR Mixed train	Bearley							10.6														Alcester
12 9.51 Passenger	Birmingham New St	10.23	10.28	10.35	10.38	10.45	10.50	10.56	11.1	11.4	11.6	11.10	11.15	11.21	11.22	11.27			11.35	11.36	11.42	Ashchurch
14 Passenger	Broom			11.30							11.15											Blisworth
15 11.0 Light Engine Saturdays only	Bournville Eng Shed	11.51		12/1		12/31	12/36	12/41														Alcester
16 GWR Auto car	Stratford							11.56														Alcester
17 11.16 Empty carriages Saturdays only	Saltley Carr. Sids.	11.55		12/4																		Redditch
18 11.30 Passenger Saturdays excepted	Birmingham New St			12/4																		Redditch
19 Passenger Saturdays only	Redditch																					Alcester
21 12/14 Passenger	Birmingham New St	12/57	1/2	1/9≠					Train 21 Motor						1/20	1/25	1/30	1/35	1/39	1/40	1/46	Ashchurch
23 GWR Auto Car	Bearley							1/48														Alcester
24 12/43 Passenger Saturdays only	Birmingham New St	1/30	1/35	1/42	1/48	1/55		2/4	2/9	2/12	2/13	2/17	2/23	2/30								Evesham
25 12/43 Passenger Saturdays excepted	Birmingham New St	1/38	1/43	1/50	2/13	2/21	2/26	2/32	2/37	2/40	2/51	2/55	3/1	3/8								Evesham
26 1/18 Passenger Saturday only	Birmingham New St	1/42	1/47	1/54	2/13	2/21	2/26	2/32	2/37	2/40	2/51	2/55	3/1	3/8								Evesham
27 Passenger	Broom										2/59											Stratford
28 GWR Mixed train Saturdays excepted	Bearley							3/36														Alcester
29 GWR Auto Car Saturdays only	Stratford							3/46														Alcester
30 Motor	Evesham														3/45	3/50	3/55	4/0	4/4	4/6	4/13	Ashchurch
31 3.6 Passenger	Birmingham New St	3/50	3/55	4/2																		Redditch
33 3/57 Empty stock Q runs when required Saturdays excepted	Saltley Carr. Sids	4/28		4/38	4/40	4/47		4/56		5/2	5/3		5/12	5/20								Evesham
34 GWR Auto Car	Bearley							5/8														Alcester
36 4/27 Passenger	Birmingham New St	4/57	5/2	5/9	5/11	5/18	5/23	5/28														Alcester
39 5/0 Passenger	Broom										6/21	6/25	6/30	6/36	6/41	6/46	6/51	6/56	7/0	7/2	7/8	Ashchurch
40 Passenger Saturday only	Birmingham New St	5/31	5/36	5/43	5/55	6/1	6/6	6/12	6/17	6/20	6/30											Stratford
41 5/20 Passenger Saturday excepted	Birmingham New St	6/8	6/13	6/20																		Redditch
42 6/12 Passenger	Birmingham New St	6/38	6/43	6/50																		Redditch
43 Perishables Q runs when required Saturday excepted	Evesham														8/20						8/34	Ashchurch
45 GWR Auto Car	Bearley							7/55														Alcester
46 7/25 Passenger	Birmingham New St	8/0	8/5	8/12	8/17	8/23	8/28	8/34	8/39	8/42	8/43	8/47	8/52	8/58	9/0	9/5		9/12	9/16	9/17	9/23	Ashchurch
47 Passenger	Stratford									8/55													Broom
49 5/2 Passenger	Peterborough	9/38	9/43	9/50																		Redditch
51 Motor Saturdays only	Redditch				10/5	10/12		10/19															Alcester
53 10/50 Passenger	Birmingham New St	11/24		11/34																		Redditch

≠ Division between two or more trains that share the same train number

Table Five

LMS Working Timetable of passenger trains 9th July to 30th September 1934

Up Direction Trains — Sunday Service

Train Number & Description	Originating Point Dept	Evesham	Harvington	Salford Priors	Broom Arr	Broom Dept	Wixford	Alcester	Coughton	Studley & Astwood Bk	Redditch Arr	Redditch Dept	Alvechurch	Barnt Green	Terminating Point
52 Passenger	Evesham	10.15	10.23	10.29	10.32	10.33	10.37	10.43		10.52	10.59	11.0		11.12	Birmingham New Street
53 Passenger	Redditch											4/10		4/23	Birmingham New Street
54 Passenger	Redditch											5/20		5/32	Birmingham New Street
56 Passenger	Evesham	7.56	8/4	8/10	8/13	8/15	8/19	8/25		8/34	8/41	8/44		8/57	Birmingham New Street
59 Passenger	Redditch											9/32		9/45	Birmingham New Street

Down Direction Trains

Train Number & Description	Originating Point	Barnt Green	Alvechurch	Redditch Arr	Redditch Dept	Studley & Astwood Bk	Coughton	Alcester	Wixford	Broom Arr	Broom Dept	Salford Priors	Harvington	Evesham	Terminating Point
56 8.20 Passenger	Birmingham New Street	8.57		9.7											Redditch
57 8.20 Passenger	Birmingham New Street					9.14		9.22	9.27	9.30	9.31	9.35	9.40	9.46	Evesham
58 3/10 Passenger	Birmingham New Street	3/47		3/57											Redditch
59 4/28 Passenger	Birmingham New Street	5/3		5/13											Redditch
61 5/50 Passenger	Birmingham New Street	6/27		6/37	6/40	6/47		6/56	7/1	7/4	7/6	7/10	7/16	7/23	Evesham
63 8/30 Passenger	Birmingham New Street	9/17		9/26											Redditch

Note: There were no Sunday passenger trains between Evesham and Ashchurch.

Timetable 5 (pages 140-144)
LMS working timetable of passenger trains 9 July to 30 September 1934
Notes on the original timetables.

Down direction trains

1 Train. Runs 10 minutes earlier when No2 (season day excursion) runs.

2 Train. Will run on 21 July, 11, 18 August and 1 September Season Day Excursion.

9 Train. Arrives Alcester at 9.41.

21 Train. Runs via the Camp Hill line.

25 and 26 Train. Arrives Studley 2/19.

41 Train. Runs via the Camp Hill line.

46 Train. The stop at Wixford was Saturday-only.

(Although shown as two separate trains, 56 and 57 would comprise the same locomotive and carriages. A similar example of two different train numbers for what is the same formation will be found with the up direction trains described below.)

56 Train. Runs via the Camp Hill line.

58 Train. This train is shown as Suspended in one section of the working timetable.

61 Train. Runs via the Camp Hill line.

63 Train. Runs via the Camp Hill line.

Up direction trains

12 Train. Arrives Beckford 9.32 and Ashton 9.38.

15 Train. Arrives Harvington 10.51.

20 Train. Runs via the Camp Hill line.

27 Train. Runs via the Camp Hill line.

32 Train. Runs via the Camp Hill line.

38 Train. Runs via the Camp Hill line.

37 Train. Arrives Bengeworth 5/30.

40 Train. Arrives Salford Priors 7/38.

42 Train. See Col. 43. (It must be said that the layout of these timetables varied and I have tried to interpret the information for readers. In the earlier timetables the column number was referred to as the train number and I have continued this practice, although later this method of train identification was to be changed. In this instance we have a train, shown in column 42, that ran from Ashchurch to Evesham. Five minutes later the same train departed for Birmingham with a new identity. Clearly there was a reason; unfortunately it is not evident to me.)

43 Train. Arrives Harvington 8/4, Salford Priors 8/13, Alcester 8/31.

46 Train. Runs via the Camp Hill line.

49 Train. Season Day Excursion. Will run on 21 July, 11, 18 August and 1 September. Arrives Alvechurch 10/47.

50 Train. Will run 5 minutes later when 49 runs.

52 Train. Runs via the Camp Hill line.

53 Train. Runs via the Camp Hill line.

54 Train. Runs via the Camp Hill line.

56 Train. Runs via the Camp Hill line.

Wartime and the 1940s

'Is your journey really necessary?' was the message during the war, and in October 1942, the services on offer were limited. The LMS public timetable gave the following trains that ran on the branch, beginning with the down direction trains.

Birmingham New Street. Dep 6.32 all stations to Ashchurch except Coughton. Ashchurch arrive 8.51. Another through train ran at 8.35, this train stopping at all stations and arriving at Ashchurch at 10.39. The 1/35 from Birmingham also stopped at all stations and arrived at Ashchurch at 3/49. The 5/0 from Birmingham stopped at all stations, arriving at Ashchurch at 7/14, while the last train, the 7/21 from Birmingham, did not stop at Wixford or any station between Evesham and Ashchurch, where it arrived at 9/30. The only other train on the line was the 12/20 Saturday only from Birmingham to Alcester.

The up direction trains began with the 7.10 from Alcester to Birmingham arriving at 8.19 and the 7.10 from Ashchurch to Birmingham. This train did not stop at Hinton and arrived at Birmingham at 9.19. The 9.30 from Ashchurch was interesting as it arrived at Evesham at 9.59 and formed the 10.44 Evesham to Birmingham, arriving at 12/25. Another through train was the 2/9 from Ashchurch to Birmingham which arrived at 4/2. This train did not stop at Hinton or Wixford. The 4/30 from Ashchurch stopped at all stations and arrived in Birmingham at 6/55. The final train was the 7/35 from Ashchurch which arrived in Birmingham at 9/51 and stopped at all stations except Wixford and Coughton.

The Sunday service was two trains in each direction, all stopping at every station except Coughton. In the down direction the trains departed at 8.5 and 6/35, arriving at Evesham at 9.31 and 8/0. The up direction trains departed from Evesham at 9.50 and 8/15, arriving in Birmingham at 11.25 and 9/41. The outward service in both the morning and evening provided both the locomotive and stock for the return working.

Although the passenger train service was somewhat basic, the freight train service contained some very interesting workings that continued into the early postwar years. In order to illustrate the variety of trains that passed over the line I have summarised the 6 May to 5 October 1946 working timetable of freight trains, beginning with the down line weekday service. Trains are listed in the order that they appear in the timetable.

Down Direction Trains

11/20 Express freight train. Washwood Heath to Gloucester. Monday and Saturday excepted.

12.50 Mineral train. King's Norton to Redditch. Monday excepted. The sidings at King's Norton were opened during World War 2 — the exact date is unknown — in order to enable some trains to bypass Washwood Heath, where they would normally be remarshalled, and to be shunted at these new sidings at King's Norton.

1.50 Freight train. Alcester to Evesham. Monday excepted.

2.5 Through freight train. Washwood Heath to Evesham. Monday excepted.

1.35 Through freight train. Exchange Sidings to Gloucester. Monday excepted.

3.15 Through freight train. Washwood Heath to Evesham. Monday only.

3.35 Express freight train. Washwood Heath to Broom.

1.30 Through freight train. Blisworth to Gloucester.

3.5 Through freight train. Bedford to Gloucester.

6.50 Through freight train. Washwood Heath to Evesham.

8.55 Mineral train. King's Norton to Gloucester.

12.0 noon Mineral train. Clifford Sidings to Gloucester. Q runs when required.

8.15 Stopping Freight train. Washwood Heath to Evesham. Saturday excepted.

9.45 Mineral train. Washwood Heath to Alcester. Saturday only.

11.0 Mineral train. Washwood Heath to Alcester. Saturday excepted.

Light engine coupled to 1/40 passenger train from Birmingham New Street. 2/36 from Alcester to Evesham.

1/35 Through freight train. Exchange Sidings to Westerleigh (Bristol).

5/50 Stopping freight train. Evesham to Ashchurch.

3/38 Mineral train. Washwood Heath to Evesham. Saturday excepted.

4/15 Mineral train. Washwood Heath to Evesham. Saturday only.

4/25 Express freight train. Horninglow Bridge (Burton upon Trent) to Gloucester. Friday/Saturday only. Runs as a through freight, Q when required Friday and Saturday excepted.

1/0 Mineral train. Toton to Gloucester. Q runs when required.

7/15 Through freight train. Washwood Heath to Stratford.

8/35 Mineral train. Washwood Heath to Westerleigh (Bristol).

8/52 Through freight train. Washwood Heath to Redditch. Saturday only.

8/10 Mineral train. Washwood Heath to Evesham.

11/10 Express freight train. Washwood Heath to Gloucester. Friday only.

11/20 Express freight train. Washwood Heath to Gloucester. Friday excepted.

Sunday Service

1.50 Freight train. Broom to Evesham.

1.30 Through freight train. Blisworth to Gloucester.

6.45 Mineral train. Washwood Heath to Evesham.

8.28 Freight train. Washwood Heath to Evesham.

10.30 Mineral train. Washwood Heath to Evesham.

11.30 Mineral train. Washwood Heath to Evesham.

Up Direction Trains

11/40 Through freight train. Stratford to Washwood Heath. Monday excepted.

1.10 Light engine. Evesham to Alcester. Monday excepted.

12.8 Through freight train. Gloucester Barnwood to Bedford. Monday excepted.

3.25 Through freight train. Gloucester Barnwood to Blisworth.

4.0 Empties. Westerleigh (Bristol) to Stratford.

7.55 Empties. Gloucester Barnwood to Olney.

8.13 Light engine. Broom to Redditch.

10.45 Empties. Redditch to Washwood Heath.

8.25 Stopping freight train. Evesham to Washwood Heath.

12.0 noon Empties. Gloucester Barnwood to Toton. Saturday only.

2/0 Express freight train. Evesham to Water Orton.

12/45 Empties. Gloucester Barnwood to Toton. Saturday excepted.

6/10 Mineral train. Redditch to Lawley Street. Saturday only.

3/35 Through freight train. Evesham to Lawley Street. Saturday excepted.

3/50 Through freight train. Evesham to Lawley Street. Saturday only.

145

No 1353 was stationed at 22B, Gloucester when photographed on 18 September 1948 at Evesham. Although this 0-4-4T is at the north end of the up platform, the photographer recorded that the engine had worked an Ashchurch to Evesham goods train. *W. A. Camwell*

2/28	Stopping freight train. Ashchurch to Evesham.
7/13	Through freight train. Evesham to Lawley Street. Saturday excepted.
7/45	Light engine. Evesham to Saltley.
8/19	Light engine. Evesham to Barnt Green. Saturday only.
8/19	Light engine. Evesham to Redditch. Coupled to the 4/35 through freight train from Gloucester Barnwood to Washwood Heath. Saturday excepted.
10/0	Empties. Redditch to Bournville (Canal Branch). Saturday excepted.
4/35	Through freight train. Gloucester Barnwood to Washwood Heath.
7/35	Empties. Gloucester Barnwood to Stratford. Saturday excepted.
9/0	Empties. Gloucester Barnwood to Stratford.
11/40	Through freight train. Stratford to Washwood Heath.

Sunday Service

1.10	Light engine. Evesham to Alcester.
12.3	Through freight train. Gloucester Barnwood to Bedford.
5.13	Light engine. Redditch to Washwood Heath.
10.55	Light engine. Evesham to Redditch (off 6.45 Washwood Heath to Evesham).
2/45	Light engine. Evesham to Saltley (off 10.30 Washwood Heath to Evesham).
4/45	Through freight train. Evesham to Washwood Heath.

The most noticeable feature of this timetable is the number of services that do not appear in other timetables and the intense

Sunday workings. My recollections of 1948/9 are that the system was closed for only a few hours each week, in particular during the winter months. The Sunday morning shift in the major marshalling yards booked on at 6.0 and would either be relieved at 2/0 by the afternoon shift or would continue on duty until the last train arrived in the late afternoon. Some trains were stored in lie-bys that were controlled by signalmen and the arrival of a light engine with a goods guard enabled the train to continue the journey on the following Monday morning.

The British Railways Era

I expect many older readers will have nostalgic memories of the 1950s, recalling with affection the times when they were able to watch steam trains. No doubt many will regard this era as the golden age of the British steam railway. To this I would say, please study the timetables and note how the volume of traffic had declined when compared with the Edwardian years. In some respects the 1940s were extraordinary as far as the amount of freight that was moved, but those were exceptional years.

The freight timetable for 1951 is shown at Table 6 and the passenger details for 1956 are in Table 7. Due to the poor condition of the track, the section between Alcester and Evesham was closed with effect from 1 October 1962. However, British Railways had not given adequate notice of closure so buses were substituted between Studley & Astwood Bank and Alcester until 17 June 1963 when closure to passenger traffic became permanent. With effect from 6 July 1964 the line was closed for goods trains and track lifting commenced shortly thereafter.

Class 3F No 43529 heads an Evesham to Washwood Heath stopping freight train at Broom Junction on 14 June 1961. The sidings and turntable seen in a number of views of Broom in Chapter 3 have been removed. *Collection R. J. Essery*

The Stanier 2-6-2T engines were employed mainly on the Birmingham to Redditch trains but sometimes they worked to Ashchurch. I recall a few days' work on the Redditch passenger service when we were allocated this class of engine, but I do not remember being impressed by them. No 171 is shown at Ashchurch on 8 September 1949 after it had arrived with a passenger train from Birmingham. *H. C. Casserley 58529*

The Fowler Class 4P 2-6-4T, later reclassified 4MT, was often used on the Birmingham to Ashchurch trains; they were excellent locomotives. This 9 September 1949 picture shows No 42326 at Ashchurch with a three-coach set, the leading vehicle being an LMS Period Two third corridor brake, the others being a Period One composite and a third brake — a rather lightweight Birmingham train. *H. C. Casserley*

Timetable 6 (pages 149-150)
British Railways London Midland Operating Area (Midland Division)
working timetable of freight trains 18 June to 23 September 1951
Notes on the original timetables.

Down direction trains
The 1.0 Monday Excepted Through Freight train from King's Norton to Gloucester requires an explanation. The small yard at King's Norton existed for many years but at some date during World War 2 about six sidings with a shunting neck were laid down. There is no record of the opening date but 1942/3 seems reasonable. The object was to act as a relief to the sidings at Washwood for West of England traffic. At this time a number of trains, generally mineral or through goods, were booked to start from King's Norton rather than Washwood Heath.

The 11.3 from Stratford terminated at Ashchurch on Saturdays.

The 7.55 from Washwood Heath arrives Alvechurch at 9.22, at Salford Priors at 12/3 and at Harvington at 12/20.

Target 20. When required Bengeworth arrives 5/10, departs 5/15, Hinton arrives 5/20 departs 5/25, Beckford arrives 5/40 departs 5/50, Ashchurch arrives 6/0.

Up direction trains
The 6.15 light engine to Saltley loco from Evesham was the path home for the locomotive and crew that had worked the 3.10 from Washwood Heath.

The 8.25 Class K from Evesham to Selly Oak ran with altered times on Saturday from Studley. The timetable gives these arrival times; the departure times are shown in the table. Harvington arrives 8.35, Salford Priors 8.55, Broom Junction 9.15, at Wixford the train was not booked to stop, Alcester 10.45, Coughton 11.23, and Studley 11.43. The train ran later on a weekday, the departure from Studley was 12/20 instead of 12/10 on a Saturday, 1/0 from Redditch, 32 minutes after the weekday time of 12/28. The timetable shows that the stop at Barnt Green on a Saturday, arrive 12/50 depart 1/0, was to change crews or engine. While I cannot rule out the latter, I think it was unlikely and the change was of enginemen. The arrival times at Selly Oak were weekday 2/8, Saturday 1/55.

The light engines that arrived at Evesham at 12/55 on a Saturday and 1/20 during the week were to work the Evesham-Water Orton Class D trains.

The 6/0 Class H from Beckford to Lawley Street was, when required, timed to arrive at Ashton-under-Hill at 6/5 and to depart at 6/10 and to arrive at Bengeworth at 6/20 and depart at 6/30; the Evesham arrival time was 6.35. This was 15 minutes later than shown in the working timetable and the matter is further confused by the note that states 'dept. 6/52 as booked'.

The 7/35 light engine from Evesham to Saltley loco was the path home for the engine that had worked the 3/30 from Washwood Heath.

The 6.0 light engine working on Sunday morning was the path home for the engine that had worked the 2.35 from Washwood Heath.

A 1962 view of Evesham, showing a down train headed by Fowler Class 4MT 2-6-4T No 42421. The train appears to comprise entirely LMS Period Three corridor coaches. *M. Mensing*

British Railways London Midland Operating Area (Midland Division)
Working Timetable of Freight Trains 18th June to 23rd September 1951   Down Direction

Class	Train	Classification of train	Barnt Green	Alvechurch	Redditch Arr	Redditch Dept	Studley & Astwood Bk	Coughton	Alcester Arr	Alcester Dept	Wixford	Broom North Junc. Arr	Broom North Junc. Dept	Broom West Junc. Arr	Broom West Junc. Dept	Salford Priors	Harvington	Evesham Arr	Evesham Dept	Bengeworth Hinton	Ashton under Hill	Beckford	Ashchurch
E	11/30	Washwood Heath to Gloucester Monday excepted‡	12.9			12.24	12.33			12.45	12.52		12.55		12.57		1.6	1.20w	1.30				2.5
H	1.0	Kings Norton to Gloucester Mondays excepted	1.16			1.36	1.45			1.55	2.1		2.4		2.6		2.15	2.25w	2.30				3.0
H	1.50	Washwood Heath to Evesham Mondays excepted	2.40		2.58	3.18	3.27			3.39	3.45	3.48	4.0		4.4		4.12	4.24					
H	1.35	Exchange sidings to Westerleigh Mondays excepted	3.20			3.39	3.47			4.2	4.8		4.12		4.15		4.26	4.36w	4.41				5.11
J	3.10	Washwood Heath to Evesham Mondays only	4.7			4.24	4.35			4.48	4.55	5.1	5.12		5.16		5.27	5.40					
H	3.15	Washwood Heath to Evesham Mondays only	4.7		4.23	4.35	4.47			4.57	5.3	5.8	5.20		5.25		5.35	5.48					
J	4.5	Washwood Heath to Gloucester Mondays only	4.55		5.15w	5.25	5.36			5.49	5.56		5.59		6.1		6.9		6.21				6.54
J	5.0	Kings Norton to Gloucester Mondays only	5.20		5.37w	5.42	5.53			6.6	6.12		6.16		6.18		6.28		6.38				7.16
H	6.50	Stratford to Gloucester													7.17		7.25	7.35w	7.50				8.26
G	10.5	Light engine from Stratford toGloucester. Saturday only												10.35	10.42		10.51	11.1	11.1				11.30
F	10.5	Stratford to Gloucester Saturday excepted												10.35	10.42		10.51	11.1	11.11				11.40
H	11.13	Stratford to Gloucester													11.39		11.48	12/2	12/12				12/43
K	7.55	Washwood Heath to Evesham Saturdays excepted	9.15	9.38	9.53	10.8	10.18		10.30	11.30	11.36	11.40	11.55		11.59	12/13	12/32	12/47					
G	1/2	Light engine to Tewkesbury loco Saturdays excepted																	1/2				1/27
G	2/5	Stratford to Gloucester												2/32	3/4		3/14	3/24w	3/29				4/2
H	2/10	Washwood Heath to Broom	3/8		3/25w	3/35	3/47			3/57	4/3		4/8										
K	5/5	Evesham to Ashchurch Target 20																	5/5				5/40
J	1/50	Exchange Sidings to Westerleigh	3/40			4/2	4/11			4/21	4/28	4/32	5/35		5/38		5/48	5/58w	6/3				6/35
J	3/30	Washwood Heath to Evesham	5/8		5/27	6/5	6/16			6/29	6/36		6/39		6/41		6/50	7/3					
J	7/5	Clifford Sidings to Gloucester													7/57		8/7	8/17w	8/22				8/55
H	8/52	Washwood Heath to Redditch	9/49		10/7																		

Note: There were no goods trains that served Bengeworth, Hinton, Ashton under Hill or Beckford. See up direction table for details of the goods services at this time.

Sunday Service   Down Direction

Class	Train	Classification of train	Barnt Green	Redditch Arr	Redditch Dept	Studley & Astwood Bk	Alcester Dept	Wixford	Broom North Junc.	Broom West Junc.	Harvington	Evesham
J	2.15	Washwood Heath to Evesham	3.28	3.57	4.12	4.26	4.39	4.46	4.49	4.51	5.1	5.14

w Water stop

‡ It is not clear from the Working Timetable if this train ran on a Saturday.

With effect from 5 June 1950 a new Passenger and Freight train classification came into effect in respect of headlamp codes and block bell codes. To assist understanding of the letter-codes, the details of these trains were as follows:

D — Express freight, livestock, perishable or ballast train partly fitted with the automatic brake operative on not less than one one third of the vehicles.
E — Express freight, livestock, perishable or ballast train partly fitted with not less than four vehicles connected by vacuum pipe to the engine; or Express freight, livestock, perishable or ballast train with limited load of vehicles not fitted with continuous brake.
F — Express freight, livestock, perishable or ballast train not fitted with continuous brakes.
G — Light engine or engines coupled. Engine with not more than two brake vans.
H — Through freight or ballast train not running under Class 'C', 'D', 'E' or 'F' headcode.
J — Mineral or empty wagon train.
K — Freight, mineral or ballast train stopping at intermediate stations. Branch freight train. Freight, ballast or Officers Special train, requiring to stop in section.

Table Six

British Railways London Midland Operating Area (Midland Division)
Working Timetable of Freight Trains 18th June to 23rd September 1951   Up Direction

w Water Stop

Classification of trains	Ashchurch	Beckford Arr	Beckford Dept	Ashton under Hill	Hinton	Bengeworth	Evesham Arr	Evesham Dept	Harvington	Salford Priors	Broom West Junc. Arr	Broom West Junc. Dept	Broom North Junc. Arr	Broom North Junc. Dept	Wixford	Alcester Arr	Alcester Dept	Coughton	Studley & Astwood Bk	Redditch Arr	Redditch Dept	Alvechurch	Barnt Green
J 12.18 Redditch to Washwood Heath Mondays excepted																					12.18		12.37
H 3.10 Barnwood to Stratford	3.54						4.25	4.50	5.0			5.10											
G 6.15 Light Engine Evesham to Saltley Loco. Mondays excepted								6.15	6.25			6.33		6.35	6.38	6.43	7.47		8.2		8.11		8.27
H 4.8 Empties Westerleigh to Stratford	6.11						6.40w	6.52	7.3			7.14											
K 8.25 Evesham to Selly Oak Saturdays excepted								8.25	8.50	9.10		9.13	9.15	10.35	10.38	10.45	11.15	11.33	12/20	12/28w	1/0		1/23
K 8.25 Evesham to Selly Oak Saturdays only								8.25	8.50	9.10		9.13	9.15	10.35	10.38	10.45	11.15	11.33	12/10	12/18w	12/32		12/50
H 7.20 Empties Barnwood to Clifford Sidings	7.55						8.35w	9.0	9.15			9.25											
H 9.5 Empties Barnwood to Stratford	9.45						10.15w	10.23	10.33			10.41											
G 12/5 Light engine Gloucester to Evesham Saturdays only	12/33						12/55																
G 12/30 Light engine Gloucester to Evesham Saturdays excepted 12/56	12/56						1/20																
D 2/0 Evesham to Water Orton Saturdays excepted								2/0	2/10			2/18		2/20	2/22		2/27		2/39	2/48	2/51		3/5
H 1/55 Evesham to Water Orton Saturdays only								1/55	2/6			2/17		2/20	2/22		2/27		2/42	2/53	2/57		3/13
H 5/45 Broom to Lawley Street														5/45	5/48	5/53	6/31		6/57	7/7	7/20		7/40
K 2/38 Ashchurch to Evesham Target 20+	2/28	2/38	3/30	3/49	4/8	4/23	4/27																
H 3/30 Barnwood to Stratford	4/40						5/11w	5/16	5/26			5/33											
G 5/0 Light engine. Ashchurch to Beckford Saturdays excepted 5/0	5/0	5/10																					
H 6/0 Beckford to Lawley Street Saturdays excepted			6/0				6/20	7/5	7/18			7/27		7/29	7/32		7/37		7/50		8/0		8/18
G 7/35 Light engine to Saltley Loco from Evesham								7/35	7/43			7/49		7/51	7/53		7/57		8/7		8/14		8/29

Sunday Service Up Direction

Classification of trains	Ashchurch	Beckford Arr	Beckford Dept	Ashton under Hill	Hinton	Bengeworth	Evesham Arr	Evesham Dept	Harvington	Salford Priors	Broom West Junc. Arr	Broom West Junc. Dept	Broom North Junc. Arr	Broom North Junc. Dept	Wixford	Alcester Arr	Alcester Dept	Coughton	Studley & Astwood Bk	Redditch Arr	Redditch Dept	Alvechurch	Barnt Green
J 12.18 Redditch to Washwood Heath																					12.18		12.27
G 6.0 Light engine Evesham to Saltley Loco								6.0	6.10			6.18		6.20	6.23		6.28		6.43	6.53	6.55		7.9

+Target 20 was the only goods train to stop, detach or attach wagons at Ashton under Hill, Hinton and Bengeworth. This train called at Ashton-under-Hill between 3/36 and 3/49, Hinton between 3/54 and 4/8 and Bengeworth between 4/13 and 4/23.

Class 5MT No 45448 hauls a down Class C fitted freight train past Redditch South up distant signal on 29 September 1962. While I cannot be certain, I believe this is the 1962 version of 'The Cabbage' whose 1956 timings are set out below.

The train ran every day except Sunday, but the Saturday times (shown in brackets) were different from weekdays. The engine was prepared at Gloucester motive power depot and ran light to Barnwood sidings where the locomotive was coupled to a goods brakevan. The engine and brake departed from Barnwood at 12.25pm (12 noon) and arrived at Ashchurch at 12.56pm (12.35pm). The train arrived at Evesham at 1.20pm (12.57pm) and departed at 2pm (1.55pm) passing Barnt Green at 3.5pm (3.13pm). The weekday train did not stop at Broom Junction; the Saturday train did and was booked to arrive at 2.15pm and to depart at 2.19pm. The weekday train ran via the Birmingham West Suburban line, passing New Street at 3.29pm and Landor Street Junction at 3.35pm. The Saturday-only train ran via the Camp Hill line and passed Landor Street Junction at 3.35pm. Both trains were booked to run main line to Water Orton where they were due to arrive at 3.48pm. At Water Orton the wagons would be sorted and no doubt trains such as the 4.50pm Class C to Glasgow College and the 5.15pm Class D to Carlisle conveyed much of the traffic forward. *M. Mensing*

This picture was taken c1947 and shows a Johnson 0-4-4T, No 1251, with an ordinary passenger train and a single non-corridor brake carriage at Tewkesbury Junction Ashchurch. The large building to the left is part of the provender stores, while the line curving away behind the coach leads to the level crossing and the Evesham and Ashchurch line. At about this date passenger train services between Ashchurch and Great Malvern were limited. The 6 May to 6 October 1946 timetable shows the through train service as departing from Ashchurch at 9.20am, 12.30pm, 5.10pm and 7.45pm, with additional Ashchurch to Tewkesbury trains at 8.40am, 10.55am and 4.30pm. There was a similar service from Malvern to Ashchurch with a journey time of 32 minutes. *Collection D. F. Tee*

Timetable 7 (page 152)
British Railways London Midland Operating Area (Midland Division)
Working timetable of passenger trains 19 September 1955 to 10 June 1956
Notes on the original timetables. AT-Accelerated timings. This applied to the 5/10 down and 7/14 and 2/25 up trains.

Down direction trains
Sunday service. The 7.55 from Saltley called at all stations except Studley from 19 September until 23 October 1955 and from 1 April 1956. The 7.55 that did not stop at Studley, Alcester, Salford Priors and Harvington, ran from 30 October until 25 March 1956.
The 6/35 light engine from Saltley loco to Evesham was to work the 8/10 to Birmingham.

Up direction trains
The 10.5 Sunday train from Evesham to Birmingham ran until 23 October 1955 and from 1 April 1956.
The 10.5 light engine was the path home for the engine that had worked the 7.55 from Saltley.
The 8/10 from Evesham was the return working of the 7.55 and was subject to the same periods and station stops as the down working.

British Railways London Midland Operating Area (Midland Division)

Working Timetable of Passenger Trains 19th September 1955 to 10th June 1956   Up Direction Trains

Train No. & Description	Ashchurch	Beckford	Ashton under Hill	Hinton	Evesham Arr	Evesham Dept	Harvington	Salford Priors	Broom Junc. West	Broom Junc. North Arr	Broom Junc. North Dept	Studley & Alcester	Astwood Bk	Redditch Arr	Redditch Dept	Alvechurch	Barnt Green
6.30 Passenger Redditch to Birmingham New St															6.30	6.39	6.45
7.5 Passenger Alcester to Birmingham New St												7.5	7.14	7.21	7.26	7.35	7.41
8.0 Passenger Redditch to Birmingham New Street															8.0	8.9	8.15
7.14 Passenger Ashchurch to Birmingham New Street	7.14	7.21	7.26		7.34	7.39	7.47	7.53	7.55	7.57	7.59	8.6	8.18	8.25	8.27	8.36	8.42
9.14 Passenger Ashchurch to Birmingham New Street	9.41	9.49	9.54	9.59	10.5	10.10	10.18	10.24	10.26	10.28	10.29	10.36	10.45	10.52	10.55	11.4	11.10
12/50 Passenger Saturday only Redditch to Birmingham															12/50	12/59	1/5
2/31 Passenger Saturday only Redditch to Birmingham New St															2/31	2/40	2/46
2/25 Passenger Ashchurch to Birmingham New St	2/25	2/32	2/37	2/42	2/48	2/52	3/0	3/6	3/8	3/10	3/11	3/18	3/27	3/34	3/37	3/46	3/52
4/20 Passenger Ashchurch to Birmingham New St	4/20	4/28	4/33	4/38	4/45	4/57	5/5	5/11	5/13	5/15	5/20	5/27	5/39	5/46	5/55	6/4	6/10
7/35 Passenger Redditch to Barnet Green															7/35	7/44	7/50
8/15 Passenger Saturdays excepted Evesham to Birmingham New St						8/15			8/24	8/26	8/29	8/36	8/45	8/52	9/2	9/11	9/17
8/3 Passenger Saturdays only Ashchurch to Birmingham New St	8/3	8/11	8/16	8/21	8/27	8/32	8/40	8/46	8/48	8/50	8/53	9/0	9/14	9/21	9/33	9/42	9/48

Sunday Service Up Direction

Train No. & Description	Evesham Arr	Evesham Dept	Harvington	Salford Priors	Broom Junc. West	Broom Junc. North Arr	Broom Junc. North Dept	Studley & Alcester	Redditch Arr	Redditch Dept	Alvechurch	Barnt Green
10.5 Passenger Evesham to Birmingham New St until 23 October 1955 and from 1 April 1956	10.5	10.5	10.13	10.19	10.21	10.23	10.24	10.31	10.47	10.50	10.59	11.5
10.5 Light Engine Evesham to Saltley loco from 30 October 1955 until 25 March 1956	10.5	10.5		10.19	10.21	10.23	10.24	10.31		10.53		11.9
8.10 Passenger Evesham to Birmingham New St until 23 October 1955 and from 1 April 1956	8/10	8/10	8/18	8/24	8/26	8/28	8/29	8/31	8/49	8/52	9/1	9.7
8.10 Passenger Evesham to Birmingham New St from 30 October 1955 until 25 March 1956	8/10	8/10			8/26	8/28	8/29		8/49	8/52	9/1	9.7

British Railways London Midland Operating Area (Midland Division)

Working Timetable of Passenger Trains 19th September 1955 to 10th June 1956   Down Direction Trains

Train No. & Description	Barnt Green	Alvechurch	Redditch Arr	Redditch Dept	Astwood Bk	Studley & Alcester	Broom North Junc. Arr	Broom North Junc. Dept	Broom West Junc.	Salford Priors	Harvington	Evesham Arr	Evesham Dept	Hinton	Ashton under Hill	Beckford	Ashchurch
6.35 Passenger Redditch to Alcester				6.35		6.50											
6.32 Passenger Birmingham New St to Ashchurch	7.8	7.13	7.20	7.28	7.35	7.46	7.52	7.59	8.1	8.4	8.10	8.17	8.22	8.29	8.34	8.39	8.46
8.27 Passenger Birmingham New St to Ashchurch	8.55	9.0	9.7	9.12	9.19	9.27	9.33	9.34	9.36	9.39	9.45	9.52	9.57	10.4	10.9	10.14	10.21
11.50 Passenger Saturdays only Birmingham New St to Redditch	12/22	12/27	12/34														
12/50 Passenger Saturdays excepted Birmingham New St to Ashchurch	1/22	1/27	1/34	1/40	1/47	1/58	2/4	2/24	2/26	2/29	2/35	2/42	2/47	2/54	2/59	3/4	3/11
1/5 Passenger Saturdays only Birmingham New St to Ashchurch	1/38	1/43	1/50	1/55	2/2	2/10	2/16	2/18	2/20	2/23	2/29	2/36	2/41	2/48	2/53	2/58	3/5
1/42 Passenger Saturdays only Birmingham New St to Redditch	2/9	2/14	2/21														
4/20 Passenger Birmingham New St to Redditch	4/55	5/0	5/7														
5/10 Passenger Birmingham New St to Ashchurch	5/41	5/46	5/53	5/58	6/4	6/12	6/18	6/19	6/21	6/24	6/29	6/35	6/39	6/46	6/51	6/56	7/2
5/32 Passenger Birmingham New St to Redditch	6/11	6/16	6/23														
6/20 Passenger Saturdays excepted Birmingham New St to Evesham	6/52	6/57	7/4	7/8	7/15	7/23	7/29	7/31	7/33			7/44					
8/0 Passenger Saturdays only Birmingham New St to Ashchurch	8/32	8/37	8/44	8/48	8/55	9/3	9/9	9/11	9/13	9/16	9/22	9/29	9/34	9/41	9/46	9/51	9/58
8/0 Passenger Saturdays excepted Birmingham New St to Redditch	8/32	8/37	8/44														
10/30 Passenger Birmingham New St to Redditch	10/58	11/3	11/7														
10/30 Passenger Saturdays only Birmingham New St to Redditch	10/58		11/10														

Sunday Service Down Direction

Train No. & Description	Barnt Green	Alvechurch	Redditch Arr	Redditch Dept	Astwood Bk	Studley & Alcester	Broom North Junc. Arr	Broom North Junc. Dept	Broom West Junc.	Salford Priors	Harvington	Evesham Arr
7.55 Passenger Saltley to Evesham	8.38	8.50	8.54			9.6	9.12	9.13	9.15	9.18	9.24	9.31 (until 23 October 1955 and from 1 April 1956)
7.55 Passenger Saltley to Evesham	8.38	8.50	8.54						9.15			9.31 (from 30 October 1955 until 25 March 1956)
6.35 Light engine Saltley loco to Evesham	7/7	7/12	7/18				7/40	7/43				7/54 (to work 8/10 to Birmingham)
6/40 Passenger Birmingham New St to Evesham	7/7		7/19	7/21	7/33		7/39	7/40	7/42	7/45	7/51	7/58 (until 23 October 1955 and from 1 April 1956)

Appendices

Appendix I. Extracts from the LMS Sectional Appendix to the Working Timetable LMS Midland Division March 1937 and Midland Railway Appendix 1908

Various sections from these appendices have been combined in order to present a single table. This part of the appendix is useful and gives the official LMS mileage between places in miles and yards; the Midland Railway recorded distances in miles and chains.

In addition, it confirms the existence of the catch point at Barnt Green, the absence of any lie-by sidings, speed restrictions in force and the directional engine whistles. The code provided by engine whistles during the steam railway era was most important and amongst other things advised the signalmen the route that the driver wished to take.

Local Instructions

Redditch
Not more than 10 wagons may be taken in front of an engine from Redditch goods yard to Redditch Gas Sidings signalbox. A guard's brake, in which a guard must ride, must be taken in front of the wagons. After sunset, and in foggy weather or during falling snow, a lamp showing a white light must be carried on the front of the brake.

An engine must be in front, and a guard's brake, in which a guard must ride, must be in the rear of all wagons conveyed from the Redditch Gas Sidings signalbox to Redditch goods yard, proper tail and side lamps being carried in accordance with the company's regulations.

Between Redditch and Studley
Drivers must keep a good look out, and sound their whistles when approaching in either direction the occupation level crossing leading to the brickyard, about three-quarters of a mile on the Studley side of Redditch.

Evesham South Box
Before any vehicles are placed on the transfer siding, or before any vehicles which may be standing on the transfer siding are set back towards the GW Railway, a man must go towards the Great Western Railway in order to ascertain that the siding is clear, and that vehicles are not being placed upon it by the GW Co's servants at the opposite end. Vehicles must not, under any circumstances, be pushed foul of the connection between the transfer siding and the GW Railway.

GLOUCESTER AND BIRMINGHAM, AND BRANCHES—continued.

ADDITIONAL RUNNING LINES.	STATIONS AND SIGNAL BOXES.	Distance from place next above.		DIRECTION OF UP LINE.	Lie-by Sids. and holding capacity. No. of Wagons.		RUNAWAY CATCH POINTS.			Approximate Gradient 1 in	ENGINE WHISTLES.					SPEED RESTRICTIONS. MILES PER HOUR.	
											UP		DOWN				
		Miles.	Yards.		Up. Side.	Down Side.	WHERE SITUATE.	LINE.			Main, Fast or Passenger Line.	Slow or Goods Line.	Main, Fast or Passenger Line.	Slow or Goods Line.	TO	UP.	DOWN.
	BARNT GREEN AND ASHCHURCH BRANCH.																
	Ashchurch—Junction,	—	—										1		Evesham Branch Platform through crossover road.		
	„ Level Crossing	—	192										2		Ashchurch Junction		
													3		Tewkesbury		
	Over Curve to and from Ashchurch Junction															20	20
	Beckford—Station	3	1404														
	Ashton-under-Hill—§Station	1	1562														
	Hinton—Station	1	1716														
	Bengeworth—Station	1	1056														
	Over curves between 73¾ and 74½ mile posts between Bengeworth and Evesham															15	15
	Evesham—Station	1	890														
	Harvington—Station	3	1002														
	Salford Priors—§Station	1	1672														
	Broom Junction—Junction	1	662										1		Evesham		
													3		Stratford		
	Wixford—§Station	—	1874														
	Drivers must whistle when approaching in either direction the occupation level crossing near 65¾ mile post, about ¾ mile on Alcester side of Wixford Station.																
	Alcester—Station	2	94										2		Redditch		
													3		G.W. line		
	Coughton—§Station	1	1754														
	Studley & Astwood Bank—Station	2	896														
	BETWEEN STUDLEY AND REDDITCH.—Drivers of up and down trains must sound the engine whistle when approaching the occupation level crossing, situated about 400 yards on the Studley side of Redditch Tunnel, and Drivers of up passenger trains must also reduce speed to ten miles an hour when approaching the crossing.																
	Redditch—South	3	132														
	„ North	—	484						p4						Stop King's Norton for traffic purposes	Freight trains	
	Alvechurch—§Station	3	44														
	Barnt Green—Single Line Junction	1	748			*Near signal box	Up loop	74								
	„ Main Line Junction	—	867														
	Over the curve and through the Junction to and from main line															15	15

Appendix II. Details of Locomotives Known to Have Worked Over the Line

As far I am aware, no records exist of the engines that first worked over the line, so I can only speculate. Clearly the goods workings were in the hands of the various 0-6-0 tender engines, at first the double-frame Kirtley and later the Johnson single-frame locomotives, but the power for the passenger trains is less certain. The Midland Railway was not a tank engine line and so it is likely that old 2-4-0 tender engines displaced from main line work were employed, together with suitable goods engines. However, I believe that 0-4-4Ts Nos 1732 and 1734 (post 1907 Nos 1325 and 1327) went to Redditch when new.

Although the information from the Midland era is sparse, I am fortunate because I have details of engine numbers that worked on the line and were taken from the train register book at Redditch North signalbox at various dates.

Locomotives recorded between 2 October 1937 and 17 April 1938

Class 3P Fowler 2-6-2T. Nos 9, 11, 16, 54, 67, 69.

Class 3P Stanier 2-6-2T. Nos 91, 92, 96, 97, 110, 112, 115, 116, 117, 118, 119, 143, 144, 165, 173, 174, 177.

Class 2P 4-4-0 Midland. Nos 325, 326, 368, 369, 397, 439, 486, 505, 508, 509, 511, 512, 513, 517, 519, 521, 522, 524, 527, 528, 530, 536.

Class 2P 4-4-0 Standard. No 633.

Class 3P 4-4-0 Midland. Nos 710, 712, 715, 716, 745.

Class 4P 4-4-0 Compound. No 1000.

Class 1P 0-4-4T. Nos 1348, 1361.

LT&S Section 4-4-2T. Nos 2105, 2106.

Class 4P Standard 2-6-4T. Nos 2337, 2357, 2372, 2373. 2554, 2555, 2556, 2557, 2559.

Class 5P5F Standard. 2-6-0. Nos 2724, 2812, 2824, 2911.

Midland Class 2F, shown as *, and 3F 0-6-0. Nos 3016*, 3062*, 3074*, 3078*, 3102*, 3180, 3181, 3185, 3186, 3191, 3197*, 3203, 3205, 3210, 3213, 3216*, 3223, 3225, 3227*, 3232, 3236*, 3237, 3247, 3250, 3251, 3254, 3257, 3258, 3263, 3265, 3273, 3277, 3278, 3305, 3312, 3316, 3317, 3318, 3321, 3323, 3331, 3335, 3336, 3338, 3339, 3340, 3344, 3355, 3359, 3372*, 3373, 3395, 3400, 3401, 3411, 3419, 3427, 3429, 3432*, 3433, 3434*, 3435, 3436, 3439, 3441, 3444, 3446, 3452, 3453, 3455*, 3462, 3463, 3464, 3484, 3485*, 3490, 3491, 3504*, 3506, 3507, 3516*, 3519*, 3520, 3521, 3522, 3523, 3525*, 3526*, 3527*, 3529, 3531, 3533*, 3535*, 3536*, 3540, 3543*, 3544, 3551*, 3553, 3556, 3562, 3568, 3575, 3579, 3583, 3593, 3594, 3598, 3604, 3608, 3616*, 3618, 3620, 3621, 3623, 3624, 3627, 3628, 3629, 3635*, 3640*, 3644, 3645, 3648, 3655*, 3656, 3658, 3667, 3668, 3673, 3674, 3675, 3677*, 3678, 3680, 3782, 3683, 3684, 3686, 3687, 3688*, 3689*, 3690, 3691*, 3693, 3694, 3695*, 3696*, 3698, 3699*, 3712, 3724, 3727, 3729, 3751, 3754, 3763, 3769, 3780, 3788, 3791, 3799, 3812, 3816, 3817, 3821, 3822, 3823, 3826, 3827.

Midland and LMS Class 4F 0-6-0. Nos 3835, 3836, 3839, 3855, 3858, 3860, 3861, 3863, 3866, 3869, 3871, 3872, 3873, 3876, 3878, 3879, 3883, 3895, 3898, 3905, 3907, 3911, 3912, 3913, 3924, 3926, 3927, 3928, 3929, 3933, 3939, 3948, 3949, 3950, 3958, 3969, 3974, 3978, 3982, 3983, 3984, 3986, 4013, 4022, 4024, 4028, 4035, 4037, 4038, 4040, 4045, 4046, 4048, 4055, 4068, 4071, 4084, 4085, 4088, 4092, 4101, 4102, 4103, 4108, 4113, 4122, 4133, 4134, 4135, 4136, 4138, 4139, 4141, 4146, 4157, 4160, 4166, 4167, 4169, 4176, 4178, 4180, 4184, 4192, 4199, 4200, 4203, 4206, 4207, 4214, 4217, 4224, 4225, 4226, 4227, 4234, 4236, 4241, 4242, 4246, 4248, 4264, 4269, 4270, 4272, 4276, 4277, 4278, 4290, 4297, 4299, 4332, 4371, 4373, 4376, 4405, 4406, 4408, 4411, 4415, 4416, 4421, 4424, 4427, 4433, 4437, 4439, 4446, 4457, 4458, 4467, 4469, 4490, 4502, 4503, 4515, 4516, 4519, 4520, 4521, 4523, 4524, 4525, 4526, 4527, 4528, 4532, 4534, 4535, 4536, 4537, 4538, 4540, 4551, 4566, 4569, 4571, 4591.

Class 5 Standard 4-6-0. No 5276.

LNWR Class 7F 0-8-0. No 9208.

Midland Class 1P 2-4-0. No 20157 *Engineer Walsall*.

Midland Class 2F 0-6-0. Nos 22630, 22818, 22834.

Midland Class 1F 0-6-0. Nos 22921, 22935, 22953, 22977.

Locomotives recorded between 5 July and 20 December 1947

Class 3P Stanier 2-6-2T. Nos 97, 115, 116, 117, 120, 147, 162, 165, 168, 171, 173, 175, 179.

Class 2P 4-4-0 Midland. Nos 325, 364, 383, 385, 395, 407, 411, 416, 432, 436, 437, 438, 439, 456, 482, 485, 500, 501 *Engineer Walsall*, 508, 511, 512, 516, 517, 519, 523, 525, 526, 528, 530.

Class 2P 4-4-0 LMS Standard. Nos 618+, 631, 632, 633, 682+. (+The allocation of these engines at this date suggests that perhaps the register is incorrect. Signalmen were only human and it is impossible to guarantee that all the numbers are correct. For example, No 618 was at Hurlford and No 682 at Accrington.)

Class 3P 4-4-0 Midland. Nos 711, 719, 728, 739, 745, 756.

Class 4P 4-4-0 Compound. Nos 928, 934, 1014, 1017, 1019, 1024, 1027, 1029, 1033, 1035, 1039, 1046, 1051, 1061, 1063, 1064, 1074, 1078.

Class 4P Standard 2-6-4T. Nos 2324, 2326, 2327, 2329, 2334, 2336, 2337, 2338, 2339, 2342, 2372, 2373, 2577, 2685.

Class 5P5F Standard 2-6-0. Nos 2700, 2754, 2757, 2758, 2762, 2764, 2767, 2768, 2770, 2784, 2790, 2793, 2799, 2814, 2818, 2822, 2824, 2825, 2826, 2827, 2829, 2832, 2850, 2857, 2890, 2898, 2900, 2903, 2922, 2927, 2963, 2969, 2970.

Midland Class 2F, shown as *, and 3F 0-6-0. Nos 3073*, 3161*, 3178, 3180, 3181, 3201, 3203, 3204, 3210, 3213, 3214, 3217*, 3223, 3225, 3247, 3257, 3258, 3260, 3263, 3264*, 3267, 3273, 3274, 3277, 3284, 3321, 3324, 3335, 3336, 3338, 3339, 3343*, 3344, 3352*, 3355, 3359, 3367, 3369, 3373, 3374, 3381, 3419, 3427, 3435, 3436, 3439, 3441, 3442, 3443, 3444, 3464, 3484, 3485*, 3490, 3491, 3506, 3507, 3520, 3521, 3528*, 3531, 3540, 3544, 3548, 3562, 3568, 3572, 3582, 3583, 3594, 3604, 3608, 3620, 3621, 3623, 3624, 3627, 3644, 3645, 3667, 3668, 3673, 3675, 3680, 3681, 3686, 3687, 3690, 3691*, 3693, 3698, 3712, 3754, 3767, 3779, 3780, 3791, 3796, 3797, 3799, 3812, 3821, 3822, 3826, 3830.

Midland and LMS Class 4F 0-6-0. Nos 3836, 3838, 3843, 3845, 3846, 3847, 3851, 3853, 3858, 3861, 3865, 3870, 3871, 3873, 3875, 3876, 3879, 3887, 3890, 3891, 3911, 3912, 3917, 3924, 3928, 3929, 3930, 3932, 3938, 3940, 3941, 3945, 3946, 3949, 3951, 3953, 3954, 3957, 3965, 3968, 3969, 3972, 3978, 3982, 3983, 3986, 3988, 3995, 4001, 4002, 4013, 4017, 4025, 4026, 4027, 4030, 4045, 4049,

4051, 4066, 4076, 4084, 4085, 4088, 4092, 4093, 4095, 4100, 4101, 4103, 4106, 4108, 4109, 4112, 4117, 4129, 4132, 4137, 4138, 4139, 4143, 4145, 4148, 4150, 4167, 4169, 4170, 4174, 4175, 4176, 4179, 4180, 4182, 4185, 4186, 4190, 4200, 4201, 4202, 4203, 4204, 4207, 4213, 4224, 4226, 4227, 4229, 4232, 4235, 4248, 4266, 4267, 4268, 4269, 4270, 4272, 4275, 4287, 4289, 4304, 4317, 4332, 4333, 4376, 4385, 4404, 4406, 4413, 4414, 4419, 4422, 4424, 4426, 4427, 4429, 4430, 4466, 4470, 4475, 4515, 4516, 4520, 4524, 4525, 4526, 4527, 4528, 4532, 4534, 4537, 4538, 4539, 4545, 4553, 4560, 4563, 4566, 4567, 4568, 4575, 4576, 4580, 4581, 4583, 4584, 4586, 4587, 4589, 4591, 4596, 4599, 4604, 4606.

Class 5 Standard 4-6-0. Nos 4801, 4802, 4804, 4805, 4806, 4811, 4812, 4813, 4814, 4824, 4826, 4829, 4832, 4837, 4840, 4843, 4844, 4848, 4852, 4853, 4855, 4857, 4861, 4876, 4906, 4919, 4940, 4943, 4945, 4951, 4963, 4964, 5056, 5081, 5088, 5186, 5223, 5264, 5273, 5274, 5337, 5440, 5447.

Class 5XP Standard 4-6-0. Nos 5543, 5587, 5610, 5652.

LNWR Class 1P 2-4-2T. No 6661 (A Walsall engine).

LNWR Class 7F 0-8-0. Nos 9329, 9360, 9377 (These engines were stationed at Saltley).

Midland Class 2F 0-6-0. No 22630.

Class 8F Standard 2-8-0. Nos 8008, 8010, 8017, 8026, 8041, 8043, 8053, 8083, 8093, 8102, 8125, 8129, 8158, 8195, 8206, 8207, 8225, 8236, 8270, 8271, 8336, 8337, 8338, 8339, 8351, 8353, 8386, 8388, 8389, 8400, 8401, 8402, 8403, 8405, 8406, 8410, 8411, 8417, 8420, 8427, 8230, 8524, 8539, 8549, 8614, 8647, 8654, 8665, 8669, 8687, 8690.

Locomotives recorded between 17 September 1955 and 10 February 1956

Class 3P Stanier 2-6-2T. Nos 40115, 40119.

Class 2P 4-4-0 Midland. No 40540.

Class 4P 4-4-0 Compound. Nos 40927, 41050.

Class 4P Standard 2-6-4T. Nos 42052, 42053, 42054, 42056, 42083, 42186, 42322, 42326, 42327, 42334, 42337, 42338, 42340, 42373, 42374, 42383, 42527, 42583, 42599.

Class 6P5F Standard 2-6-0. Nos 42728, 42754, 42758, 42761, 42764, 42769, 42812, 42816, 42846, 42857, 42872, 42883, 42884, 42889, 42890, 42900, 42903, 42947, 42962.

Class 4MT Standard 2-6-0. Nos 43010, 43013, 43017, 43027, 43036, 43046, 43047, 43073, 43077, 43118.

Class 3F Midland 0-6-0. Nos 43210, 43213, 43219, 43223, 43246, 43258, 43337, 43339, 43355, 43373, 43374, 43433, 43435, 43441, 43444, 43464, 43506, 43521, 43523, 43594, 43599, 43607, 43620, 43627, 43645, 43673, 43675, 43682, 43684, 43690, 43698, 43712, 43734, 43754, 43762, 43771, 43786, 43798.

Midland and LMS Class 4F 0-6-0. Nos 43837, 43843, 43845, 43853, 43855, 43864, 43865, 43878, 43879, 43885, 43898, 43911, 43912, 43917, 43924, 43932, 43938, 43939, 43940, 43941, 43946, 43949, 43951, 43963, 43985, 43986, 44004, 44026, 44035, 44047, 44087, 44092, 44108, 44123, 44137, 44138, 44139, 44165, 44166, 44167, 44171, 44175, 44176, 44179, 44185, 44187, 44201, 44202, 44203, 44204, 44211, 44213, 44226, 44227, 44230, 44235, 44248, 44263, 44266, 44268, 44296, 44327, 44333, 44338, 44356, 44406, 44411, 44413, 44515, 44516, 44520, 44534, 44567, 44569, 44571, 44572, 44580, 44583, 44587, 44591, 44599, 44601.

Class 5XP Standard 4-6-0. Nos 45601, 45690, 45699.

Class 8F Standard 2-8-0. Nos 48061, 48063, 48081, 48101, 48143, 48149, 48197, 48211, 48213, 48266, 48268, 48272, 48311, 48336, 48357, 48417, 48424, 48507, 48523, 48618, 48619, 48647, 48650, 48669, 48687, 48700, 48728.

Note. During the periods under review some locomotive classifications were changed. However, I have used power classifications that generally applied and suggest that readers refer to the locomotive running number in order to establish the locomotive's identity.

Appendix III. Train Classification and Loading

Barnt Green, Evesham and Ashchurch

Class of Engine	No 1			No 2		
	Minerals	Goods	Empties	Minerals	Goods	Empties
Barnt Green to Alcester	25	35	50	30	42	50
Alcester to Evesham	35	50	50	42	50	50
Broom Junction to Evesham			60*		59*	60*
Evesham to Ashchurch		54*	60*		60*	60*
Evesham to Ashchurch	38	50	50	46	50	50
Ashchurch to Evesham	38	50	50	46	50	50
Evesham to Alcester	35	50	50	42	50	50
Alcester to Barnt Green	21	30	45	25	35	50

Only passenger and goods engines of the No 1 class, and goods engines of the No 2 class (engines of the American type excepted) must be worked over the section of line between Barnt Green Junction and Ashchurch via Evesham.

7.15pm Class 'B' goods Evesham to Birmingham is, when required, worked by two engines in front Evesham to Barnt Green, and 15- or 20-ton brake in the rear, and conveys 50 wagons of goods.

*Applies to Saturday and Sunday nights only. Through goods trains will be allowed 20 minutes to run Broom Junction to Evesham, and 30 minutes Evesham to Ashchurch when conveying these loads.

Loads for Engines, Barnt Green to Alcester. Wagons containing empty fruit and vegetable hampers and not exceeding 5cwt per wagon, must be reckoned the same as empties; Birmingham to Evesham trains to convey 50 wagons of goods from Barnt Green to Alcester, when the wagons are not loaded with more than 5cwt of empty fruit or vegetable hampers.

Source: *Midland Railway 1908 Appendix*

By 1945 the instructions in respect of loading of passenger and freight engines on branch lines were more complex. Set out below are the passenger train details:

Between Redditch and Barnt Green in the up direction a Class 1 passenger engine could take 150 tons, Class 2 — 200 tons, Class 3 — 245 tons, Class 4 — 270 tons, Class 5 — 310 tons, Class 5X — 350 tons. Freight engines could take greater loads when working passenger trains: Class 2 — 220 tons, Class 3 — 270 tons, Class 4 — 300 tons, and Class 5 — 340 tons.

Between Barnt Green and Redditch on the down line and between Evesham and Redditch on the up line the loads were: Passenger engines Class 1 — 160 tons, Class 2 — 220 tons, Class 3 — 260 tons, Class 4 — 290 tons, Class 5 — 335 tons, Class 5X — 375 tons. The freight engine loads were: Class 2 — 220 tons, Class 3 — 270 tons, Class 4 — 300 tons, Class 5 — 340 tons.

Between Redditch and Evesham on the down line the loads were: Passenger engines Class 1 — 180 tons, Class 2 — 245 tons, Class 3 — 295 tons, Class 4 — 330 tons, Class 5 — 380 tons, and Class 5X — 430 tons. The freight engine loads were: Class 2 — 270 tons, Class 3 — 325 tons, Class 4 — 365 tons, Class 5 — 415 tons.

Between Ashchurch and Evesham in either direction the loads were: Passenger engines Class 1 — 160 tons, Class 2 — 220 tons, Class 3 — 260 tons, Class 4 — 290 tons, Class 5 — 335 tons, Class 5X — 375 tons. The freight engine loads were: Class 2 — 240 tons, Class 3 — 285 tons, Class 4 — 320 tons, Class 5 — 365 tons.

Although various loadings applied to different sections of the line, through train loading was determined by the Redditch to Barnt Green loading in both the up and down directions.

The freight train loading was based upon the power class of the train locomotive and the type of wagon being hauled. For example, when calculating equivalent loading of freight trains 3½ wagons of goods or 5 empty wagons were equal to two wagons of mineral, based upon a 13-ton or less mineral wagon as being equivalent to one.

The other factor was the class of train. The more quickly the train was scheduled to cover a given length of railway the less weight was hauled by the same class of locomotive.

Freight train loads, express freight trains. Wagons of goods or empty wagons.

The load for the section between Alcester and Barnt Green in the up direction is shown in brackets, the other loading applied to the entire down line and the up line from Ashchurch to Alcester. Class 1 — 33 (30), Class 2 — 40 (36), Class 3 — 48 (43), Class 4 — 58 (52), Class 5 — 63 (57), Class 6 — 69 (63), Class 7 — 76 (69), Class 8 — 84 (76).

Through freight trains (or empty wagon trains signalled as through freight).

The load for the section between Alcester and Barnt Green in the up direction is shown in brackets, the other loading applied to the entire down line and the up line from Ashchurch to Alcester. Class 1 — 40 (30), Class 2 — 48 (36), Class 3 — 58 (43), Class 4 — 69 (52), Class 5 — 76 (57), Class 6 — 84 (63), Class 7 — 90 (69), Class 8 — 99 (76).

The loading for mineral trains.

	Up line: class of engine								Down line: class of engine							
	1	2	3	4	5	6	7	8	1	2	3	4	5	6	7	8
Ashchurch to Evesham	32	38	46	55	61	67	74	81	32	38	46	55	61	67	74	81
Evesham to Alcester	29	35	42	50	55	61	67	74	29	35	42	50	55	61	67	74
Alcester to Redditch	18	22	26	31	34	38	41	45	21	25	30	36	40	44	48	53
Redditch to Barnt Green*	18	22	26	31	34	38	41	45	21	25	30	36	40	44	48	53

*20-ton brakevan required in the up direction only. There was no specification for brake vans over the rest of the branch.

In addition to the restriction that applied with regard to the power of the locomotive and the weight and speed of the train, there was also a restriction to the length of the train. On the Evesham branch the maximum number of wagons that was authorised was 76 between Ashchurch and Evesham, and 60 over the remainder of the branch. Therefore, although a Class 8 2-8-0 was able to haul 74 mineral wagons between Evesham and Alcester, the maximum number that was permitted in a train was 60.

Finally, there are the point-to-point times. When a train was running 'out of course' or had 'lost its path', in other words it was not able to keep to the times laid down in the working timetable and was running late, the driver was expected to run to the point-to-point times. These times were also used by signalmen to decide if a late running train could be sent forward without causing delay to other trains that were running to time.

Class of train: up trains

	Express freight	Through freight	Mineral
Ashchurch to Evesham	24	26	33
Evesham to Harvington	9	10	11
Harvington to Broom	8	9	10
Broom to Alcester	7	8	10
Alcester to Studley	12	13	14
Studley to Redditch	9	10	11
Redditch to Redditch North	3	3	3
Redditch North to Barnt Green	14	15	16

Class of train: down trains

	Express freight	Through freight	Mineral
Barnt Green to Redditch North	10	11	14
Redditch North to Redditch	3	3	3
Redditch to Studley	9	9	11
Studley to Alcester	12	13	14
Alcester to Broom	8	9	10
Broom to Harvington	9	9	10
Harvington to Evesham	9	10	11
Evesham to Ashchurch	24	26	33

Appendix IV. Tariff Van Traffic

Tariff traffic was conveyed by a series of booked services and I have described those that ran on the Evesham branch in 1935. Tariff vans were used to convey all small consignments for the stations they served and the vans ran daily, irrespective of weight of traffic carried, except where otherwise stated in the company's instructions. The traffic was conveyed in covered goods vehicles and the Midland Railway designed a van for this traffic. The LMS never built any replacement vehicles, preferring to use ordinary covered goods vans.

There were six services each day and each service was numbered:

No 58. Labelled to Evesham
Departs 3.15 Birmingham Lawley Street goods station to Ashchurch. Serves Ashton-under-Hill, Hinton, Bengeworth. Departs 1/30 from Ashchurch to Evesham.

No 203. Labelled to Birmingham
Departs 4/0 from Evesham to Birmingham Lawley Street. Arrives 8/35.
Serves Harvington, Salford Priors, Broom Junction, Wixford, Alcester, Studley & Astwood Bank, Redditch, Birmingham. Redditch traffic goes forward to Lawley Street and is delivered by motor the following morning. This suggests that the Redditch stop was to load traffic only.

No 210. Labelled to Alvechurch
Departs 4.20 Gloucester to Evesham. Departs 8.25 Evesham to Alvechurch, arrives 2/30. Serves Evesham, Broom Junction, Harvington, Salford Priors, Wixford, Alcester, Coughton, Studley & Astwood Bank, Redditch, Alvechurch.

No 213. Labelled to Evesham
Departs 4.20 Gloucester to Evesham. Serves Ashchurch, Beckford, Ashton-under-Hill, Hinton, Bengeworth, Evesham.

No 337. Labelled to Broom and Redditch
Departs 11/10 St Pancras goods station to Olney. Dep 2.0 Olney to Stratford-upon-Avon. Departs 7.22 Stratford on Avon to Redditch via Broom Junction. dept. 9.36 Broom to Redditch. Serves Stratford-upon-Avon, Binton, Bidford-on-Avon, Broom Junction, Wixford, Alcester, Coughton, Studley & Astwood Bank, Redditch.

No 536. Labelled to Redditch
Departs 11/25 Worcester to Evesham and then forward to Redditch. Departs 8.25 Evesham to Redditch, arrives 1/55. Serves Evesham, Harvington, Salford Priors, Broom Junction, Wixford, Alcester, Coughton, Studley & Astwood Bank, Redditch.

The goods were loaded in the vans in station order and the vans were labelled on both sides with the authorised road van labels. The invoices for the goods went with the Tariff vans.

Appendix V. Hours of Opening of Signalboxes

1875

	Weekdays Time of closing	Time of opening
Ashchurch, Evesham Junction	8/15	7.0
Redditch station	8/15	7.0
Studley station	6/30	7.0
Evesham station	8/0	7.0

1908
The branch was closed on Sundays and Sunday nights and this applied to all the signalboxes.

These signalboxes were closed each night: Wixford, Salford Priors, Bengeworth, Hinton, Ashton-under-Hill, Beckford. The other boxes remained open at night.

1922
Ashchurch, Evesham Junction — Closed on Sunday and Sunday night.
Beckford — Closed on Sunday and Sunday night.
Ashton-under-Hill — Not a block post.
Hinton — Open for freight trains stopping at the station for traffic purposes.
Bengeworth — Closed each night and on Sundays.
Evesham, South and North — Closed on Sunday and Sunday night.
Harvington — Closed on Sunday and Sunday night.
Salford Priors — Not a tablet station.
Broom Junction, South and North — Closed on Sunday and Sunday night

Wixford — Not a tablet station.
Alcester Station and Junction — Closed on Sunday and Sunday night.
Studley & Astwood Bank — Closed on Sunday and Sunday night.
Redditch South, Redditch North and Gas Works Sidings. — Closed between the running of trains on Sunday and on Sunday night

1944
Barnt Green Single Line Junction, Redditch North, Redditch South, Studley & Astwood Bank, Alcester station, Broom Junction North, Harvington and Evesham were open continuously. Broom Junction West was closed from 5.25 Sunday until 5.30 Monday, or after passage of 1.30 from Blisworth.

	Weekdays closed from	Weekend closed from
Bengeworth	6/55 to 3/30	6/55 Saturday to 3/30 Monday
	5/0 to 5/45	
Hinton	6/30 to 3/0	6/30 Saturday to 3/0 Monday
	4/15 to 6/0	
Beckford	10/0 to 6.0	10/0 Saturday to 6.0 Monday
Ashchurch East		6.0 Sunday to 8.30 Sunday
		5/30 Sunday to 6.0 Monday

Appendix VI. Extracts from the SMJR Appendix

Cattle Trucks Attached to Passenger Trains

If at any time a stationmaster receives the traffic manager's special permission to attach a cattle wagon to one of the passenger trains the stationmaster must see that a screw coupling is used for the purpose.

Two screw couplings are provided in each passenger break van for this purpose.

Through Cattle Traffic from Midland Railway via Broom Junction to Blisworth & LNW Stations

The stationmaster at Stratford-on-Avon may attach trucks of cattle received from the Midland Railway for Blisworth and beyond to the first up passenger train ex-Stratford-on-Avon, provided the trucks are fitted with the continuous break or break pipe in use on the train, in accordance with the instructions on Pages 31, 32 and 33 of this Appendix.

Screw couplings must be used for cattle trucks on passenger trains, and for this purpose four screw couplings will be kept in the lamp room at Stratford-on-Avon station, two spare screw couplings also being kept in each passenger break for use in emergency.

When the stationmaster at Stratford-on-Avon finds it is probable that he may require to attach cattle trucks to the above passenger train he must at once find out, from all stations to Blisworth, whether they want to attach 'unbreaked' piped horse boxes to the train, and if he finds that the number of 'unbreaked'

vehicles would then exceed the limits set out on Page 26 of this Appendix, he must arrange for the cattle trucks to be worked specially.

All stations must wire this office and the stationmaster at Stratford-on-Avon immediately they know that they will require to attach horse boxes or other vehicles to the first up passenger train ex-Stratford-on-Avon, and it the vehicles are on hand they must say whether breaked or unbreaked.

In attaching cattle trucks to the above passenger train the Stratford-on-Avon stationmaster must bear in mind that the G.C. coach will be detached at Byfield, so that the number of unbreaked vehicles must only be in proportion to the number of Breaked vehicles which will proceed from Byfield to Blisworth.

This Order does *not* sanction the conveyance of cattle charged at goods train rates by passenger trains, except through cattle traffic from the Midland Railway via Broom Junction to Blisworth and L. & N.W. stations.

Engine Turntables

Turntables are provided at the following stations:

Blisworth	40ft diameter
Towcester	41ft 9in diameter
Stratford-on-Avon	51ft 8in diameter
Broom Junction (SMJ & Midland)	40ft 10in diameter
Banbury (LNWR)	41ft 6in diameter
Olney (Midland)	50ft diameter
Woodford and Hinton (GCR)	53ft 9in diameter

Sources Consulted

Birmingham New Street — LMS Days, Richard Foster, Wild Swan Publications
British Railway Journal
LMS and British Railways Hours of Opening of Signal Boxes
LMS Country Lorry Services 1939
LMS General Appendix to the Working Timetables 1937
LMS Engine Sheds Volume 2, C. Hawkins and G. Reeve, Wild Swan Publications
LMS Instructions respecting the working of Rail Motors and Motor Trains 1946
Midland and British Railways Routes over which engines may run
The Midland Railway: A Chronology, John Gough, Railway and Canal Historical Society, 1989
Midland Railway Distance Diagrams
Midland Record
Numerous Midland, LMS and British Railway Working and Public Timetables, Appendices, etc
The Official Guide to the Midland Railway, 1912
A Pictorial Record of LMS Signals, L. G. Warburton, OPC, 1972
Public Record Office Kew, MT6 files
Railway Clearing House *Official Hand Book of Railway Stations*, various editions
The Railway Magazine
The Railway Yearbook, various issues
Various Ordnance Survey maps

Index

Much of this book is self-indexing but where subjects appear or are mentioned elsewhere I have included them below. To do otherwise would probably have not been to make the best use of space available and it would have made the index rather unwieldy.

Postscript

An overall view of Ashchurch Junction looking north. The empty coach, on the left, stands on the Tewkesbury branch. *Lens of Sutton*

Although the line has been closed south of Redditch, some of the structures still remain. To the best of my knowledge, the following is a summary of structures which can still be seen on the course of the line:

Alvechurch: the original stationmaster's house remains in commercial use.
Redditch: now the terminus of the existing line. The original station has disappeared but a new station has been built to the south of the original site.
Studley & Astwood Bank: buildings remain in residential and commercial use.
Coughton: the stationmaster's house is in residential use.
Salford Priors: buildings have been taken over by Bromford & Evershed.
Harvington: the stationmaster's house remains in residential use.
Hinton: the stationmaster's house remains in residential and commercial use.
Ashton-under-Hill: the stationmaster's house remains in residential use.
Beckford: the stationmaster's house remains in residential use.
At least one overbridge, near Studley, remains and part of the embankment and trackbed can be seen but other than the buildings above, the line no longer exists. The connection into the MoD depot at Ashchurch is still in place, with access through the sidings and not off the Evesham and Ashchurch line.

No 41097 works a Birmingham-Gloucester ordinary passenger service through Ashchurch Junction having passed a freight train in the lie-by. Note that the tender of No 41097 still carries LMS lettering. A train waits in the Evesham branch platform. The date is c1949. *Joe Moss*